EUROPEAN REGIONALISM AND THE LEFT

MANCHESTER
1824
Manchester University Press

European regionalism and the Left

Edited by Gerard Strange and Owen Worth

Manchester University Press

Manchester and New York

*distributed in the United States exclusively
by Palgrave Macmillan*

Copyright © Manchester University Press 2012

While copyright in the volume as a whole is vested in Manchester University Press, copyright in individual chapters belongs to their respective authors, and no chapter may be reproduced wholly or in part without the express permission in writing of both author and publisher.

Published by Manchester University Press
Oxford Road, Manchester M13 9NR, UK
and Room 400, 175 Fifth Avenue, New York, NY 10010, USA
www.manchesteruniversitypress.co.uk

Distributed in the United States exclusively by
Palgrave Macmillan, 175 Fifth Avenue, New York,
NY 10010, USA

Distributed in Canada exclusively by
UBC Press, University of British Columbia, 2029 West Mall,
Vancouver, BC, Canada V6T 1Z2

British Library Cataloguing-in-Publication Data
A catalogue record for this book is available from the British Library

Library of Congress Cataloging-in-Publication Data applied for

ISBN   978 07190 8573 4   hardback

First published 2012

Typeset
by Carnegie Book Production
Printed in Great Britain
by MPG Books Group, Bodmin

Contents

List of figures and tables

Figures

Tables

Acknowledgements

The collection has its roots in a Special Issue in *Capital and Class* called 'The Left and Europe' that was published just before the onset of the financial crisis in 2007. It also benefited greatly from a panel put together for the International Studies Association annual conference at San Francisco in 2008. We would in particularly like to thank Alan Cafruny and Stephen Gill for their contributions to the panel. We would also like to thank Tony Mason and Sarah Hunt at Manchester University Press. Special thanks to Jackie, Harry, Perys and Rosa for their personal support throughout the completion of this book.

Notes on the contributors

David J. Bailey is lecturer in political science at the University of Birmingham. His research focuses on social democratic parties and European integration. He recently published articles in the *Journal of International Relations and Development*, the *British Journal of Politics and International Relations* and the *Journal of European Social Policy*. He also co-edited *The European Union and Global Governance: A Handbook* (Routledge, 2010).

Andreas Bieler is Professor of Political Economy and Fellow of the Centre for the Study of Social and Global Justice (CSSGJ) in the School of Politics and International Relations, University of Nottingham, UK. His main research interest deals with neoliberal globalisation and the possibilities for resistance, including the potential role of trade unions. He is author of *Globalisation and Enlargement of the European Union* (Routledge, 2000) as well as *The Struggle for a Social Europe: Trade Unions and EMU in Times of Global Restructuring* (Manchester University Press, 2006). He is also co-editor (with Ingemar Lindberg and Devan Pillay) of *Labour and the Challenges of Globalisation: What Prospects for Transnational Solidarity?* (Pluto Press, 2008) and (with Ingemar Lindberg) of *Global Restructuring, Labour and the Challenges for Transnational Solidarity* (Routledge, 2010).

Randall Germain is Professor of Political Science at Carleton University, Ottawa, Canada. His most recent book is *Global Politics and Financial Governance* (Palgrave, 2010). The principal focus of his work is on the political economy of global finance and disciplinary debates within the field of international political economy.

Michael Holmes is a Senior Lecturer in European Politics at Liverpool Hope University. His main interests are European politics and Irish politics. Within European politics, he has specialised in the study of the impact of European integration on political parties and party systems. He is the author of *The Development of the Irish Labour Party's European Policy: From Opposition to support* (Edwin Mellen Press, 2006)

Simon Lightfoot is a Senior Lecturer in European Politics. His area of research is European social democracy, especially the Party of European Socialists. He is author of *Europeanising Social Democracy?* (Palgrave, 2005).

Neil Robinson teaches in the Department of Politics and Public Administration at the University of Limerick, Ireland. His publications include *Russia: A State of Uncertainty* (Routledge, 2002), *The Sage Handbook of Comparative Politics* (with Todd Landman, Sage, 2009) and *The Political Economy of Russia* (Rowman & Littlefield, forthcoming).

Ben Rosamond is Professor of Political Science and Deputy Director of the Centre for European Politics at the University of Copenhagen. He co-edits the journal *Comparative European Politics*. His books include *Theories of European Integration* (Palgrave Macmillan, 2000), *Handbook of European Union Politics* (co-editor, Sage, 2007) and most recently *New Regionalism and the European Union: Dialogue, Comparison and New Research Directions* (co-editor, Routledge, 2011). His research has been published in journals such as the *European Journal of International Relations, Government and Opposition,* the *Journal of Common Market Studies,* the *Journal of European Public Policy, New Political Economy, Political Studies* and the *Review of International Political Economy.*

Magnus Ryner is a Reader at Kings College, University of London, having been Professor of International Relations at Oxford Brookes University. He is the author of *Europe at Bay: In the Shadow of US Hegemony* (Lynne Rienner, 2007) and *The European Union* (both with Alan Cafruny) and has published widely in international and comparative political economy.

Ray Silvius is an instructor in the politics department at the University of Winnipeg. He specialises in Russian political economy and international political economy.

Gerard Strange is Reader in International Political Economy at the School of Social Sciences, University of Lincoln, UK. His recent work has appeared in *New Political Economy, Government and Opposition* globalisations, *The British Journal of Politics and International Relations* and *Political Studies*.

Lawrence Wilde is Professor of Political Theory at Nottingham Trent University. He is the author of *The Marx Dictionary* (with Ian Frasier) (Continuum, 2011), *Erich Fromm and the Quest For Solidarity* (Palgrave, 2004), *Ethical Marxism and its Radical Critics* (Palgrave, 1998) and *Modern European Socialism* (Dartmouth, 1984). He has published widely in a number of leading journals in the areas of solidarity, cosmopolitanism and on new social movements.

Owen Worth is a lecturer in International Relations at the University of Limerick, Ireland. He is the author of *Hegemony, International Political Economy and Post-Communist Russia* (Ashgate, 2012) and *Resistance in the Era of Austerity* (Zed, 2012). His recent work has appeared in the *Review of International Studies*, the *Journal of International Relations and Development*, *International Politics*, *Capital and Class* and the *Third World Quarterly*.

List of acronyms and abbreviations

ASEAN	Association of Southeast Asian Nations
ATTAC	Association for the Taxation of Financial Transactions for the Aid of Citizens
BRIC (countries)	Brazil, Russia, India, China
CDU	Christian Democratic Union (Germany)
CEE	Central and Eastern Europe
Comecon	Council for Mutual Economic Assistance (Warsaw Pact)
CSP	Common Foreign and Security Policy (EU)
CSU	Christian Social Union (Germany)
DGB	Confederation of German Trade Unions
EC	European Community
ECB	European Central Bank
ECJ	European Court of Justice
Ecofin	Economic and Financial Affairs Council (EU)
ECSC	European Coal and Steel Community
ECT	European Constitutional Treaty
EEC	European Economic Community
EFC	Economic and Finance Committee
EFSF	European Financial Stabilisation Facility
EGP	European Green Party
EIF	European Industry Federations
EMF	European Metalworkers' Federation
EMS	European Monetary System

EMU	European Monetary Union
ENP	European Neighbourhood Policy
EP	European Parliament
EPSU	European Federation of Public Service Unions
ERM	Exchange Rate Mechanism (EU)
ESF	European Social Forum
ESM	European Stabilisation Mechanism
ESRB	European Systemic Risk Board
ETUC	European Trade Union Confederation
EU	European Union
EUCOB@	European Collective Bargaining Information Network
Eurogroup	finance ministers of the eurozone
eurozone	17 EU nations using the euro
FPD	Free Democratic Party (Germany)
FSAP	Financial Services Action Plan
FSBG	Framework for Sustainable and Balanced Global Growth (G20–IMF)
FTAA	Free Trade Agreement for the Americas
G20	group of finance ministers and central bank governors of the leading developed countries
GATT	General Agreement on Tariffs and Trade
GATS	General Agreement on Trade in Services
GDP	gross domestic product
GFC	global financial crisis (2007–8)
GUE	Group of the United European Left
IFI	international financial institution
ILO	International Labor Organization
IMF	International Monetary Fund
IPE	International Political Economy
IR	International Relations
IT	information technology
LACC	Latin American and Caribbean Community
MDG	Millennium Development Goal
MEP	Member of the European Parliament
Mercosur	Common Market of the South (South America)
MNC	multinational corporation
NAFTA	North American Free Trade Agreement

NATO	North Atlantic Treaty Organisation
NGL	Nordic Green Left
NGO	non-governmental organisation
OAS	Organization of American States
OECD	Organisation for Economic Cooperation and Development
ÖGB	Austrian Trade Union Federation
PCA	Partnership and Cooperation Agreement (EU)
PEL	Party of the European Left
PES	Party of European Socialists
PIGS (countries)	Portugal, Italy, Greece, Spain
PIIGS	Portugal, Ireland, Italy, Greece, Spain
QMV	qualified majority voting
SAP	Social Democratic Party (Sweden)
SDP	Social Democratic Party (Germany)
SEA	Single European Act
SGP	Stability and Growth Pact
SWF	sovereign wealth fund
TEU	Treaty on European Union
TNC	transnational corporation
UK	United Kingdom
UN	United Nations
UNICE	Industrial and Employers' Confederations of Europe
US	United States
USSR	Union of Soviet Socialist Republics (pre-1991)
WSF	World Social Forum
WTO	World Trade Organization

Introduction: global change, European regionalism and the Left

Gerard Strange and Owen Worth

Introduction

Writing in 1973, on the eve of the entry of the UK, Ireland and Denmark into the Common Market, Tom Nairn argued that European integration, both as an ideal and a process, had always divided the left (Nairn, 1973). While Trotsky and later Spinelli favoured greater European integration as a vehicle for socialism, after the Second World War the Left more generally became sceptical about grand projects for European unity. In the decades following the war the Left tended to prefer 'settlements' focused on *national* social democratic political economy whose efficacy had been enhanced by new government commitments to the mixed economy, comprehensive national welfare systems and Keynesian tools of macroeconomic management aimed at securing full employment within a stable economic frame. All this seemed to favour the advance of labour. Social democracy developed many national variants in post- war western Europe but was grounded in a wider *international* political economy framed by the Bretton Woods agreement, famously described by Ruggie (1982) as 'embedded liberalism'. Despite the decisive role played by the Soviet Red Army, alongside the Allies, in the defeat of European fascism, as well as the diplomatic and intellectual efforts of Keynes, Britain's leading negotiator at Bretton Woods, this new international political economy came to be determined by (distinctly) American multilateral leadership.

Against this backdrop, European political parties on the Left were able to rebuild as serious political players in the post-war period. Some, like the British Labour Party, enjoyed new pre-eminence as policy agenda setters as well as parties of government. However, the Labour Party, the German Social Democratic Party and the Communist and Socialist Parties of

France and Italy initially took defensive positions towards European integration as promoted by its founding fathers, notably Schuman, Monnet and Adenauer. While advocates of integration regarded a European customs union as a priority objective in the rebuilding of a peaceful and prosperous Europe, the left was concerned that social democratic principles and institutions established at the national level after the war would become hostage to an expanding free market beyond the control of democratic governments.

Yet, the decline of US multilateral leadership within the Bretton Woods frame, post-1971, uprooted embedded liberalism and like the later collapse of Soviet communism fundamentally changed the context in which European political economy developed and has subsequently been evaluated by the Left. While many on the Left remained (and indeed remain) anchored to the perspective of national political economy, others began to re-evaluate the role and potential of European unity as a means of preserving and developing social democracy (and, by extension, socialism) in the absence of more pervasive hegemonic leadership and in face of the growing challenge of neoliberalism (see, for example, Milward, 1992; Holland, 1993). The break-up of eastern bloc 'socialisms' in the late 1980s and early 1990s (often, as in the case of Yugoslavia, leading to catastrophic civil wars) and the seemingly decisive collapse of the Soviet Union reinforced the need for the Left to rethink Europe and the project of European union.

Since these events much of the wider discussions on global change have placed the analysis of the European Union (EU) and European integration within the wider context of 'new regionalism'. Although the 'European Model' could by no means be uncritically endorsed by the Left, it was also to be acknowledged that in an era of neoliberal globalisation 'Europe' seemed to represent, for many, 'the only [alternative] card game in town'. While in one sense Europe as a form of 'open regionalism' (Gamble and Payne, 1996) helped facilitate neoliberal globalisation by freeing up markets for trade and investment, at another level it represented, also, a distinct political *response* to that process (Hettne, 1997). European integration held out the possibility of defending social democracy from external constraints and pressures associated with globalisation, be it through a 'fortress' policy of 'social Europe' or by a more globally orientated projection of socially focused macroeconomic as well as rule-based regulation which retained a commitment to openness.

In practice, European integration has come to be dominated by the EU's drive to extend and consolidate a distinctly neoliberal *form* of open regionalism, notably through the management and prioritisation of its own eastward expansion around liberal democratic and market-focused conditional accession. Deep integration, focused especially on the euro project and the launch of the single currency in 1999 has, in turn, given priority to price stability at low rates of inflation in order to secure external credibility with key global actors for the new currency while seeking to manage the internal social and economic dislocations this has generated. Although the euro crisis which erupted in 2010 has generated uncertainty and significant policy change, both forms of integration have been pursued in the absence of a coherent strategy aimed at forging a cohesive political identity for the EU and its erstwhile 'citizens'. The result has been that in the post-Delors period, 'social Europe', in particular, has survived primarily as the shadow discourse of Europe's internal 'other', evoked by the Left as a point of critique in the face of welfare retrenchment and the advance of neoliberal reform.

As a consequence the contemporary EU finds itself at a crossroads marked by the convergence of three related crises. First, both prior to and after the global financial crisis (GFC) of 2007–8, the EU has suffered crises of political identity and legitimacy, most evident in the failure to agree a constitutional treaty in the mid 2000s. While the ratification of the Lisbon Treaty and its passing into EU law in 2009 resolved aspects of this crisis, it did so by studiously avoiding the problem of political identity and democratic deficit (Gamble, 2006). Second, European regionalism has come up against what can be regarded as a deep-seated division between western Europe on the one hand and the former Soviet bloc economies, states and societies on the other. Since the collapse of the Soviet Union in the early 1990s and despite an initial optimism among EU enthusiasts that this afforded an historic opportunity to extend the EU project to the borders of Asia and the Middle East, this division has proved to be enduring if not altogether stable or unchanging. The division between west and east Europe is rooted in different state structures between the two regions, which has continued and will continue to frustrate the EU's longer-term ambition to expand open regionalism eastwards. Third, European regionalism has been marked by and/or has developed concomitantly with a crisis of social democracy, as party ideology, national-state-level government strategy and as supranational regionalist ambition. The political crisis of social democracy has been linked to globalisation but also more specifically to the EU's prioritising of a neoliberal economic model of open regionalism. More recently it has been heightened by crises of regional economy around the eurozone and the broader euro project, crises widely acknowledged as structurally rooted in fundamental macroeconomic asymmetries between eurozone member states. Not surprisingly, therefore, the crisis of the euro remains ongoing.

These different contexts have important implications for both the future of European regionalism and for Left theorisations and analyses of it. For many on the left, including many of the contributors to this volume, there is, in particular, an intimate connection between the EU's drive to consolidate open regionalism and the decline of social democracy at the party, national and supranational level. As part of what neo-Gramscian scholars (more specifically those who follow the reading of Gramsci associated with the so-called 'Amsterdam school') identify as a 'constitutionalising' project of global neoliberalism, the EU's open regionalism has, according to many critics, systematically closed off the key structures and policy spaces around which social democracy had been articulated (Gill, 1998; van Apeldoorn *et al.*, 2003). This is not to say that opportunities to counter this process have not been forthcoming. Certainly, the GFC and the wider processes that led to it have put neoliberalism on the back foot and on the defensive in many respects (Gamble, 2009). However, social forces supportive of neoliberalism have not gone away and they remain deeply entrenched in the EU and elsewhere.

World order and Europe

The Marxist neo-Gramscian critique of the EU associated with the 'Amsterdam school' has been important in helping make sense of European regionalism not least because it immediately draws attention to the EU's place within wider *capitalist* world order transformations. European *regional* integration made its most important advances during a period (the last thirty-five years) also dominated by neoliberal *globalisation*. This period has seen a remarkable freeing up of trade and investment flows globally and regionally. For many years or even decades this project appeared to be highly successful in its own terms in both achieving its core objectives of freeing up capital and re-embedding market order and discipline around new governance regimes that constrained state agency, and in its wider capacity to disorganise – or, alternatively, incorporate into the neoliberal project – potential social forces and institutionalised vectors of opposition.

But crucial to this success was a global economic boom dating from the early 1990s and sustained through to the late 2000s. A critical dimension of the neoliberal period beyond Europe, and one from which it drew strength and legitimacy, was the incorporation of much of the developing world during the boom period into the global neoliberal order through both regional economic integration (for example through Mercosur in Latin America and ASEAN in south east Asia) and through membership of the World Trade Organization (WTO), regarded by many critics on the Left as the pinnacle institution of global neoliberalism. Against this backdrop of regional and global integration and global economic boom, the neoliberal period also saw the rise of new regionally embedded but increasingly global powers, notably Brazil, Russia, India and China, the so-called BRIC powers.

However, the story of the neoliberal period was not one of unqualified success *for* neoliberalism. Africa, although at one level strongly integrated into the world trading system and despite renewed efforts over the past two decades to build its own regionalisms (efforts which have tended to be supported by the 'neoliberal' dominated international elite policy communities), nevertheless stands out as an unmitigated failure of neoliberalism. Neoliberalism's active encouragement of the weakening of state power has produced 'fragile' and 'failed' states throughout Africa which, though weak in developmental terms, have proved to be strong bases for the entrenchment of rival patrimonial forms of power and, associated with this, corruption. This has contributed to the strengthening of patrimonial forms of the 'state', the embedding of civil conflict and extreme poverty for the majority of the sub-continent's 650 million people. Endemic social instability, in some cases leading to societal collapse, has been common even while power-holding state elites purportedly engage in democratic reform processes.

With regard to the BRICs, radical and orthodox research continues to contest the *meaning* of their rise. While there are strong elements of neoliberalism evident here, especially reliance on trade and investment sectors characterised by the dominance of foreign direct investment (FDI) and the enforcement of low-wage regimes, so that the BRICs can, for some radicals, be legitimately portrayed as neoliberal 'competition states' *par excellence*, this has not been one-way traffic for neoliberalism. China, India and Brazil all have strong and growing sectors and sub-sectors of independent or semi-independent (often state dominated) economic capability in manufacturing, services (including banking and international technology (IT)), the knowledge economy and high technology and energy, alongside the foreign dominated sector, with the state maintaining overarching and strategic control at the macroeconomic level (this is particularly true of China; see Strange 2011a). Russia stands out as more dependent on the energy sector. But, overall, integration with the global economy has enabled the BRICs to accumulate unprecedented and sustained trade surpluses over the past twenty years (and particularly the last ten years), which have contributed to the accumulation and augmentation of sovereign wealth funds alongside asymmetrical income and profit flows associated with FDI. The strong demand for energy and resources coming from the developed *and* developing countries, alongside the shift in traded production towards the BRICs, means that the augmentation of sovereign wealth by developing countries is set to continue for the foreseeable future. How this new sovereign wealth comes to be used will help to determine judgments made about the meaning and nature of these rising states (Beeson, 2010; Taylor, 2011).

Finally, the BRICs and developing world countries more generally have integrated into the world economy through membership of the WTO. For some, this has been a difficult, controversial and protracted process. For example, China joined in 2001 only after a lengthy process of negotiation. For radical critics, China's integration into the WTO regime will constrain her development trajectory in neoliberal, path-dependent terms (Wade, 2003; Harvey, 2005). Yet WTO membership also provides new opportunities for developing countries. China has subsequently become a pivotal power within the WTO, as well as the G20, the longer-term consequences of which remain far from clear, as hawkish voices in the US are fully aware (Strange, 2011a). Again, China's rise within global governance might signal nothing more than a changing of the guard from US to Chinese leadership or to a more generic form of neoliberal or free market hegemony where there is a lack of a distinct state leader in the international political economy. Equally, China's 'state capitalist' model may provide renewed opportunities for challenging neoliberalism and carving out developmental and social democratic 'space' within world order.

Importantly for Europe within world order, Russia has remained outside the WTO, despite making many attempts to restructure its economic base to attract foreign investment since the oligarchic character of its state became clear in the 1990s. Indeed, it is tempting to regard the former Soviet states, including Russia, as 'basket case' economies, the failure of which, though perhaps rooted in the Soviet era, is every bit as damning for neoliberalism as the catastrophes visited upon Sub-Saharan Africa (Simon, 2009). Neoliberalism proved incapable of (or interested in) mobilizing a 'quick fix' for eastern Europe when the historic opportunity arose following the collapse of the Soviet Union in 1991 and the arrival into power of a leader, Boris Yeltsin, who was willing, initially, to embrace the path of radical pro-market reform. Instead, the Soviet economies collapsed into the nadir of the 'lost decade', gradually recovering (in some regions) only once global demand for energy began to boom (while supply became more constrained) and only once reformers had long since lost the political initiative. But if this is so, oil wealth dependence, alongside nuclear capability and alongside the dominance of an oligarchic and authoritarian state, will continue, for the foreseeable future, to determine Russia's strategic orientation to the west and the world economy. This will reinforce a development trajectory that favours the survival of the 'natural' state in Russia and many of its dependent satellite states, which at one level put it at odds with the neoliberal model. Many recent studies have highlighted Russia's continuing pursuit of multinational investment through the state-endorsed liberalisation of its financial- and service-based sectors in a bid to improve its stature in the neoliberal global economy (Worth, 2009; Simon, 2010). Equally, however, Russia can be expected to continue resisting attempts to deregulate the global energy sector if this threatens energy-based state rents and concomitant sovereign wealth on which the ruling oligarchs depend.

'After' neoliberalism?

World order is therefore arguably a very different 'beast' now than it was when the neoliberal project first began to be articulated four decades ago. In particular it has come to be characterised not only by powerful global formations of capital, in the form of influential global money market actors, multinational corporations and transnational capitalist class formations, but also by the emergence of new and often highly assertive state and regional powers. China is the most obvious example of a newly developed and assertive *state* global actor (Beeson, 2009, 2010; Strange, 2011a). But regional integration has enabled the EU, too, to emerge as a more coherent, unified and assertive global actor in important power and policy domains (Bretherton and Vogler, 2006). Most effectively, this has been the case in the domains of trade and environmental regulation. But the EU has also entered the global stage as a monetary power with the arrival of the euro in 1999, albeit that the euro project is still far from complete and its future, after a first decade marked by a succession of cumulative crises, far from certain. Reflecting this uncertainty, the nature, efficacy and future of European monetary power has been the subject of often polarised debates on the Left, debates that are reflected in some of the contributions to this volume.

Caveats and debates such as these notwithstanding, the emergence of new global actors represents an important structural change in world order which, according to many critical scholars, has ushered in a new global conjecture under which power relations, once focused unambiguously on US state and societal dominance, have become increasingly diffused, making the future of world order uncertain, less hegemonic and less stable. The greater diffusion of global power, it should be stressed, is itself a relative and uncertain phenomenon, whose impact, should it continue, would be felt over future decades. Moreover, as Ben Cohen has stressed, shifts in structural power do not automatically translate into decisive changes in the purposive and active *exercise* of power or in the specific purposes for which power, once gained at the structural level, is exercised (Cohen, 2006; see also Bretherton and Vogler 2006). Power may or may not be effectively *projected* onto others as leverage and influence, or if it is may not serve, necessarily, to challenge neoliberalism so much as to change the configuration of actors exercising power on its behalf. Indeed, one of the attractions and strengths of Gramsci's understanding of hegemony (an understanding followed by many of the contributors to this volume) is that it focuses attention on the complex configuration of power and power relations beyond the dominance of one specific state to include vectors such as class and ideology in interaction with states and the international state system. The relative decline of the US as the dominant state power does not necessarily signal the decline of neoliberalism as a broader power matrix in the contemporary political economy.

That said, it is already apparent that structural changes *have* fed through into the way power is exercised globally. This has been most evident, perhaps, in the growth of tension and conflict between the US and China over trade and monetary policy and over regional hegemonic leadership in Asia in recent years. But Europe's growing capacity for global actorness is also an important dimension of the diffusion of power, with many commentators anticipating a much less stable relationship between Europe and the US over the coming decades. As a trade as well as an environmental policy actor, the EU has been both assertive and effective in refusing to subordinate its own interests and leadership capabilities to those of the US. Evidence for this is to be found in the EU's global leadership of the Kyoto process aimed at the regulation and reduction of carbon gas emissions (albeit that the future of the Kyoto process post-2012 is uncertain) despite US unilateralism and recalcitrance; and in the fact that many of the formalised trade disputes subject to WTO rulings have been between the EU and the US. The EU has been less effective and less unified in the military domain, not least because, despite the Common Foreign and Security Policy (CFSP), the EU continues to lack decisive structural capability in terms of personnel and military hardware and software. Nevertheless, tensions between the US and EU, and consequently policy change, have also been evident here. Beyond Britain, key powers in the EU, notably Germany and France (famously dubbed 'old Europe' by former US Defense Secretary Donald Rumsfeld) refused to support the war in Iraq on American terms. More recently, Germany refused to sanction military intervention by the US and some of its European allies, this time under a UN agreement, aimed at supporting anti-Gaddafi forces and protecting civilian populations in Libya in 2010–11. Interestingly, a core source of tension between the US and Europe over Libya was America's own concerns about hegemonic 'overstretch' at a time of domestic weakness and uncertainty following the GFC. This has led to growing US frustration at Europe's failure to take on a more decisive military leadership role in its own 'backyard'. Similar frustration has been evident in US criticisms of the EU's apparent failure to deal decisively with the euro crisis.

Against this backdrop of structural world order change, much of it instigated by the neoliberal revolution of the past three decades, neoliberalism itself has, for the first time, begun to show more clearly its own contradictions, weaknesses and limits. This has been most dramatically demonstrated by the GFC and its still unravelling aftermath. But the weaknesses of neoliberalism had already become apparent well before the GFC. The WTO, regarded by many supporters and critics alike as the crowning achievement of neoliberalism at the global level, has become increasingly moribund, at least in its neoliberal formation, as is evidenced by the failure of the so-called Doha round, which has now been 'stalled' for over a decade. At the heart of this failure is a common unwillingness on the part of developed and developing countries, regions and blocs to embrace further moves towards market deregulation. For developed countries, the stumbling block has been unwillingness, *contra* neoliberal ideology, to sanction the liberalisation of long-protected markets in which they no longer exercise comparative advantage – agricultural products, commodities and textiles as well as primaries and minerals processing – but which have remained strategically important both for employment and social stability in the neoliberal heartland. Defence of these sectors has become a critical issue for developed countries because they have lost pre-eminence, also, in the manufacturing sector where free trade has generally prevailed. For developing countries the stumbling block is developed country demands for the further liberalisation of FDI and high-end technologies and services, sectors where developing countries are now increasingly pursuing independent capacity building. Demands for the deregulation of energy sectors have also been resisted by developing countries, including Russia, whose recent development has been driven by unprecedented income flows from these sectors. Faced with deadlock at the WTO, developed countries have pursued more limited multilateral and bilateral deals in an effort to consolidate neoliberalism by other means. But these, too, have been subject to deadlock, failure and even reversal in recent years. For example, the EU's long-running attempt to negotiate a bilateral free trade agreement with Brazil has become indefinitely stalled, not least as a consequence of Brazil's renewed commitment to a relaunched and increasingly politicised Mercosur. Similarly, efforts by the US to seed the further expansion of the North American Free Trade Agreement (NAFTA) through the bilateral Free Trade Agreement for the Americas (FTAA) project has come up against growing Latin American unity around both Mercosur and most recently the launch in 2010 of the Latin American and Caribbean Community (LACC), a project explicitly opposed to both the FTAA and its US leadership under the auspices of the Organization of American States (OAS). By contrast, the past ten years has witnessed a boom in intra-developing world finance, trade and investment deals, with 'state capitalist' China featuring as the conspicuous driver and principal paymaster of that process.

These global power shifts and the concomitant weakening, if not unravelling, of actually existing global neoliberalism, provide new opportunities for the Left around the relaunching of state developmentalism and social democracy, including in the regionalist heartlands of neoliberalism, notably the still evolving and contested EU project. But such new opportunities, if they are to be understood and grasped, require, first, a careful reconsideration and further development of the terms on which the Left has sought to understand regional and global neoliberalism and challenge it.

Europe and the Left

This volume represents a relatively early attempt to contribute to such a reappraisal of Left thinking. Despite the important contribution of the 'Amsterdam school' and of 'new constitutionalism' to Left understandings of the neoliberal period, there is currently no overall agreement on the Left – including among critical scholars influenced by Gramscian theory – about continuing processes of and the potential limits to neoliberalism as a hegemonic project. Thus, while some on the Left discern new opportunities for rearticulating social democratic reform in an emerging 'post-neoliberal' era, others have begun to reposition their critique away from the peculiarities of neoliberalism and towards a more fundamentalist focus on global capitalism, regardless of the specificity of legitimising hegemonic projects, be they neoliberal, post-neoliberal, social democratic, or whatever. Against new opportunities for the Left, which hardly come with gilt-edged guarantees, neoliberalism may seek to rearticulate itself as a coherent project, albeit that the defeats it has suffered as well as the structural changes it has itself wrought means that it will do so from a position of weakened legitimacy, underpinned by significant doubts surrounding the future growth trajectory of the global economy. The immediate impulse for some in the neoliberal camp, as has been partly evident in the response of the eurozone authorities to the euro crisis, will be to mobilise for retrenchment around core market principles and policies and to promote such retrenchment around a universal legitimising discourse or discourses. 'There is no alternative to the "age of austerity"' is one such discourse with particular resonance in the crisis-hit EU. The contemporary Left in Europe has yet to decide whether a *systemic* regional or global alternative to austerity is possible or desirable, a sign of profound weakness for it. As the next phases of the GFC and the euro crisis unfold, European social democracy will in all likelihood be torn between the politically expedient but economically destructive pull of protectionism, on the one hand, and moves to stabilise open regionalism around new regulatory liberal frameworks, on the other. Having failed to articulate radical or feasible alternatives to social democracy during the neoliberal era, the broader Left, likewise, is in danger of finding itself once again divided between the immediate (but ultimately self-defeating) palliatives and securities promised by protectionists and the commitment to openness and economic integration characteristic of regulatory liberalism. Under the latter, solidarity and social democratic outcomes can be advanced but with few guarantees in an uncertain world. Whether, and if it does, *how*, the EU is able to survive the crisis will help determine which of the alternatives ultimately prevails. Modernising social democracy through interaction with the opportunities structures made available as a consequence of regional integration offers some hope for the Left, not least because social democracy itself, as a broad and relatively open body of ideas, remains the most potent source of a popular counter-hegemony. But a renewed social democracy must also interact more effectively with ecological critiques of capitalism that have provided the cutting edge for radical and fresh thinking and ideas about alternatives in recent decades, ideas that neoliberalism has struggled to accommodate to its own project.

The chapters in this book both articulate and reflect some of the divisions on the Left about the possible futures of world order and how the Left might express itself during a period likely to be marked by fundamental changes and transformations. This can be seen in Part I, where Ryner, Rosamond and Strange offer different accounts of the nature and potential of the EU. Ryner's Chapter 1 links strongly to the 'Amsterdam' tradition in terms of its historical analysis and the emphasis given to the role played by US power in the construction of the EU. But in making this argument Ryner utilises Poulantzas' often-neglected analysis of internationalism structured around a Marxist account of accumulation regimes. The perception is that European regional expansion and integration in the neoliberal period was heavily influenced by and subordinated to US structural power – a position that, for Ryner, only seems set to continue in the current environment of crisis. For Ryner, subordination to American power has imposed 'self-limitation' on EU integration and the purposes it can serve, evident particularly in a 'monetarist' project of monetary union and concomitant processes of economic crisis and welfare retrenchment. European integration cast in this context, Ryner suggests, has undermined the feasibility of a 'social' or social democratic EU, leaving the EU hostage to American power, externally, and reactionary political forces, internally.

Rosamond's Chapter 2 critically scrutinises the claim that the EU can be adequately described as a neoliberal entity primarily seeking to develop a transnational market regime. When such claims are made about the EU, they lack an engagement with European economic space and spatiality as a socially constructed and contested discourse. The history of European economic integration should not be seen wholly in terms of de-politicised, technocratic processes, by means of which neoliberalism necessarily prevails, but as the historical unfolding of contrasting spatial narratives that offer distinct understandings of what Europe and the EU is or could be. In the constructivist tradition, Rosamond gives primacy to agency and reminds us that the governmental process within the EU has never been one constructed solely around a 'neoliberal' agenda. Instead, it has been built around competing sets of ideas drawn from a variety of technical and normative discourses. While 'neoliberal ideology' has been an influential source of ideas for economic governance within the EU, there is no *necessary* linkage between these ideas and the EU's core technologies of governance, such as monetary union. The EU's governance forms have built new spaces capable of hosting a plurality of ideational constructs and yielding alternative policy priorities and outcomes.

Finally in Part I, Strange in Chapter 3 foregrounds what he regards as relatively declining US power as the context in which EU integration has evolved since the 1970s. He highlights European monetary union as a critical structural dimension of this decline, alongside other recent structural power shifts in the broader international political economy, such as the rise of China. Against this backdrop, while not denying the continuing importance of US power and neoliberalism within the EU and globally, Strange focuses on the policy significance of the EU's complex 'constellation of governance' during a period of deep crisis and policy change. European integration has contributed to the diffusion of power within world order. But the EU has struggled to utilise its new structural power strategically or to translate this power into global political influence and leverage, particularly in the monetary domain. The consequence has been the further marginalisation of the EU's 'shadow' project of 'social Europe' within open regionalism. But monetary union and the power it brings, Strange contends, remains the best basis on which to build a regional social democracy in Europe and to project it globally. It is also, he contends, the EU's main safeguard against a resurgence of national protectionism.

The book's Part II looks at the transformation of the directly power-seeking Left in the era of neoliberalism. Both Holmes and Lightfoot, and Bailey, highlight the problems that exist in any attempt to construct a social Europe at the EU level. Holmes and Lightfoot argue in Chapter 4 that some aspects of EU integration, in terms of the expansion of the human rights, poverty reduction and environment policy agendas – where the EU can legitimately claim a degree of global leadership – alongside progressive social and employment policies, provide potential platforms for building a popular social Europe. Holmes and Lightfoot foreground party political 'Europeanisation', including increased *cooperation* between Greens and Social Democrats in the building of European-level political parties, as an important form of leadership here. Nevertheless, they also highlight Left party *competition* as well as policy divergence, especially between Greens and Social Democratic Euro-enthusiasts, on the one hand, and Socialist sceptics, on the other, as significant barriers to more decisive and unified Left mobilisations for a different, less neoliberal, form of European integration.

Bailey, on the other hand, outlines in Chapter 5 how the very notion of 'social democracy' has unravelled during the neoliberal era. He argues that attempts to 're-social democratise' at a supranational European level reflect this but still leave social democracy on the back foot. Despite the regionalist turn the trend decline of European social democracy will be maintained if it continues to work within the boundaries of the EU's current political and regulative apparatuses. This can be illustrated by reference to the acceptance by social democratic parties across Europe (with the exception of Sweden) of policies of austerity in the light of the GFC and the euro crisis. For Bailey, this is indicative of and in line with a more long-standing 'downscaling' of reformist and redistributive policies and demands by erstwhile social democratic parties during the neoliberal era under perceived political and economic constraints associated with the EU and neoliberal capitalist globalisation more generally.

If, as Bailey argues, new forms of radical strategy are required to break this downward spiral of social democratic retreat and defensiveness, then Bieler, and Worth provide different ways of understanding where such a transformation might come from. Both argue from a Gramscian perspective that a counter/alternative hegemonic movement can be realised at the European level through a radical overhaul to contest the processes of neoliberalism. The GFC and the euro crisis provide opportunities for such an overhaul. Bieler's Chapter 6 concentrates on trade union activity and strategy, while Worth in Chapter 7 looks more generally at the possibilities for political renewal created by European regionalism. However, both argue that any form of new radical contestation must build upon post-national forms as fostered over the past thirty years by European integration and enlargement.

Part III of the book looks at the potential problems and shortcomings faced by any form of new thinking from the Left focused on the European level. Foregrounding cosmopolitanism, Wilde's Chapter 8 looks in detail at Habermas' influential work on the 'post-national constellation' and its use as a potential model for Left renewal. Wilde argues that while the left can take much from Habermas' visions, his understandings of civic engagement and European unity negate the primacies of class struggle and social solidarity that were central to labour and social welfare advancements in the past. Thus, a future trans-European Left vision should be wary of idealist forms in promoting a new agenda, especially elite fixations on Europe. More substantially, as Robinson argues in his Chapter 9, the reality for any form of European regional project is that Europe is still ultimately a divided entity. The consolidation of Russia and the post-Soviet space has arguably seen a re-drawing of a new East–West boundary across the physical area of Europe. This negates any substantial claims to a truly 'open' regionalism in Europe as strategic political divisions remain that provide significant obstacles for a supranational form of action.

In view of the global financial crisis and its impact on Europe, the Conclusion to this volume by Silvius and Germain reflects back on the different contributions to distil a set of unifying themes around which future critical research on the political economy of Europe, as well as (more importantly) progressive Left political interventions, can hopefully build. The themes – 'ideas, political parties and social movements' – yield, according to Silvius and Germain, a 'deep sociological classification' from which to understand Left politics in and of Europe and its capacity for renewal. Within this framework, the contested role of neoliberalism, as the 'central ideational glue of global capitalism', emerges as the overarching theoretical and practical concern for all the authors. A global crisis and its dramatic impact on Europe signals the need to revisit, clarify and refine left critical theorisations of Europe especially as pioneered by Stephen Gill in developing the conceptual framework of global 'new constitutionalism' as a way to understand the dynamics and trajectory of neoliberal capitalism. While this framework has offered much that is of lasting value in advancing critical understanding of how neoliberal ideas became institutionally anchored and how the global capitalist order functions organisationally, its very strength has also been a barrier to a critical understanding of Europe and the International Political Economy (IPE) and the immanent possibilities for transformation. As Silvius and Germain contend, 'new constitutionalism' has overestimated the ability of neoliberalism to mobilise policy consensus and 'capture' the levers of global power. Nevertheless, recognising these weaknesses opens up a fruitful terrain of engagement between scholars working from within the multiple traditions that make up critical IPE.

In many respects, this volume represents an early attempt to open up this terrain of engagement. In planning the book we, as editors, consciously eschewed any specific Left theoretical narrative or research programme in favour of a more open-ended critical engagement with the political economy of contemporary Europe. This, we believe, better reflects the pluralism of critical theory to which Silvius and Germain point as well as the reality of Europe as a contested and still evolving dialectical political economy, one embroiled in a rapidly changing world order whose future is increasingly uncertain. Our decision to embrace the eclecticism of 'the Left' and of critical theory has arguably been vindicated by the turn of events that has so changed the world since this project first emerged in 2007 out of an earlier edited collection published as a special edition of the journal *Capital and Class* (Strange and Worth 2007). The GFC and the series of crises that have subsequently afflicted the EU did not help the production schedule for this book and we appreciate the patience of its contributing authors. But of course this is of nothing by comparison to the devastating impact the crisis has had and will continue to have on the lives of ordinary working people in Europe and around the globe. On the critical Left, 'pessimism of the intellect' has been pervasive during the neoliberal era but it is now an informed 'optimism of the will' that is most required to secure progressive forms of transformation. We hope this volume offers elements of both and is at least suggestive of how these two pillars of critical praxis identified by Gramsci can be more effectively combined to signpost the possibilities for progressive change.

16   Introduction

References

Van Apeldoorn, B., Horn, L. and Drahokoupil, J. (eds) (2003) *Contradictions and Limits of Neoliberal European Governance – From Lisbon to Lisbon*. Basingstoke: Palgrave.

Beeson, M. (2009) 'Hegemonic Transition in East Asia? The Dynamics of Chinese and American Power', *Review of International Studies*, Vol. 35, 95–112.

Beeson, M. (2010) 'There *Are* Alternatives: The Washington Consensus Versus State Capitalism', in Beeson, M. and Bisley, N. (eds), *Issues in Twenty-first Century World Politics*. Basingstoke: Palgrave Macmillan, 81–92.

Bretherton, C. and Vogler, J. (2006) *The European Union as a Global Actor*, 2nd edn. London: Routledge.

Cohen, B. (2006), 'The Macrofoundations of Monetary Power', in Andrews, D. (ed.), *International Monetary Power*. Ithaca, NY: Cornell University Press, 31–50.

Gamble, A. (2006) 'The European Disunion', *British Journal of Politics and International Relations*, Vol. 8 (1), 34–49.

Gamble, A. (2009) *The Spectre at the Feast: Capitalist Crisis and the Politics of Recession*. Basingstoke: Palgrave Macmillan.

Gamble, A. and Payne, A. (1996) *Regionalism and World Order*. Basingstoke: Macmillan.

Gill, S. (1998) 'European Governance and New Constitutionalism: EMU and Alternatives to Disciplinary Neo-liberalism in Europe, *New Political Economy*, 3 (1), 5–26.

Gill, S. (2008) *Power and Resistance in the New World Order*, 2nd edn. Basingstoke: Palgrave Macmillan.

Harvey, D. (2005) *A Brief History of Neoliberalism*. Oxford: Oxford University Press.

Hettne, B. (1997) 'The Double Movement: Global Markets versus Regionalism', in Cox, R. W. (ed.), *The New Realism: Perspectives on Multilateralism and World Order*. New York: United Nations University Press, 223–44.

Holland, S. (1993) *The European Imperative*. Nottingham: Spokesman.

Milward, A. (1992) *The European Rescue of the Nation State* London: Routledge.

Nairn, T. (1973) *The Left Against Europe?* London: Penguin.

Ruggie, J. G. (1982) 'International Regimes, Transactions and Change: Embedded Liberalism in the Post-war Economic Order', *International Organization*, Vol. 36 (2), 379–415.

Simon, R. (2009) '"Upper Volta with Gas"? Russia as a Semi-Peripheral State', in Worth, O. and Moore, P. (eds), *Globalization and the 'New' Semi-Peripheries*. Basingstoke: Palgrave Macmillan, 120–37.

Simon, R. (2010) 'Passive Revolution, Perestroika and the Emergence of the New Russia', *Capital and Class*, Vol. 34 (3), 429–48.

Strange, G. (2011a) 'China's Post-Listian Rise: Beyond Radical Globalisation

Theory and the Political Economy of Neoliberal Hegemony', *New Political Economy*, iFirst, April.

Strange, G. (2011b) 'Saving the Euro – and Social Democracy', *Social Europe Journal*, www.social-europe.eu.

Strange, G. and Worth, O. (eds) (2007) *Europe and the Left: Capital and Class Special Issue*, Issue 93.

Taylor, A. M. (2011) 'The Financial Rebalancing Act', *Foreign Affairs*, Vol. 90 (4), 1–99.

Wade, R. (2003) 'What Strategies are Viable for Developing Countries Today?: The World Trade Organization and the Shrinking of Development Space', *Review of International Political Economy*, Vol. 10 (4), 621–44.

Worth, O. (2009) 'Unravelling the Putin Myth: Strong or Weak Caesar?', *Politics*, Vol. 29 (1), 53–61.

PART I

European regionalism, neoliberalism and world order

1

US power and the crisis of social democracy in Europe's second project of integration

Magnus Ryner

Before the sub-prime financial crisis, it was commonplace to argue that the completion of the European Monetary Union (EMU), *inter alia*, reinvigorated Europe's 'social models' and challenged US world economic supremacy. The sentiment remained early on in the crisis, when the 'decoupling thesis' construed it as a distinctly American disease. Nothing is more illustrative of this having been an untenable thesis than Charles Kupchan's remarkable U-turn. Having previously been a leading voice postulating the 'European challenge' (2003), he now argues (2010) that the EU is 'slowly dying'.

This extreme oscillation of predictions rests on a failure to appreciate the nature of the structural power relations that underpin transatlantic political economy, which I have critiqued elsewhere (Cafruny and Ryner, 2007a, 2007b). By contrast, this chapter returns to major insights of Poulantzas in order to analyse the implications of Europe's 'second project of integration' for European social democracy. The 'second project of integration' commenced with the Fontainebleau Summit of 1984, which followed in the wake of Mitterand's U-turn in 1983, and facilitated a *modus vivendi* of social and Christian democrats with the neoliberal paradigm of economic management. The cornerstones of this project are the single market, EMU (which followed the realignment of the European Monetary System (EMS) and Exchange Rate Mechanism (ERM) in 1983) and the Lisbon and Cardiff Agendas, most notably containing the Financial Services Action Plan (FSAP). Currently, this project is undergoing desperate crisis management with an uncertain future. What is certain, however, is the marginal role that social democracy has played in this unfolding drama, in no little measure because of the dynamics outlined in this chapter.

European social democracy entails above all two things: first, it entails a 'historic compromise' with capital, based on production and distribution of relative surplus value, which makes mass consumption, welfare state expansion and even a fair degree of decommodification of labour possible. This 'politics of productivity' is essential in ensuring what T. H. Marshall called 'social citizenship', which in turn stabilises 'political' and 'civic' citizenship (*inter alia*, Lipietz, 1987; Esping-Andersen, 1990). This brings us to the second defining feature of European social democracy. As the 'historic compromise' was forged after the Second World War, European social democratic parties became what in German is called *Volksparteien* – that is, 'mass-', 'catch-all', or 'people's' parties. While still depending on an industrial working-class core of support, social democratic parties no longer sought to challenge the political construction of subjects on terms other than class. Instead, they sought to appeal to a broader range of social identities to thus address a broad range of social (economic, religious, linguistic) cleavages, and in this process they sought to mediate between these. The immediate cause for this was consistent defeats at the hands of, for the most part, Christian democratic parties and attempts to copy the latter's winning strategies. In truth, social democratic parties never consistently outperformed Christian democracy in this 'politics of mediation'. The 'established Left' remained a junior partner in most European societies throughout the Second World War period (van Kersbergen, 1995). Be this as it may, the conditions of these two defining features of social democracy have been undermined by the second project of European integration. Hence European social democracy, along with Christian democracy, is facing a crisis from which it seems unlikely to recover. At the same time, the conditions are not ripe in Europe for a neoliberal social hegemony. Consequently, there is a crisis of social representation, which has given increased room of manoeuvre for author-itarianism and populism, in which the Far Right increasingly thrive, either directly through electoral success, or indirectly as established parties address their own crisis of representation by adopting Far-Right policies in a more 'respectable' guise.

The 'interiorisation' of European capital

Caricatures and stereotyped understandings of Poulantzas' social theory have led to its dismissal, and this at great cost for critical analysis (Bruff, 2011). Panitch (1994) has demonstrated that closer attention to a brief essay by Poulantzas (1974) could have avoided the inhibiting 'either-or-isms' in the 'globalisation debate' that follow from poorly posed questions such as 'has the power of the nation state waned as a result of the globalisation of markets?'. In capitalism, state power is always exercised through its structural relation to the capitalist economy, and a necessary function of such power is to reproduce the social conditions of the latter's existence. Hence the question is not so much about the 'retreat' of the state as it is about its structural transformation. What is more, in advanced capitalism, social reproduction is so fundamentally dependent on state intervention that any transnationalisation is dependent on state action for that purpose.[1] 'Globalisation' is fundamentally 'authored' through the sovereignty that resides in nation-states (Panitch, 1994; Panitch and Gindin, 2005).

However, Poulantzas' essay offers not only enduring insights about the role of, and implications for, the state in the transnationalisation of capital. Being one of the very few sustained and comprehensive Marxist analyses of European integration, it also offers clues of a more concrete kind concerning the nature of European integration in a transatlantic context, which are critical for understanding the prospects of European social democracy.

Poulantzas developed his argument in juxtaposition to two dominant tendencies of Marxist theorising at the time. He contrasted his position with the 'Kautskyite ultra-imperialist' position of Sweezy and Baran (1968) and Magdoff (1968) who (as precursors to the strong globalisation thesis), according to Poulantzas, implied that the dominant role of the US among the capitalist countries had eliminated inter-imperialist contradictions to such an extent that the only relevant 'line of demarcation within the imperialist chain is between "centre" and "periphery"' (Poulantzas, 1974: 145). As more empirically careful studies indicate is indeed still the case (Ruigrok and van Tulder, 1995; Hirst and Thompson, 1999; Dicken, 2003), these kind of arguments vastly underestimate the extent to which distinct individual European, and indeed Asian, capitals maintain an autonomous base of capital accumulation in a context of 'monopolistic' (oligopolistic) competition.

But this did not, for Poulantzas, validate the other theoretical tendency, i.e. that which argued that these distinct centres of capital accumulation were indicative of a qualitative continuity of inter-imperialist rivalry between distinct monopoly-capitalist/state blocs that had been characteristic of capitalism since the late nineteenth century. Mandel (1970) had published a provocative book that argued that the development of the forces of production in Europe was resulting in the concentration of a distinct, integrated, European monopoly capital emerging as a rival to American capital. The tendencies towards supranationality in the

European Community (EC) were, for Mandel, superstructural expressions of this. Apart from pointing to obvious gaps and contradictions in Mandel's political analysis (with its curious mix of inter-imperialist continuity on the world level and complete ultra-imperialist transcendence on the European level), Poulantzas argued that Mandel underestimated the qualitative transformations resulting from the US post-Second World War hegemony.

Poulantzas (1974: 161–9) argued that a peculiar European dependence on American capital had developed despite European capital having its own base for capital accumulation. This dependence was due to the novel way in which American capital had become imbricated directly in the social relations of European capital. Clearly influenced by the French industrialist intellectual Jean-Jacques Servan-Schreiber (1967) on this point, Poulantzas pointed towards the particular form of FDI, which the export of American capital had taken after 1945. This was not only a matter of the official percentages of American FDI in Europe (Mandel had used such figures against the Servan-Schreiber thesis). Even though official statistics underestimated these (by not taking into account the extent to which investments through the euro-dollar market and intermediaries actually expressed direct strategic control of American capital), far more significant was the extent to which US direct investments were dominant in leading sectors: that is, sectors that were leading in the (Fordist) socialisation of labour and sectors that fed strategic inputs to other sectors, hence defining the standardisation of base materials and articulating other sectors in terms of sub-contracting arrangements. To this, Poulantzas added the US-centred international concentration of money-capital, which at that time was beginning to have an effect on the terms under which access to credit was granted. Finally, Poulantzas argued that this imbrication of US capital in European capital determined a whole series of corporate 'practices, know-how, modes and rituals to do with the economic sphere', that is, 'ideology' in a broad and materialist sense (Poulantzas, 1974: 164). Hence, while the existence of distinct, competitive, European groupings by no means justified an understanding of the European bourgeoisie as a peripheral 'comprador bourgeoisie', these dependencies nevertheless indicated that we were no longer talking about the 'national bourgeoisie' of old either (or a European supranational bourgeoisie in Mandel's sense). Instead, Poulantzas suggested the category of 'interior bourgeoisie' to describe a European capital that was increasingly articulated with American capital and its distinct American social formation and power bloc (1974: 164–7). The result of this was a complex disarticulation of distinct and autonomous European circuits of (industrial, banking, and commercial) capital and their complex articulation into a US-centred circuit. In addition, this imbrication with American capital increasingly alienated European capital from the specificities of the various European social formations, exacerbating the problems for European states to perform their functions as 'factors of social cohesion': that is, their function of reproducing the distinct European power blocs through the mediation of capital accumulation and social legitimation imperatives.

In retrospect, it can be argued that Poulantzas overestimated the implications of US FDI and underestimated the prospects of European capital developing internally cohesive, distinct as well as competitive groupings. Since the launching of the single market, interlocking directorships of strategic control have assumed less of a transatlantic fix. Instead, more distinctly European configurations, congealing around German capital, can be discerned (van der Pijl *et al.*, 2011). However, at the same time, these European groupings no longer seek – as seemed to be the case in the early 1980s – to compete on the basis of ideologically distinct 'Rhineland-capitalist' accumulation strategies, but rather on the basis of Anglo-American neoliberal strategies (see also van Apeldoorn, 2002: 78–82, 132–57). This is not a 'purely ideological' development. It has rather to do with another development that Poulantzas identified but that has become much more important since his time: the tendential increase of the dominance of financial capital over productive capital (Duménil and Lévy, 2004a: 69–142), even within the very corporate organisation of the latter (Grahl, 2001; Aglietta and Rebérioux, 2005). Hence, while the interpersonal links of directors have a more cohesively European fix, they operate within a context that is determined by US-centred finance-led capital accumulation.

Implications for social democracy

Poulantzas' analysis was undertaken at a turning point. The early stages of 'interiorisation' of European capital into American capital had, if anything, been beneficial for European social democracy. The diffusion of Fordist techniques and norms facilitated propitious conditions for capital accumulation based on relative surplus value and a reorientation of European capital towards *ex ante* integration of mass production with mass consumption. US-led agreements (such as the Bretton Woods, the General Agreement on Tariffs and Trade (GATT), the Marshall Plan), or agreements forged with the good memory of the US (the European Coal and Steel Community (ECSC), the European Economic Community

(EEC)) created the international conditions for this development (Cocks, 1980: 24–35; van der Pijl, 1984: 138–77). However, equally importantly, these agreements deliberately regulated transnationalising capital so as to enable discretionary policy action on the national level, so as to facilitate the regulation of Fordist constellations, and the build-up of the welfare state, in a manner consistent with the distinct character of distinct social formations (Aglietta, 1982: 6–19; Ruggie, 1983: 209–14). In this regard, US hegemony was an *integral hegemony*, which in the process of forging consent redistributed benefits and provided certain autonomy to subordinate social formations.

However, at the time of Poulantzas' analysis, Bretton Woods had just collapsed as the US unilaterally decoupled the dollar from gold in 1971. What is more, whether because of socio-technological exhaustion (Lipietz, 1987: 32–40), or the effects of east Asian competition (Brenner, 2006: 27–40), or both, Fordist capitalism had at this time entered a crisis as productivity and profit rates fell, ushering in a period of 'stagflation'. In retrospect, it is clear that the structural relations between American and European capital that Poulantzas began to discern (albeit misinterpreting the relative significance of its elements) shaped the response to the crisis. US-centred financial capital has decisively favoured a 'flexible-liberal' organisation of 'post-Fordist' productive forces as the pressure of shareholder value and lean corporate organisation has undermined corporate strategies based on 'own resource' (Grahl, 2001: 32, 39), which was an essential precondition for Europe's productivity bargains (labour's acquiescence to technological change, in exchange for training and wage rises *ex ante* integrated with productivity growth). This has made it increasingly difficult to maintain the conditions of relative surplus value augmentation and redistribution, upon which social democracy depends. But in addition, the American state increasingly used the structural power it could mobilise from finance-led transnational capital circuits to displace contradictions from its own transformation to other parts of the world, including Europe. This has intensified contradictions in Europe, since the second project of integration – through the single market, EMU to the FSAP – is constructed on these structures (Gill, 1998), serving Europe's interiorised capital, but this is deeply problematic in relation to what is required to reproduce the terms of legitimacy as defined by the distinct social accords and power blocs of Europe's national societies.

American structural power; European self-limitation

During the post-war era, US monetary and financial power derived in large part from industrial supremacy. But after 1971 such power resulted increasingly from America's extraordinary ability to create capital through credit. The size and power of the US economy made it possible to pursue economic policies according to the logic of domestic politics – a capability connected with the progressive dominance of financial over industrial capital. America's structural power enabled it to transform indebtedness into a strength by creating the necessity to develop financial innovation, thereby enabling the US essentially to tax the resources of major holders of US debt. Expansion of the euro-dollar market 'provided a way of increasing the attractiveness of dollar holdings to foreigners' while facilitating the spread of off-shore financial markets. The US 'sought to avoid undertaking adjustment measures by encouraging foreign governments and private investors to finance these deficits' (Seabrooke, 2001: 10). Beginning in the 1980s the US began to attract massive capital inflows from the rest of the world. By the end of 2004 the US current account deficit had grown to $650 billion. American financial and monetary power, while still institutionalised in the formal monetary regime, is exercised through a combination of 'international passivity and national activism', resulting from the 'interactive embeddedness' of Washington, Wall Street and the 'main-street' of retail credit and debit of the US upper middle class (Seabrooke, 2001: 19; Duménil and Lévy, 2004b).

According to Seabrooke, the origins of US structural power lie in the advantages that the Dollar's *numéraire* status gave US international banks in the Bretton Woods period. This offered these banks the opportunity to monopolise the issue of dollar-denominated liabilities with zero exchange risk, increasingly demanded on the commercial loan, investment services and foreign exchange markets because of the expansion of international trade (Seabrooke, 2001: 48). At the same time, in sharp contrast to most European states, the more market-orientated Fordist settlement in the US encouraged the development of a securitised domestic financial market (encouraging 'ordinary' Americans to invest in the stock market and to take on personal debt). Significantly, the US government created incentives for US banks to set up foreign subsidiaries in order to exercise control over domestic monetary policy while providing reserve currency for international trade and also ensure US control over the emerging transnational financial networks (Seabrooke, 2001: 60). Consequently, US banks came to dominate the euro-dollar markets, which made it possible to expand dollar-denominated assets on a sufficient scale to facilitate international trade without imposing adjustment constraints on the US economy (Seabrooke, 2001: 64, 66–70). The uncertainties of exchange rates and interest rates favoured the US social formation in part because the dollar remained the world's reserve currency and in part because market uncertainties promoted direct financing and favouring the social formation with the 'deepest' and most capitalised domestic financial market. Deep market capitalisation had a social base in the US which was lacking in European states, given their Christian and social democratic social accords. The latter were based on relatively decommodified pay-as-you go incomes-replacement programmes and, following the Bismarckian legacy, were emphatically *not* to have a role as financial actors. Nevertheless, America's highly capitalised market progressively became an attractive place for Japanese and European banks, given the exchange and interest rate risks associated with the debt crisis. Asian and European corporations were progressively attracted towards the US stock market as a source of finance, as an alternative to their traditional house-bank links at home (Seabrooke, 2001: 73–106, 111, 118).

In this context, US assets are seen as less risky. From the large government deficits of Reagan to the massive expansion of private debt under Clinton, and even greater governmental deficits under Bush II, capital accumulation was sustained, despite relatively low yields on capital invested in the US compared to the return of US investments abroad (Duménil and Lévy, 2004b: 664–5), and despite the credit crises in Latin America, the former Communist states and East Asia. Indeed, the American-centered system managed to turn these crises into opportunities to extend their control over weakened and particularistic domestic financial systems (Grahl, 2001: 45–7). Nevertheless, the crisis that started in 2007 points to the limits of this regime of finance-led accumulation. The imperatives of profitable deployment of an ever-expanding mass of capital compelled lending into ever more risky market segments, including sub-prime mortgages. When defaults on these loans began to shatter the assumptions of business plans, and when the complex securitised financial products made it impossible to separate good loans from bad, rapid contagion ensued, resulting in a dramatic loss of confidence in outstanding investments, a destruction of values and a deterioration of balance sheets of the most blue-chip companies that threatened a meltdown of the entire financial system. The result was a massive contraction of liquidity and a deep recession, and only public bailouts on an unprecedented scale could prevent a total collapse.

One central objective of Europe's second project of integration was to copy America's finance-led regime of accumulation (Bieling, 2003).

However, by not challenging a structural configuration that was articulated so as to serve the particular imperatives of the American social formation, the result was a self-limiting mode of regulation. The European economy lacked, *inter alia*, the seigniorage status of the dollar as the world's reserve and vehicle currency and institutional complementarity between the global financial markets and their system of corporate governance and retail finance via 'residual' welfare state arrangements.

The self-limitation was hard-wired into the very monetarist design of EMU, which in turn underpinned its credibility in financial markets. The result has been stagnation of output and productivity growth in the eurozone as a whole (OECD, 2010, Annex Tables 1 and 12), and severe problems of uneven development, that took on an acute and, for EMU, life-threatening form in the course of development of the financial crisis. Economies in the north have pursued 'competitive austerity', whereby export-orientated macroeconomic and wage policy undercut demand in the eurozone as a whole (although at various junctures this or that small economy would enjoy 'success' and hence healthy growth). Insofar as there was any demand pull in the eurozone, it was due to unintended consequences resulting from it not being an optimal currency area. Southern European economies enjoyed lower interest rates resulting from adopting a currency with higher credibility on money markets than their old national currencies. This led to capital inflows in expectation of high returns especially in the housing sector. Since the monetary policy of the European Monetary Bank (ECB) was set also with northern economies in mind, this resulted in relatively lax monetary policies in the south, and current account deficits, financed by further inflows of capital in search of high returns especially in the housing market (*The Economist*, 2009). In the course of the financial crisis and ensuing deep recession, monetary contraction and increased doubt that southern European states could meet their payments led to an acute payments crisis. This threatened the viability of the eurozone and a polarisation between southern and northern member states. At the time of writing, extraordinary emergency loan facilities that explicitly breach ECB rules concerning direct lending to member states, and which have involved the International Monetary Fund (IMF), have stabilised the situation. However, the EU is deeply divided between southern states that have been forced to undertake savage cuts amid widespread mass protests and northern states where southern bailouts are deeply unpopular. The EU is divided between those who argue that the crisis points to the need of fiscal federalism, and those who reduce the problem to a breach of the Stability and Growth Pact (SGP). Commissioner Olli Rehn's current proposed package of economic reforms clearly favour the latter, but one wonders where demand stimulus is going to come from in the future (demand pull from China imports is surely not sufficient) and how future asymmetric shocks are going to be addressed.

Welfare retrenchment and the crisis of social democracy

The foregoing account might raise the question of why the EU actively and at their own volition constructed a single market and monetary union that was consistent with Europe's subordination to America. This is less of a puzzle than at first sight, if we follow another major insight of Poulantzas (1976, 1978), namely that the state is not a 'thing' but rather a particular crystallisation of social relations manifesting itself as a complex ensemble of distinct state apparatuses, and that the configuration of this ensemble itself reflects prevailing power relations. As the 'factor of social cohesion' in a social formation that mediates capital accumulation and legitimation imperatives, the state must counteract the potentially disintegrative functions of the commodity-economic logics in order 'to save capitalism from itself' through practices of 'socialisation' (what Marx, in the *Grundrisse*, called *Vergesellschaftung* (Marx, 1857[1973]: 161, 832, cited in van der Pijl, 1998: 8–21)). However, the state does not do so in a neutral manner, but rather state socialisation reflects, *inter alia*, the prevailing structure and power relations in the capitalist economy, as well as prevailing power relations among social forces in society at large, and these forces determine the configuration of the ensemble of apparatuses that constituted the state.

In this context, the central role given to the European Commission, and especially the Competition Commission and Directorate General in the forging of the Single Market, and central bankers in the forging of EMU, is of central importance. Given Europe's problem with competitiveness and inflation in the 1970s (Sandholtz and Zysman, 1989), an overarching 'ideology of authorisation' (Therborn, 1980) assigned such state agencies a monopoly of competence in addressing these questions (van Apeldoorn, 2002: 69–71). These apparatuses have always been particularly geared towards capital accumulation imperatives, with a particular emphasis on transatlantic openness, as opposed to mass legitimation imperatives (Cocks, 1980: 29). If one adds the direct agential pressure that organisations such as the European Roundtable of Industrialists exerted, increasingly dominated by Atlanticist corporations (van Apeldoorn, 2002: 142–57; MacCartney, 2010), it is no wonder that the design has primarily been in accordance with the interests of Europe's interiorised transnational capital. Its room of manoeuvre for mergers, and its healthy profit rates, that contrast sharply with the sluggish figure of Europe's national accounts, also suggests that these interests have been well served (European Commission, 1996). In this context we should also add that monetarist monetary policy norms were integral to the 'social mercantilist' stance of the economically most powerful state in the EC, West Germany, and had served to anchor a corporatist incomes policy based on export-led growth of industrial input goods, which reproduced a rather labour-inclusive welfare state in that country (Lankowski, 1982).

The active participation of European social democracy in the second European project of integration has also been based on the premise that 'progressive competitiveness' strategies, such as that of West Germany in the 1980s, are sustainable in the long term and that they provide the basis of a general concept of governance. However, while uneven development makes it possible to pursue such strategies in certain locales in certain conjunctures – apart from West Germany one can point to the Dutch 'Polder Model' in the early 1990s, the 'Nordic models' in the late 1990s and early 2000s, and social policy expansion in Portugal and Spain on the back of capital inflows from their housing boom, aggregate development trends clearly point to the limits of these policies. For the most part, they are 'beggar-thy-neighbour' policies in the sense that they undercut aggregate demand growth and promote surplus production. What is more, as Dutch and above all German developments in the late 1990s showed, these corporatist growth strategies are to an increasing extent unstable. Stagnant aggregate output and productivity growth has also gone hand in hand with mass unemployment as well as with a marked retrenchment of welfare state entitlements in Europe (Korpi, 2003: 592–7).

The concurrence of increased profit rates and room of expansion of mergers for European transnational corporations (TNCs), with declining growth and output rates, high unemployment and welfare state retrenchment, is an expression of current EU arrangements serving a European capital, increasingly interiorised with American capital, but also increasingly alienated from European social formations. This in turn feeds into the second dimension of the crisis of European social democracy, namely the narrowing room for manoeuvre for its politics of mediation, whereby it has engaged in electoral political competition with Christian democracy, in order to maximise an electoral appeal among the range of groups that constitute the electorate. This competition has been essential for the reproduction of social–political legitimacy in Europe, and the narrowing scope to pursue this competition goes beyond social democracy and expresses a crisis of political society as a whole.

Strains in the politics of mediation

Successful political and electoral strategies of mass parties have been based on the management of the various dimensions of socio-political cleavages (especially of class, religion and language). However, as economic growth slows, and as welfare state retrenchment proceeds, the scope of such politics of mediation is restricted, thereby reducing the range of social forces that can be integrated into the political mainstream. This in turn requires a change in the politics of mediation itself. Parties are compelled either to redefine the terms of redistributive coalitions, or to change the politico-economic framework, or sometimes both. Here we show how this political dynamic has unfolded in Germany and France.

It is exceedingly difficult to implement the abstract and uncompromising neoliberal reforms of 'flexibility'. Such reforms contravene the very nature of compromise and mediation, and threaten highly entrenched status groups as well as the claims of social protection of the most vulnerable in society. Electorally, implementing these reforms is a hazardous exercise for political movements whose success has been based on constructing complex and composite coalitions such as the Social Democratic Party (SPD), and quintessentially, the Christian Democratic Union (CDU) in Germany (Ryner, 2003). French Presidentialism seems to give the state more 'executive authority' to take 'hard decisions' in a 'Bonapartist' mould. However, there are powerful counter-tendencies: the 'dual executive' nature of the French system; electoral laws that encourage the formation of composite coalitions; the semi-autonomous status given to professional groups and unions in the management of French social insurance, connected to the 'Jacobin' tradition of street protests when the executive goes 'too far.' As the mass demonstrations of 1995, 2005 and 2006 showed, French unions and other social movements have developed skills in strategically harnessing such outbursts (*'greviculture'*) (Ross, 2004: 95).

Since the 1983 Mitterrand 'U-turn', French politics has been characterised by a series of neoliberalisation and welfare retrenchment thrusts that have provoked organised resistance, which has in turn led to reversals, symbolic calls for a compensatory 'social dimension' to European restructuring and a European 'economic government,' and more cautious retrenchment by stealth, which increasingly challenges the incomes-replacement principle to essential to French conceptions of Republican solidarity and social citizenship (Beland and Hansen, 2000). This cycle has produced some rather spectacular phenomena, including periodic mass demonstrations, Jospin's surprise election as Prime Minister in 1997, his equally surprising ousting in the first round Presidential elections in 2002 by Jean-Marie Le Pen and the 'non' in the referendum on the EU Constitution. The politics of austerity and retrenchment has made *Front Nationale* a mainstay in French political society, with strong support in the white French working class, and it has fragmented the Left. President Sarkozy's expulsion of the Roma in France indicates the temptation of playing xenophobic cards in French politics amid political paralysis and unpopularity. France has returned to a political economy of stagnation, where neoliberal reform is resisted by strong social groups, but the commitments of the EMU and the impossibility of economic nationalism prevent demand-led recovery.

France has always had an ambivalent and difficult relationship with monetarism, the EMS and EMU because of the difficulties of mediating its economic rationality with social and political legitimacy. French monetary politics is often characterised in terms of a 'long game', where France acquiesces to monetarist integration pragmatically from a defensive position of weakness, in order to push for further integration in a more interventionist direction at opportune moments (Clift, 2003). But this 'long game' affirms a sort of post-modern neoliberalism, where the promise of a 'social Europe' remains forever absent and affirms its opposite.

Germany had a much less problematic relationship with the EMS and EMU. However, since the late 1990s the German mass parties have found it increasingly difficult to pursue successful electoral and governance strategies that reproduce their coalitions. The CDU and the SPD fought over the allegiance of east German voters, still in the throes of post-socialist restructuring, and white-collar middle classes, both of which value their social benefits, protections and pensions, but also support 'economic competence'. Hence, the parties have tried to appeal to these groups together with their core constituencies (the blue-collar working class in the case of the SPD and market-orientated business groups, 'value conservatives' and Catholic workers in core regions in the case of the CDU). The cutbacks of transfer payments by Kohl in 1996 and 97, as Germany faced pressures to meet the Maastricht convergence criteria, enabled the SPD to win the votes of the latter groups in 1998. However, the abandonment of Lafontaine's Keynesianism effectively deepened Kohl's retrenchment. The SPD lost power even in its 'safest' state of North Rhine-Westphalia and suffered massive losses of party membership, interrupted only temporarily by Schröder's tactical opposition to the US invasion of Iraq. Nostalgia for stability and the 'competence factor' propelled the CDU first into tenuous leadership of a Grand Coalition and then, amid the financial crisis, a return to coalition with the FDP. However, current malaise in opinion polls indicates how difficult it has become for incumbent mass parties to retain popularity; and it is not the SPD that has benefited from this. Currently the two mass parties poll about 55 per cent of the electorate together. In Germany, it is rather the Left Party and currently the Greens that are filling the representational vacuum. But also here, the Far Right has shown in State elections that they should not be discounted as a political force.

The fragmentation in Germany and France appears to be part of a broader trend away from the established parties in EU member states (Mair, 2006). Examples abound of populist mavericks who thrive in the political vacuum left when economic stagnation and welfare retrenchment sharpen policy tradeoffs that make the appeal to multifarious groups increasingly difficult. Charismatic populist political figures, claiming to speak directly to 'the people', and not through any official party and movement, have been increasingly successful in playing on people's fear amid increased uncertainties and exposures to risks (real and imagined): Haider in Austria; Fortuyn and Wilders in the Netherlands; Berlusconi in Italy and the range of Far-Right parties that have entered Parliament in Scandinavia.

Conclusion

This chapter has argued that the consolidation of Europe's subordination to a US-centred finance-led accumulation regime, as implied in Europe's second project of integration, has undermined the prospects of relative surplus value augmentation in Europe, and that this is undermining the material basis of European social democracy. This, in turn, is undermining the prospects of European social democratic parties, along with the Christian democratic ones, to pursue their 'politics of mediation'. However, the chapter has also argued that there is a deeper structural context for this, namely the 'interiorisation' of European capital with American capital and the attendant alienation of the former from the distinct European social formations. I have used insights from Poulantzas to make this point.

Of course, social formations are not static, political parties even less so. Indeed, one can interpret the 'Third Way' turn of European social democracy precisely as an attempt to respond to the difficulties entailed in the 'politics of mediation'. However, the fortunes of the administrations of Schröder in Germany, Jospin in France and Wim Kok in the Netherlands point to the difficulties in appealing to the unemployed, industrial working-class interests, welfare state constituencies, as well as the potential 'winners' in Europe's articulation with US-centred, finance-led, accumulation. If anything, Christian democratic and centre-right parties are more likely to be successful in reconfiguring their politics of mediation in a manner that is successful in this context, and the current political absence of social democracy is symptomatic of their failure to do so (Ryner, 2010).

Note

1 Since the late nineteenth century, and the breakdown of extended agrarian-based extended family and communal networks, the national welfare state has served essential reproductive functions for capitalist society (Wilensky, 1975; Bendix, 1977; Therborn, 1987). Even beyond the rather obvious case of the tax system, it is hard to find evidence of these mechanisms geared towards mediating antagonisms between classes, and distancing political rule overtly from the class structure, decisively abandoning their distinctly national 'spatio-temporal' fixes (Panitch and Gindin, 2005: 102–4).

References

Aglietta, M. (1982) 'World Capitalism in the Eighties', *New Left Review*, Vol. 136, 5–41.

Aglietta, M. and Rebérioux, A. (2005) *Corporate Governance Adrift: A Critique of Shareholder Value.* Cheltenham: Edward Elgar.

Van Apeldoorn, B. (2002) *Transnational Capitalism and the Struggle Over European Integration.* London and New York: Routledge.

Beland, D. and Hansen, R. (2000) 'Reforming the French Welfare State: Solidarity, Social Exclusion and the Three Crises of Citizenship', *West European Politics*, Vol. 23 (1), 47–64.

Bendix, R. (1977) *Nation Building and Citizenship.* Berkeley, CA: University of California Press.

Bieling, H.-J. (2003) 'Social Forces in the Making of the New European Economy: The Case of Financial Market Integration', *New Political Economy*, Vol. 8 (2), 203–24.

Brenner, R. (2006) *The Economics of Global Turbulence.* London: Verso.

Bruff, I. (2011) 'The Relevance of Nicos Poulantzas for Contemporary Debates on "The International"', *International Politics* (forthcoming).

Cafruny, A. and Ryner, M. (2007a) 'Monetary Union and the Transatlantic and Social Dimensions of Europe's Crisis', *New Political Economy*, Vol. 12 (2), 141–65.

Cafruny, A. and Ryner, M. (2007b) *Europe at Bay: In the Shadow of US Hegemony.* Boulder, CO: Lynne Rienner.

Clift, B. (2003) 'The Changing Political Economy of France: *Dirigisme* under

Duress', in Cafruny, A. and Ryner, M. (eds), *A Ruined Fortress? Neoliberal Hegemony and Transformation in Europe.* Lanham, MD: Rowman & Littlefield, 173–200.

Cocks, P. (1980) 'Towards a Marxist Theory of European Integration', *International Organization*, Vol. 34 (1), 3–40.

Dicken, P. (2003) *Global Shift: Reshaping and Global Economic Map in the 21ˢᵗ Century*, 4ᵗʰ edn. London: Sage.

Duménil, G. and Lévy, D. (2004a) *Capital Resurgent: Roots of the Neoliberal Revolution.* Cambridge, MA: Harvard University Press.

Duménil, G. and Lévy, D. (2004b) 'The Economics of US Imperialism at the Turn of the 21ˢᵗ Century', *Review of International Political Economy*, Vol. 11 (4), 657–76.

The Economist (2009) *Special Report on the Euro Area: 'One Size Fits None'*, 11 June.

Esping-Andersen, G. (1990) *The Three Worlds of Welfare Capitalism.* Cambridge: Polity.

European Commission (2006) *The European Economy.* Brussels: European Commission, Spring.

Gill, S. (1998) 'European Governance and New Constitutionalism: Economic and Monetary Union and Alternatives to Disciplinary Neoliberalism in Europe', *New Political Economy*, Vol. 3 (1), 5–26.

Grahl, J. (2001) 'Globalized Finance: The Challenge to the Euro', *New Left Review*, Vol. 8, 23–47.

Hirst, P. and Thompson, G. (1999) *Globalization in Question*, 2ⁿᵈ edn. Cambridge: Polity.

Van Kersbergen, K. (1995) *Social Capitalism: Study of Christian Democracy and the Welfare State.* London: Routledge.

Korpi, W. (2003) 'Welfare State Regress in Western Europe: Politics, Institutions, Globalization and Europeanization', *Annual Review of Sociology*, Vol. 29, 589–609.

Kupchan, C. (2003) *The End of the American Era: US Foreign Policy and the Geopolitics of the Twenty-First Century.* New York: Vintage Press.

Kupchan, C. (2010) 'As Nationalism Rises, Will the European Union Fall?', *Washington Post*, August 29, www.washingtonpost.com/wp-dyn/content/article/2010/08/27/AR2010082702138.html?referrer=emailarticle (accessed 28 September 2010).

Lankowski, C. (1982) 'Modell Deutschland and the International Regionalization of the West German State', in Markovits, A. (ed.), *The Political Economy of West Germany: Modell Deutschland.* New York: Praeger, 90–115.

Lipietz, A. (1987) 'The Globalization of the General Crisis of Fordism, 1967–84', in Holmes, J. and Leys, C. (eds), *Frontyard/Backyard.* Toronto: Between the Lines, 23–55.

MacCartney, H. (2010) *Variegated Neoliberalism: EU Varieties of Capitalism and International Political Economy.* London: Routledge.

Mair, P. (2006) 'Ruling the Void: The Hollowing of Western Democracy', *New Left Review*, Vol. 42, 25–51

Magdoff, H. (1968) *The Age of Imperialism*. New York: Monthly Review Press.

Mandel, E. (1970) *Europe versus America? Contradictions of Imperialism*. London: New Left Books.

Marx, K. (1857 [1973]) *The Grundrisse: Foundations of the Critique of Political Economy*. New York: Vintage Press.

OECD (2003) *Economic Surveys: The Euro-Area 2002*. Paris: OECD.

OECD (2010) *Economic Outlook*, 87. Paris: OECD.

Panitch, L. (1994) 'Globalisation and the State', in Miliband, R. and Panitch, L. (eds), *The Socialist Register*. London: Merlin Press, 60–93.

Panitch, L. and Gindin, S. (2005) 'Superintending Global Capital', *New Left Review*, Vol. 35, 101–23.

Van der Pijl, K. (1984) *The Making of an Atlantic Ruling Class*. London: Verso.

Van der Pijl, K. (1998) *Transnational Classes and International Relations*. London and New York: Routledge.

Van der Pijl, K., Holman, O. and Raviv, O. (2011) 'The Resurgence of German Capital in Europe: EU Integration and the Restructuring of Atlantic Networks of Interlocking Directorates after 1991', *Review of International Political Economy*, 18 (3), 384–408.

Poulantzas, N. (1974) 'Internationalisation of Capitalist Relations and the Nation State', *Economy and Society*, Vol. 3 (2), 145–79.

Poulantzas, N. (1976) 'The Capitalist State: A Reply to Miliband and Laclau', *New Left Review*, Vol. 95, 63–83.

Poulantzas, N. (1978) *Political Power and Social Classes*. London: New Left Books.

Ross, G. (2004) 'Monetary Integration and the French Model', in Martin, A. and Ross, G. (eds), *Euros and Europeans*. Cambridge: Cambridge University Press, 76–102.

Ruggie, J. G. (1983) 'International Regimes, Transactions and Change: Embedded Liberalism in the Postwar Economic Order', in Krasner, S. (ed.), *International Regimes*. Ithaca, NY: Cornell University Press, 195–232.

Ruigrok, W. and Tulder, R. van (1995) *The Logic of International Restructuring*. London: Routledge.

Ryner, M. (2003) 'Disciplinary Neoliberalism, Regionalization and the Social Market in German Restructuring', in Cafruny, A. and Ryner, M. (eds), *A Ruined Fortress? Neoliberal Hegemony and Transformation in Europe*. Lanham, MD: Rowman & Littlefield, 201–30.

Ryner, M. (2010) 'An Obituary for the Third Way: Social Democracy and the Financial Crisis in Europe', *The Political Quarterly*, 81 (4), 554–63.

Sandholtz, W. and Zysman, J. (1989) '1992: Recasting the European Bargain', *World Politics*, Vol. 42 (1), 95–128.

Seabrooke, L. (2001) *US Power in International Finance: The Victory of Dividends*. Basingstoke: Palgrave Macmillan.

Servan-Schreiber, J.-J. (1967) *Le défi americain.* Paris: Denoel.

Sweezy, P. and Baran, P. (1968) *Monopoly Capital.* Harmondsworth: Penguin.

Therborn, G. (1980) *The Ideology of Power and the Power of Ideology.* London: Verso.

Therborn, G. (1987) 'The Welfare State and Capitalist Markets', *Acta Sociologica,* Vol. 30 (3/4), 237–54.

Wilensky, H. (1975) *The Welfare State and Equality: Structural and Ideological Roots of Public Expenditure.* Berkeley, CA: University of California Press.

2

The discursive construction of neoliberalism: the EU and the contested substance of European economic space

Ben Rosamond

This chapter considers the relationship between the EU and neoliberalism, and in particular the question of whether there is something ineluctably neoliberal about European integration. The thesis put forward here emphasises the contingent character of neoliberal Europe. This claim is made via the development of an argument about the 'European economy' as a recent discursive construction that tends towards, but does not necessarily imply, the naturalisation of neoliberal ideas, policies and practices in the EU context.

While EU neoliberalism requires the normalisation of the idea of European economic space, that normalisation requires rather more than the simple establishment of that space as an object in discourse. The chapter argues that for neoliberal logics of necessity and appropriateness to 'kick in' and tighten, (a) the space must be knowable and measurable and (b) that knowable space must be endowed with a 'personality' – that is, technical and normative substance that determines both its internal government and its external projections. With the EU case in mind, the chapter proposes a framework for thinking about the discursive construction of 'the economy' in terms of three phases: space–legibility–personality.

Moreover, the chapter argues that the discursive construction of space–legibility–personality of the European economy is not the knowing project of an *a priori* rational agent (as is presumed in much of the historical political sociology of market making). In the EU case, the emergence of an imagined spatial scalar order and its governing rationalities are co-constitutive, so that the emergent space of governance is constructed discursively, statistically and normatively in ways that enable the governance of that space to be undertaken by a particular (also) emergent agent. As such, while rationalities can tighten in a depoliticised neoliberal direction around space–legibility–personality, there is no necessary association because of that relative autonomy. This suggests some potential (albeit limited) for the construction of alternative possibilities for the European economy in terms of its legibility and personality, not least because the arrival of the 'European economy' as an object in discourse brings to the fore some very acute concerns about legitimacy.

The politics of EU neoliberalism

On what grounds might we argue that the EU is inevitably bound up with neoliberalism? There are two main arguments that suggest such a deep 'structural' relationship. The first derives from a series of observations about the institutional design of the EU and the 'democratic deficit' therein. While executive authority in key areas of economic governance has been transferred to the European level, runs the argument, mechanisms to ensure political accountability have not followed suit. Moreover, within the EU's institutional configuration there is no formal space for the constitution of political opposition and thus for effective contestation around matters of supranational economic policy. These points are fundamental to Gill's well-known designation of the EU as a prominent example of what he labels 'new constitutionalism': the tendency to 'separate economic policies from broad political accountability' (Gill, 2001: 47). The suggestion is not simply that the democratic lacuna in the EU's institutional design provides an opening for neoliberalism, but that there is a functional relationship between the institutional set-up and the types of policy that can be delivered. Neoliberalism thrives in the context of depoliticisation and from this standpoint the EU is a form of institutionalised depoliticisation. As well as disallowing effective contestation, the EU's institutional design lacks a central authority capable of engaging in redistributive or interventionist activity. It also facilitates alliance building between purposive institutions acting on behalf of neoliberal logics and transnational market actors seeking to develop a corresponding transnational market regime (van Apeldoorn, 2002, see also Bieler and Morton, 2001; Bieler, 2006).

The second argument suggests that, starting with the Treaty of Rome (1957), the EU's treaties are themselves charters for neoliberalism. Although the most conspicuous neoliberal moments in the EU's history date from the mid 1980s – the emphasis in the 1986 Single European Act

(SEA) on the completion of the internal market and the monetary union provisions of the Maastricht Treaty of European Union (1992) – this position would argue that the affiliation to a continental market order overseen by a negative, regulatory form of authority is deeply inscribed into the logic of European integration. The treaties are, of course, partly responsible for the institutional design described above, but have also been used by activist supranational institutions – notably the European Court of Justice (ECJ) and the Commission – as authoritative texts on which can be premised neoliberal moves.

Taken together these arguments would seem to suggest that neoliberalism is the only mode of governance possible for the EU. The treaties inscribe neoliberal logics into institutional design and policy substance, while the institutional design itself supposes neoliberalism to be the primary purpose and rationale of EU economic governance. There are, of course, several arguments to contest or qualify these views. For example, one strand in the literature draws attention to the tendency of the Commission to use its right of initiative to expand the EU's policy remit beyond the scope defined in the treaties. While this institutional activism could be used to account for the push towards greater neoliberalism, there are also cases – environmental policy and social policy being prominent examples – where the resultant EU policy competence institutionalises counter-neoliberal tendencies at the supranational level (Jabko, 2006). Likewise, scholars of the ECJ have noted the Court's tendency to use its jurisprudential powers to engage in expansive readings of the treaties (Weiler, 1991, 2002). Again, this could be understood as accelerating neoliberal tendencies. The assertion of the supremacy of European Community law over national laws could be understood as a means to depoliticise European economic governance by disallowing national-level forms of intervention to counter the thrust of EU marketmaking.[1] But the ECJ has also been notable for its habit of reading fundamental human rights provisions into the treaties (van Bogdandy, 2000). The consequence of this has been the gradual redefinition of the individual subject of EC law from a 'worker' within a single market space to a more rounded conception of a transborder 'citizen' endowed with a broader repertoire of social and political rights (Kostakopoulou, 2008). Finally the gradual growth of the European Parliament's legislative powers and recent (albeit incomplete) attempts to improve the democratic quality of EU institutions suggest that there is some scope for positive reform of the EU's institutional design.

An alternative view is Majone's (ultimately normative) defence of the EU regulatory state – a device for the delivery of a Pareto optimal market order – and the thin concept of output legitimacy on which it depends (Majone, 1994, 1996, 2005, 2009; see also Moravcsik, 2002 and see Wincott, 2006 for a critique). This also raises the question of how it is possible for such a thinly legitimated project to become the dominant form of European economic governance as well as such an apparently attractive description of it. This is important because the implication of academic knowledge production in that very move is stark (see Rosamond, 2008). Even if we treat it as a purely analytical category, the idea of the regulatory state is a largely static description of what the EU – as a form of state – has become. What is missing is a clear sense of how it has become. In short, we need to move from the analysis of pre-given objects (the EU regulatory state/the European economy) to *how* those objects emerge, while avoiding the static rationalist presumptions of orthodox political science (Korzeniewicz *et al.*, 2004).

Aside from Majone's position, these diverse counter-arguments offer largely agent-driven accounts of the EU's development in contrast to the more structural biases of the 'neoliberalism-as-inevitable' position. The standard literature on the evolution of the EU offers some guidance on how we might think about such processes.

Intergovernmentalist accounts (Moravcsik, 1998) explain the EU's neoliberal character through the convergence of domestically derived national preferences in the key member states. Supranationalist or neofunctionalist scholars propose that supranational governance capacity has an evolution dynamic autonomous of the preferences of member state principals. The drift of economic governance competence is explained instead by the convergent preferences of economic agents operating in an emergent transnational space. These powerful economic agents demand regulation and pre-existing supranational institutions, following a reasonably classic Weberian script of institutional purpose, offer to supply that regulation (Stone Sweet and Sandholtz, 1998).

This latter variant suffers from the problem of presuming pre-existing institutions that are ready made, as it were, to enact neoliberalism or to exercise a pre-given preference for the securing of greater regulatory scrutiny. More precisely, the presumption makes a straightforward linkage between an institutional interest in more Europe/the expansion of competence and the supply of neoliberalism. This is neat, but it leaves unexplained and undertheorised the mechanisms of that linkage. Together, these standard views are more interested in the dynamics of institutional evolution (and which self-interested agents are primarily responsible for the institutional form taken by the EU) than the substance of what these institutions do or how they come to be.

While not denying the gravity of claims about the democratic lacuna and treaty inscriptions and not disputing the usefulness of some of the orthodox literature on institutional evolution, this chapter suggests that what is missing from these analyses is an account of the spatial evolution of EU neoliberalism, and in particular of the discursive construction of European economic space as a precondition for the establishment of neoliberal logics.

The economy/economic space

To invoke the idea of the existence of a 'European economy' is not a simply to reiterate a material fact. Relatively little attention has been paid to the idea of 'the economy' as a political construct. To deploy the term 'the economy' as a noun is to make a series of claims about a spatial transactional arena. 'The economy' is populated by certain types of subjects (firms, consumers) who do certain types of things. It often comes with a qualifying adjective (British, German, American, European), which suggests some sort of boundedness (if not full-blown territoriality) and as such is frequently an object of comparison through concepts like 'competitiveness'. The notion of comparison requires that economies are knowable via the establishment of common measurement benchmarks and knowability presumes governability. So 'the economy' is a space that can be subjected to some kind of regulatory authority. It might be argued that through this very definition and terminology, 'the economy' as a construct represents the privileging of certain activities over others and thus presents itself as a space that can only best be governed through certain forms of economic rationality (this is suggested in Mitchell, 2005). Following from this is the logic of 'bracketing off the economy' (van der Pijl, 2006) as a depoliticised space in which the contingent, the normative and the political become instead necessary, technical and uncontroversial.

This would suggest a need to (re)activate a political economy where there is no longer a foundational fallacy of the economy as an autonomous quasi-metaphysical system with its own endogenous, timeless and inherently rational laws of motion from which follow certain non-negotiable and irrefutable logics (the point is argued variously by Daly, 1991; de Goede, 2003; Watson, 2005). Instead, argues Jessop, especially when considering changing forms of the state, the economy should be viewed as 'an imaginatively narrated system that is accorded specific boundaries, conditions of existence, typical economic agents and counter tendencies, and a distinctive overall dynamic' (1999: 2). This suggests the need for attention to those acts of 'imaginative narration' as well as recognition of the continued negotiability of the economy's tendencies (alternative spatial or scalar conceptions; alternative modes of economic rationality). Jessop's argument offers numerous possible pathways (see also Jessop, 2006). Two linked aspects in particular serve our purposes here.

Of particular interest in this chapter are the rationalities that follow from first the social fact of 'the economy' as a distinctive space and second 'the economy's' knowability. On the first of these, as already suggested, the claim of the existence of a particular spatial/scalar entity (such as 'the European economy') brings with it, at the very least, the subsidiary claim that the space can be acted upon or governed in some way. In other words, 'the economy' is part of the spatiality of the state or 'state space' (Brenner, 2004) and any discussion of 'the European economy' should be located in broader discussions of the changing geography of capitalism, particularly in terms of movements away from 'inherited nationalized and territorialized formations of political economic space' (Brenner, 2004: 5). Put more crudely, does 'the European economy' as a shift in state-space necessarily bring forth neoliberalism and are EU forms of governance necessarily neoliberal forms of governance?

On the second point, the key to a particular economic space becoming a social fact is its 'knowability'. Historically, considerable political energy has been expended upon both the definition of appropriate spaces to be governed and the development of justifications for how and why such spaces should be governed (Walters and Haahr, 2005). As Thrift (2005: 134) puts it 'to govern it is necessary to render visible the space over which government is to be exercised'. The point is argued most vividly by Scott (1998), who talks in terms of spaces being rendered 'legible' for governance. Such governing rationalities are produced through discourse and the deployment of various technologies of accountancy and measurement. So economies are both discursively and statistically constructed. Measurement through forms of accountancy and statistics renders a space knowable and contributes to its naturalisation. A space acquires legibility if it can be measured and such intellectual technologies 'render aspects of existence amenable to inscription and calculation' (Miller and Rose, 1990: 1) and establish the economy as an object of knowledge (Miller and Rose, 1990: 12; Barry, 1993). Statistical practices are methodologically central to the process of 'framing' through which policy contexts are defined and from which the choice of policy possibilities follows.

Both of these steps, the establishment of economic space/the economy as social fact and the attribution of measurable legibility to it, are bound up with serious questions about whether both are in and of themselves neoliberal steps. On the face of it, both might be regarded as necessary conditions for the achievement of EU neoliberalism. But they are perhaps not sufficient conditions. For example, if the relevant spatial field is an intersubjectively known and accepted ('backgrounded') European economy, then in some crucial ways it becomes difficult to make arguments that draw upon versions of national political economy. Yet to successfully construct an economy as neoliberal requires that knowable economic space to be accorded the 'personality traits' that might be expected of a neoliberal agora. 'Personality' in this sense refers to two elements (technical and normative) of an economy in two domains (internal governance and external representation). It refers to understandings of what is programmatically possible/technically necessary to govern the knowable economic space, as well as what must and should be done in terms of behaviour to the outside and forms of action that the economy might become involved with. This last point brings home the state-spatial character of economies. An economy is not simply a passive space to be acted upon. Once known and governed, it can acquire agent-like properties, particularly as a carrier of certain types of values that can be represented externally in different scalar-spatial arena. The process of discursively constructing an economic space tends to narrow and tighten what is possible within that space. If we think about this as a three-stage process (space–legibility–personality), the most open is the first, the actual naming of the economic space. This is a space that is potentially knowable. The second (legibility) phase renders the space known (accounted for, measured). In the third phase the space becomes known *as*. The first phase leaves open for the potentially knowable space all manner of models of political economy and a wide variety of technical and normative logics. A space becomes governable as it becomes knowable and the statistical construction of 'the economy' is of clear import here, not least because it begins to define both who the authentic/authorised subjects of this economic space are and what kind of subjects they are to be in law. But the assignment of precise subjectivities cannot really come until the third phase (the personality phase), when the programmatic and ethical substance of the economy is settled (Figure 2.1).

The tightening of technical and normative logics within 'the economy' together with its increasing knowability, is an enabler of 'government'. In addition, Figure 2.1 perhaps implies a clear sequencing over time through which the discursive construction of economic space takes place. Rather the likelihood is of a messy chronology. The sequencing implied is not about chronology, but about the tightening of rationalities and the consequent naturalisation of the economic space.

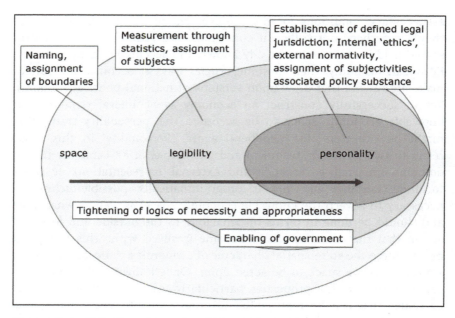

Figure 2.1 The discursive construction of European space

'The European economy'

An application of this type of framework to the case of the EU brings forth a fairly colossal research agenda that would be built around, *inter alia*, a genealogical approach to discourses that seek to naturalise the idea of 'the European economy' in one way or another, a history of European economic statistics (and the manufacture and reproduction of European statistics by others), a detailed account of the ways in which discourses of European economic integration bring forth particular subjectivities and an analysis of the recursive relationship between discourses of the European economy and forms of academic knowledge.

The chapter's ambition is necessarily more modest and as such its conclusions can only be provisional and indicative. Nevertheless, one thing is striking: the relative recency of the notion of 'the European economy' within the policy discourses of European integration. Indeed, the appearance of the term very clearly coincides with the punctuated shift from the mid 1980s into what Cafruny and Ryner (2007) call the 'second integration project' (see also Buch-Hansen and Wigger, 2010). The more or less precise coincidence of the emergence of a particular framing discourse (of 'the European economy') in the Commission with the emergence of a neoliberal push in the mid 1980s (Rosamond,

2012) is, of course, highly suggestive of some kind of functional fit between communicative discourse and practice. It is tempting to read the discursive innovation of the 'European economy' as epiphenomenal to the broader material restructuring of the European political economy under conditions of globalisation. Without wishing to dispute large chunks of this position, the argument here will not presume such an instrumental connection between discourse and material conditions and powerful social forces (see also Pistor, 2005). Rather the intention is to suggest that the emergence of discourses of 'the European economy' is at least partly a product of a ongoing 'governmental project' in which a putative governing agent positions itself as *the* rationally necessary and appropriate governing agent in the context of a newly emergent space of governance. To make this argument, the chapter identifies two broad phases of communicative discourse around European economic integration.

Phase 1: the pre-history of the European economy

Prior to the mid 1980s, the Commission and its associated advisory and working groups deployed a quite different conception of European economic integration within their communicative discourse. Integration was spoken of as a project under construction that was conforming to/ would follow a stage-by-stage logic. The idea, which owed much to the pioneering economic theory of Balassa (1962) and shared a striking resemblance to some of the arguments being developed by neofunctionalist political science theories at the time, proposed that integration progressed through a sequential process where the achievement of one stage would generate pressures towards the accomplishment of the next. Thus a customs union would beget a common market, which would in turn generate logics in favour of monetary union. Throughout the 1960s and 1970s, the Commission's communicative discourse on economic integration tended to express concern that progress towards the goals announced by the Treaty of Rome (1957) had been limited. The treaty's goals were understood to conform to the common market stage of the model. As such the policy puzzle was how, given treaty constraints, progress along this evolutionary model could be achieved. One particular discursive strategy found throughout the 1960s was the attempt to initiate discussion about monetary union – the next stage *after* the common market according to the model – as a means to deliver progress towards completion of the internal market (Maes, 2006). In this period the idea of progress and advancement was integral to the deliberative and advocacy documents produced by the Commission (Commission of the European Communities, 1966, 1973, 1975, 1976, 1978; Council/Commission of the

European Communities, 1970; Commission of the European Economic Community, 1967). The reliance on this model induced a kind of discursive path dependence that framed the policy problems of the 1960s and 1970s in a particular way and enabled discussion of (a) economic integration in terms of linear progression and (b) a state of 'becoming'. The presumption of singular economic spatiality was located at some unspecified moment in the future; the process was understood as the progressive enmeshment of extant *national* economies. It might also be suggested that public and academic discourses of integration of this time reflect two further related phenomena. The first reflects what Delanty (1998) has argued was the original underlying macro-justification of European integration: the preservation of European security, conceived in traditional, statist and militaristic terms. The second draws upon the idea that early European integration amounted to a European variant of the 'embedded liberalism' compromise, where the framework of European integration and governance was 'primarily aimed at supporting national socio-economic models and their development by providing an advantageous, growth and employment friendly economic environment' (Bieling, 2003: 205).

Phase 2: the European economy
A quite discernible shift occurred in the public discourse of European integration from the mid 1980s. What is striking is the continuing emphasis (at least in the earlier years of this second phase) upon a simple core problem: the non-achievement of the common market as laid out in the Treaty of Rome. However, what is equally remarkable is the discursive shift from (a) integration as 'work in progress' or as some at a particular point along a linear continuum to (b) an ontological claim about the existence of a 'European economy'. No doubt, this delineation between these two phases is crude, but as a heuristic device enabling the organisation of thoughts about changing patterns of economic discourse it has merit, and it is certainly possible to consider the emergence of the idea of the European economy in terms of the space–legibility–personality template outlined earlier.

Much attention has been paid to the origins of the European Community's single market programme in the 1980s that culminated in the SEA (1986) – the first major revision to the Communities' treaty basis since 1957 – which developed a timetabled programmatic blueprint and institutional mechanisms for the completion of the common market. The 1985 Commission White Paper *Completing the Internal Market* (Commission of the European Communities, 1985) represents an example of 'first phase'/'pre-history economic discourse', framing its case in terms of progress along a continuum of economic integration and developing a largely technical case for the removal of physical, fiscal and technical barriers to free factor movement within the Communities. The same cannot be said of the concerted campaign undertaken by the Commission in support of the single market initiative which, as Fligstein and Mara-Drita (1996) note, used the concept of 'Europe 1992'[2] as a 'cultural frame' in its public advocacy of the Single European Act's major provisions. The 'Cecchini Report', a 100-page analysis of the benefits of the single market (Cecchini, 1988) was the most conspicuous example of this discursive strategy. The 'Cecchini Report' condensed the findings of a Commission-funded research programme undertaken between 1986 and 1988 on the 'Costs of Non-Europe'. The job of this research programme was 'to establish the present cost of the Community's market fragmen-tation – and thus the benefits from their removal – by analyzing the impact of market barriers and by comparing with the North American experience' (Commission of the European Communities, 1988: 3). The implication is that the European economy was 'legible', albeit through the counter-factual of 'non-Europe'. The idea of a costly 'non-Europe' was an effective way to make arguments for the benefits of the single market. It was also a discursive device that enabled claims about the technical and normative correctness of a 'European economy' to be made (see also Rosamond, 2012). Thus Cecchini described the single market programme as designed to

> propel Europe onto the blustery world stage of the 1990s in a position of competitive strength and on an upward trajectory of economic growth lasting into the next century. Such additional growth following the progressive impact of EC market integration, could, in the space of a few years, put between four and seven percentage points on the *Community's domestic product*'. (1988: xvii, emphasis added)

Perhaps the most egregious example of an attempt to communicate the legibility of the 'European economy' was the 1993 *White Paper on Competitiveness, Growth and Employment* (European Commission, 1993). The White Paper contained some expansive and unambiguous invocations of an actually existing European economy. For example, '[o]ver the last 20 years the European economy's potential rate of growth has shrunk (from around 4% to around 2.5% per year)' (European Commission, 1993: 9). There were also clear attempts to attribute a personality to the economy that was being rendered legible. The White Paper spoke of 'an economy that is healthy, open, decentralized, competitive and based on solidarity'

(1993: 11). At the same time – and here it moved on from the paradoxical discourses surrounding the single market programme – the problem (the reality) to which the White Paper is responding was an economy suffering from a number of negative attributes, of which unemployment was by far the most prominent (1993: 53–67). This part of the White Paper deployed a lot of data showing 'European' figures on, for example unemployment, job creation and intensity of employment growth. Moreover, the data was presented alongside functionally equivalent information for the US and Japan. This yielded comparisons on R&D expenditures, the indebtedness of firms and the trend of profit margins (1993: 72–4).

Presenting data in this way allowed for the comparison of 'Europe' with other singular economic entities such as Japan and the US. The generation of European statistics is the main function of Eurostat,[3] an agency that might be thought of as the primary agent for the manufacture of European knowledge (Jacobsson, 2004). The contribution of Eurostat to making 'the European economy' legible is worthy of much further research, but it worth noting here how in 1992 Eurostat reclassified intra-EU trade as 'internal market' rather than as transactions between member states. Trade between EU member-states and third parties became 'foreign trade' (Fligstein, 2008: 87). This statistical anticipation of a post-national economic space is a good example of the use of data to normalise a representation of 'the European economy'. Note also that a legible 'European economy' implies the existence of equally legible European economic subjects, such as 'European firms'. Thus the 1993 White Paper mentioned one of its key objectives as 'helping European firms adapt to the new globalized and interdependent competitive situation' (1993: 81).[4] The Commission has also mobilised other categorised subjects such as the 'European consumer' (Shore, 2000: 100). The creation of European awareness among European agents became a central theme in the work of the Commission's Forward Studies Unit (*Cellule de Prospective*) from the mid 1990s (see Forward Studies Unit, n.d.).

The other effect of naming and rendering legible 'the European economy' was the sanctioning of considerable discursive effort around the idea of European 'competitiveness' (see Rosamond, 2002). The 1993 White Paper's framing of 'Europe's' dilemmas in terms of exogenous competitive threats raises several further issues. Following Brenner's (2000) vocabulary, it is clear that 'Europe' was being defined as a 'space of competitiveness' – a territorial-institutional arena – which operated within a 'space of competition' (the global economy, which itself had become more competitive). Hence, key goals for EU economic policy for the 1990s and beyond were presented as first 'helping European firms to adapt to the new globalized and interdependent competitive situation' and also 'exploiting the competitive advantages associated with the gradual shift to a knowledge-based economy' (European Commission, 1993). The Commission was not unique in using the idea of competitiveness in this way. Many discussants of the White Paper have argued that the concept was borrowed from national economic policy discourses of the 1980s, where a turn towards (de)regulatory neoliberalism was justified with reference to supposedly tangible and pressing exogenous imperatives (Tsoukalis, 1997: 59; Laffan *et al.*, 2000: 127).

At this juncture a comment might be made about the relationship between this discourse and academic analyses of competitiveness and global economic change more generally. Of course, one school of thought in political economy treats the idea of economies as competitive or uncompetitive as dangerous fiction. Krugman (1994) is perhaps the most forthright exponent of this view, with a particularly vituperative passage reserved for criticising Commission President Jacques Delors' appeal to the rhetoric of competitiveness as a complete failure to appropriately frame the real problems facing Europe. Equally famous is Reich's (1991) differentiation between the 'competitiveness of US firms' and 'American competitiveness', a theme taken up in the EU context by Strange (1998), who wrote about the fallacy of treating the EU as an entity comparable to national economies.[5]

As is the case with policy actors deploying arguments about globalisation, despite the existence of a sizable body of academic knowledge that refutes the central claims of the 'hyperglobalisation' thesis (Hay and Rosamond, 2002), the discourse around 'European competitiveness' seems to have survived such robust academic critiques – perhaps in part because there are other, arguably more influential 'professional' endorsements of the idea (notably Porter, 1990), not to mention the authenticity lent to the concept by agencies such as the Organisation for Economic Cooperation and Development (OECD).

Hitherto, the discussion has focused on the discursive practice and associated mechanisms through which 'the European economy' has been rendered into a social fact, or at least into a comprehensible signifier in the policy world of the EU. Its attributes as a legible economic entity, as a growth pole and as 'a space of competitiveness' all carry implied rationalities for action that might follow, particularly in the context of arguments about appropriate *loci* of regulatory authority. The extent to which the concept of 'the European economy' has become pervasive beyond the particular arena of EU advocacy politics is obvious. Thus we hear analysts describing the growth performance of 'the European economy', discussions of Europe's rate of GDP growth and assertions such as and the failure of the euro to 'make the European economy more dynamic' and so on. This may be attributable to lazy journalistic semantics, but in many of these cases there is rather more to the idea of 'the European economy' than a simple statistical composite of the EU member state economies.

More obviously 'professionalised' academic papers suffer from the same virus. On occasions, the concept of 'the European economy' is used as a framing device, but closer inspection reveals the analysis to be carefully sifting through national data sets. In Went's (2004) discussion, the EU is held – contrary to much prevailing wisdom – to be more advantageously positioned than the US. It might be argued that Went's presentation of numerous data comparing the economic performance of the EU15 (as an aggregated category) to that of the US, including retrospective data on real GDP *per capita* and real GDP per hour dating back to 1913 (Went, 2004: 990) commits the basic fallacy of drawing conclusions about 'Europe' from data that can be read as nothing less than a very crude arithmetic aggregation of national statistics that has little of use to say about the subtleties of the organisation and variation of European economic space. That said, Went's purpose is to re-present data that reveals patterns, which in turn create discursive space for arguments about the reorientation of the European economy away from is disciplinary neoliberal regime. This is – in effect – an attempt to recapture the idea of 'the European economy' from a technocratic (thus depoliticised), neoliberal mindset, so exposing alternative immanent possibilities for the reorientation of the European project (see also Grahl and Teague, 1990, 2003; Bieling, 2003; Hyman, 2005).

This connects to another crucial element of the recent, second phase discourse of the European economy. I have intimated already that the principal rationality that follows from the normalisation of the idea of 'the European economy' concerns the appropriate *locus* of regulatory authority. That 'Europe' is threatened by globalisation or the imperatives of competitiveness *vis-à-vis* its (national) functional equivalents is a discursive precondition for arguing for the Europeanisation of governance capacity. Of course, particularly given the normative and policy prefer-ential claims that lie within standard versions of globalisation and competitiveness discourse, then a second strand of rationality is also unleashed. This suggests a neoliberal policy substance and a regulatory (i.e. non-interventionist, non-redistributive) governance style.

This is a well-known and much-discussed pattern of argument readily found in the advocacy statements of EU policy makers. Former

Commission Vice-President Leon Brittan's recurrent neoliberal rendition of the relationship between globalisation and the EU is a case in point (see Rosamond, 1999). In his numerous speeches, Brittan (1998) spoke of 'Europe' as challenged by globalisation, which in turn was cast as a set of liberalising imperatives. The response – reflecting Brittan's logics of appropriateness and necessity – should be a project to render the EU as neoliberalism incarnate, not only internally in terms of its regulatory regime and portfolio of common policies, but also externally as a proponent of 'open regionalism' and the norms propagated by global institutions.

However, there has been, of course, a rival 'European social model' narrative of the relationship between globalisation and Europe. This was given concrete expression by the Lisbon Agenda (with its focus on employment), but has been a constant theme in the rhetorical output of some parts of the Commission over the past decade. While the position emerging from DG (Employment and Social Affairs) was careful not to characterise globalisation as *necessarily* harmful, it did place emphasis on issues such as unemployment, poverty, inequality, social and economic rights in the context of exogenous economic change. Successive Commissioners Anna Diamantopoulou, and her predecessor Padraig Flynn, were explicit in rejecting the US-style low-coverage welfare system as a feasible or desirable policy choice. The US model was presented as divisive and exclusionary. Diamantopoulou (2000) argued that '[t]he idea at the heart of the European social model is the commitment to combine competitiveness and cohesion'. The point to make here is that any engagement with the fluid 'knowledge economy' (which seemed to be part and parcel of and at times synonymous with globalisation in Commission discourse in the early 2000s) did not mean acquiescence to a particular form of capitalism (the American). In short, this analysis of globalisation provokes a response that invokes a bowdlerised 'models of capitalism' argument. The suggestion here may be that globalisation represents a form of homogenisation based upon the norms of American capitalism and that this may be a bad thing, but that the benefits of globalisation can only be delivered in Europe through a modernised version of the European social model.

Alternatively, the emphasis on the 'European social model' could be read as a response to the consequences of (globalisation as) economic openness. This is certainly how the academic literature on globalisation and labour markets understands the relationship. The appearance of cheap imports from developing economies creates unemployment in advanced economies where wage rates are higher. Consequently, demands upon the welfare state are increased and 'social exclusion' becomes a serious policy problem (see Brenton, 2000). The EU's employment strategy, that emerged from the extraordinary European Council in Luxembourg (20–21 November 1997) and which was augmented by Lisbon three years later, can be read as a substantive policy intervention stemming from this sentiment.[6]

As with the example of trade, the EU's engagement with the 'social dimension' of globalisation has an external aspect. The Commission has been engaged in dialogue with the International Labor Organization (ILO) on issues such as labour standards and corporate social responsibility (Torres, 2001). The discourse of this social dimension of globalisation is now firmly embedded in the work of DG (Employment and Social Affairs) and is now the stuff of communiqués and other agenda-setting documents (See, for example, Commission of the European Communities, 2001a, 2001b). These again suggest that the EU has a role to play in the governance of globalisation, although there is also a sense in these documents that the governance of the internal market in the EU raises precisely analogous challenges to those posed by globalisation (Lamy and Laïdi, 2002).

The point to make here is that the idea of the 'European social model' is another way in which the notion of 'Europe' as an economic space is given personality. The attribution of this personality is a function of an analysis of the context within which 'Europe' operates, together with a particular normative orientation towards that context. Thus while the neo-liberal story imagines the European economy as a spatial incarnation of globalisation, the European social model story conceptualises Europe as a space where – at the very least – globalisation is intercepted. The rationale for 'more Europe' is not bound up with a claim about the best way to enact deregulatory neoliberalism, but rather to fashion an alternative to the policy logics inherent in globalisation.

The point again is that 'the European economy' is not simply an idea that brings with it ontological claims about a particular 'space of competitiveness'. It also potentially carries with it heavy normative content and in this regard the knowable, personified, bounded European economy has no necessary normative or policy inscription. The attribution of such purpose remains a subject of contest.

Conclusions

One rather obvious point to draw from this discussion is that the discursive construction of 'the European economy' does not necessarily unleash neoliberal technical and normative logics and associated programmatic rationalities. Indeed, the imagination of a knowable space does not fully presuppose the conditions under which it is rendered legible (how it is known) and personality (what it is known as). While there is evidence of considerable effort involved in the discursive construction of 'the European economy' as neoliberal in terms of its internal governance and external representation, this is certainly not settled. The lesson for alternative versions of European economic rationality, be they neosocial democratic, sustainable, or moral is to think about and act upon and engage with the mechanisms through which economic space is made potentially knowable (space), made known (legibility) and known as (personality).

Analytically, the case of the European economy tells an interesting story about the agency through which economic space is constructed. The historical sociology of the construction of European state-space tends to rely upon an account of a pre-rational agent (centralised state building elites) whose consolidation of territorial political economies is premised upon the logic of state building. There may be (and this is stretching things considerably beyond the remit of this chapter – but see Rosamond, 2012) a case for applying a much less instrumental, constructivist lens to these historical processes, but in any case the recent history of discourses of European economic integration is suggestive of a logic of quasi-state building that draws upon extant economic knowledge in order to justify the necessity and value of government by an emerging governing agent (the Commission). The analytically interesting paradox is that the putative governing agent brings itself into meaningful existence through its discursive elaboration of the very space that it aspires to govern. One key implication here is that the emerging governing agency in Europe has never been *a priori* neoliberal. Indeed, the evidence points to substantial contestation within the Commission over technical and normative modalities of economic governance (Hooghe, 2001). This is not to say that there have not been crucial moments in the history of European integration where the Commission has aligned with neoliberalising social forces, but it does suggest a degree of relative autonomy from those social forces. At the same time the argument here is attentive to the ongoing importance of (a) forms of economic knowledge (of which neoliberalism is one) as a resource to be used in the discursive construction of economic space and (b) the degree to which forms of knowledge, and the technical and normative rationalities that they inspire, become naturalised themselves.

Notes

1 Case ECR 585 6/64, 1964 *Flaminio Costa* v. *ENFL*, 1964.
2 '1992' referred to the anticipated completion date of the single market.
3 http://epp.eurostat.ec.europa.eu/portal/page/portal/eurostat/home/ (accessed 5 June 2011).
4 Of course, the notion of the 'European firm' is not simply a floating signifier. There have been deliberate attempt by the Commission to give the idea legal personality. The tale of the European Company Statute remains one of the EC/EU's longest-running legislative sagas. This is an instrument designed to induce the creation of firms on a pan-European basis governed by EC law, thereby inducing the emergence of a European mode of corporate governance. After years of debate the idea was brought into force in 2001 (Council Regulation (EC) No. 2157/2001(4)) and was accompanied by a Directive on employee involvement (2001/86/EC) (Marginson and Sisson, 2004: 228–42).
5 More recently Hay (2007) has criticised the recurrent conception of competitiveness in Commission discourse as narrowly focused on cost competitiveness, which thereby treats markets for all goods as precisely analogous to those for cheap consumer goods.
6 Though, as Brenton (2000: 4) notes, the European-level strategy is premised on the idea that unemployment is the main form of social exclusion rather than wage inequality among the employed. Nor is there any EU-level action that targets groups or industries that are affected by changing patterns of trade. These matters remain very much in the hands of national governments.

References

Van Apeldoorn, B. (2002) *Transnational Capital and the Struggle Over European Integration*. London and New York: Routledge.
Balassa, B. (1962) *The Theory of Economic Integration*. London: Allen & Unwin.
Barry, A. (1993) 'The European Community and European Government: Harmonization, Mobility and Space', *Economy and Society*, Vol. 22 (3), 314–26.
Bieler, A. (2006) *The Struggle for a Social Europe: Trade Unions and EMU in Times of Global Restructuring*. Manchester: Manchester University Press.
Bieler, A. and Morton, A. D. (eds) (2001) *Social Forces in the Making of the New Europe: The Restructuring of European Social Relations in the Global Political Economy*. Basingstoke: Palgrave.
Bieling, H.-J. (2003) 'Social Forces in the Making of the New European Economy: The Case of Financial Market Integration', *New Political Economy*, Vol. 8 (2), 203–24.
Van Bogdandy, A. (2000) 'The European Union as a Human Rights Organisation:

Human Rights and the Core of the European Union', *Common Market Law Review*, Vol. 37, 1307–38.

Brenner, N. (2000) 'Building "Euro-regions": Locational Politics and the Political Geography of Neoliberalism in Post-unification Germany', *European Urban and Regional Studies*, Vol. 7 (4), 317–43.

Brenner, N. (2004) *New State Spaces*. Oxford: Oxford University Press.

Brenton, P. (2000) 'Globalisation and Social Exclusion in the EU: Policy Implications', CEPS Working Document, 159, *Centre for European Policy Studies*. Brussels, November.

Brittan, L. (1998) *Globalisation versus Sovereignty: the European Response*. Cambridge: Cambridge University Press.

Buch-Hansen, H. and Wigger, A. (2010) 'Revisiting 50 Years of Market-Making: The Neoliberal Transformation of EC Competition Policy', *Review of International Political Economy*, 17 (1), 20–44.

Cafruny, A.W. and Ryner, M. (2007) *Europe at Bay: In the Shadow of US Hegemony*. Boulder, CO: Lynne Rienner.

Cecchini, P. (with Catinat, M. and Jacquemin, A.) (1988) *The European Challenge: 1992*. Aldershot: Wildwood House.

Commission of the European Communities (1966) *The Development of a European Capital Market: Report of a Group of Experts Appointed by the EEC Commission*. Brussels: Commission of the European Communities.

Commission of the European Communities (1973) *European Economic Integration and Monetary Unification*. Brussels: Commission of the European Communities.

Commission of the European Communities (1975) *Report of the Study Group 'Economic and Monetary Union 1980'*. Brussels: Commission of the European Communities.

Commission of the European Communities (1976) *Optica Report '75: Towards Economic Equilibrium and Monetary Unification in Europe*. Brussels: Commission of the European Communities, COM 11/909/75-E final.

Commission of the European Communities (1978) *The Customs Union: Today and Tomorrow. Record of the Conference Held in Brussels on 6,7 and 8 December 1977*. Luxembourg: Office for Official Publications of the European Communities.

Commission of the European Communities (1985) *Completing the Internal Market: White Paper from the Commission to the European Council (Milan, 28–29 June 1985)*. Brussels: Commission of the European Communities, COM(85) 310 final. http://europa.eu.int/comm/off/pdf/1985_0310_f_en.pdf (accessed 5 June 2011).

Commission of the European Communities (1988) *Research on the 'Cost of Non-Europe': Basic Findings Volume 1. Basic Studies: Executive Summaries*. Luxembourg: Office for Official Publications of the European Communities.

Commission of the European Communities (2001a) *Promoting Core Labour Standards and Improving Social Governance in the Context of Globalisation*.

Communication from the Commission to the Council, the European Parliament and the Economic and Social Committee, Brussels 18.7.2001, COM(2001) 416 final.

Commission of the European Communities (2001b) *Promoting a European Framework for Corporate Social Responsibility – Green Paper* COM(2001) 366 final, http://eur-lex.europa.eu/LexUriServ/site/en/com/2001/com2001_0366en01.pdf (accessed 5 June 2011).

Commission of the European Economic Community (1967) *Tenth General Report on the Activities of the Community (1 April 1966–31 March 1967)*. Brussels: Commission of the European Economic Community.

Council/Commission of the European Communities (1970) *Report of the Council and Commission on the Realisation by Stages of Economic and Monetary Union in the Community: 'Werner Report'*. Luxembourg: Office for Official Publications of the European Communities.

Daly, G. (1991) 'The Discursive Construction of Economic Space', *Economy and Society*, Vol. 20 (1), 79–102.

De Goede, M. (2003) 'Beyond Economism in International Political Economy', *Review of International Studies*, Vol. 29 (1), 79–97.

Delanty, G. (1998) 'Social Theory and European Transformation: Is There a European Society?', *Sociological Research Online*, Vol. 3 (1), www.socresonline.org.uk/3/1/1.html (accessed 5 June 2011).

Diamantopoulou, A. (2000) 'The European Identity in a Global Economy', Speech to the Europe Horizons Conference, Sintra, 18 February.

European Commission (1993) *White Paper on Competitiveness, Growth and Employment: The Challenges and Ways Forward into the 21st Century*, COM(93) 700 (final), http://aei.pitt.edu/1139/01/growth_wp_COM_93_700_Parts_A_B.pdf (accessed 5 June 2011).

Fligstein, N. (2008) *Euroclash: The EU, European Identity, and the Future of Europe*. Oxford: Oxford University Press.

Fligstein, N. and Mara-Drita, I. (1996) 'How to Make a Market: Reflections on the Attempt to Create a Single Market in the European Union', *American Journal of Sociology*, Vol. 102 (1), 1–33.

Forward Studies Unit (n.d.) 'Five-year Work Programme: Four Major Challenges for 1995–2000', http://europa.eu.int/comm/cdp/programme/index_en.htm (accessed 20 March 2008, address now obsolete).

Gill, S. (2001) 'Constitutionalising Capital: EMU and Disciplinary Neo-liberalism', in Bieler, A. and Morton, A.D. (eds), *Social Forces and the Making of the New Europe: The Restructuring of European Social Relations in the Global Political Economy*. Basingstoke: Palgrave, 47–69.

Gill, S. (2003) 'A Neo-Gramscian Approach to European Integration', in Cafruny, A. and Ryner, M. (eds), *A Ruined Fortress? Neoliberal Hegemony and Transformation in Europe*. Lanham, MD: Rowman & Littlefield, 47–70.

Grahl, J. and Teague, P. (1990) *1992 – The Big Market : The Future of the European Community*. London: Lawrence & Wishart.

Hay, C. (2007) 'What Doesn't Kill You Can Only Make You Stronger: The Doha Development Round, The Services Directive and The EU's Conception of Competitiveness', *Journal of Common Market Studies*, Vol. 45 (Annual Review), 25–43.

Hay, C. and Rosamond, B. (2002) 'Globalisation. European Integration and the Discursive Construction of Economic Imperatives', *Journal of European Public Policy*, Vol. 9 (2), 147–67.

Hooghe, L. (2001) *The European Commission and the Integration of Europe: Images of Governance*. Cambridge: Cambridge University Press.

Hyman, R. (2005) 'Trade Unions and the Politics of the European Social Model', *Economic and Industrial Democracy*, Vol. 26 (1), 9–40.

Jabko, N. (2006) *Playing the Market: A Political Strategy for Uniting Europe, 1985–2005*. Ithaca, NY: Cornell University Press.

Jacobsson, K, 2004, 'Soft Regulation and the Subtle Transformation of States: The Case of EU Employment Policy', *Journal of European Social Policy*, Vol. 14 (4), 355–70.

Jessop, B. (1999) 'Narrating the Future of the National Economy and the National State? Remarks on Remapping Regulation and Reinventing Governance', Department of Sociology, University of Lancaster, www.lancs.ac.uk/fass/sociology/papers/jessop-narrating-the-future.pdf (accessed 5 June 2011).

Jessop, B. (2006) 'The European Union and Recent Transformations in Statehood', in Puntscher-Riekmann, S., Lazter, M. and Mokre, M. (eds), *The State of Europe: Transformations of Statehood from a European Perspective*. Frankfurt: Campus Verlag, 75–94.

Korzeniewicz, R.P., Stach, A., Patil, V. and Patrick, T. (2004) 'Measuring National Income: A Critical Assessment', *Comparative Studies in Society and History*, Vol. 16 (3), 535–86.

Kostakopoulou, D. (2008) 'The Evolution of European Union Citizenship', *European Political Science*, Vol. 7 (3), 285–95.

Krugman, P.R. (1994) 'Competitiveness: A Dangerous Obsession', *Foreign Affairs*, Vol. 73 (2), 28–44.

Laffan, B., O'Donnell, R. and Smith, M. (2000) *Europe's Experimental Union: Rethinking Integration*. London: Routledge.

Lamy, P. and Laïdi, Z. (2002) 'Governance or Making Globalisation Meaningful', Report for the Conseil d'Analyse Économique, www.laidi.com/papiers/governance.pdf (accessed 5 June 2011).

Maes, I. (2006) 'The Ascent of the European Commission as an Actor in the Monetary Integration Process in the 1960s', *Scottish Journal of Political Economy*, Vol. 53 (2), 222–41.

Majone, G. (1994) 'The Rise of the Regulatory State in Europe', *West European Politics*, Vol. 17 (3), 77–101.

Majone, G. (ed.) (1996) *Regulating Europe*. London: Routledge.

Majone, G (2005) *Dilemmas of European Integration: The Ambiguities and Pitfalls of Integration by Stealth*. Oxford: Oxford University Press.

Majone, G. (2009) *Europe and the Would-be World Power: The EU at Fifty*. Cambridge: Cambridge University Press.

Marginson, P. and Sisson, K. (2004) *European Integration and Industrial Relations: Multi-level Governance in the Making*. Basingstoke: Palgrave Macmillan.

Miller, P. and Rose, N. (1990) 'Governing Economic Life', *Economy and Society*, Vol. 19 (1), 1–31.

Mitchell, T. (2005) 'The Work of Economics: How a Discipline Makes its World', *European Journal of Sociology*, Vol. 46 (2), 297–320.

Moravcsik, A. (2002) 'In Defence of the "Democratic Deficit": Reassessing Legitimacy in the European Union', *Journal of Common Market Studies*, Vol. 40 (4), 603–24.

Van der Pijl, K. (2006) 'A Lockean Europe', *New Left Review* Vol. 37 (second series), 9–37.

Pistor, M. (2005) 'Agency, Structure and European Integration: Critical Political Economy and The New Regionalism In Europe', in Jones, E. and Verdun, A. (eds), *The Political Economy of European Integration: Theory and Practice*. London: Routledge, 108–27.

Porter, M. (1990) *The Competitive Advantage of Nations*. New York: Free Press.

Reich, R. (1991) 'Who is US?', *Harvard Business Review*, Vol. 68 (1), 107–26.

Rosamond, B. (1999) 'Globalization and the Social Construction of European Identities', *Journal of European Public Policy*, Vol. 6 (4), 652–68.

Rosamond, B. (2002) 'Imagining the European Economy: "Competitiveness" and the Social Construction of "Europe" as an Economic Space', *New Political Economy*, Vol. 7 (2), 157–77.

Rosamond, B. (2006) 'Disciplinarity and the Political Economy of Transformation: The Epistemological Politics of Globalisation Studies', *Review of International Political Economy*, Vol. 13 (3), 516–32.

Rosamond, B. (2008) 'Open Political Science, Methodological Nationalism and European Union Studies', *Government and Opposition*, Vol. 43 (4), 599–612.

Rosamond, B. (2012) 'Supranational Governance as Economic Patriotism? The European Union, Legitimacy and the Reconstruction of State Space', *Journal of European Public Policy*, 17 (3), 324–41.

Scott, J. C. (1998) *Seeing Like a State: How Certain Schemes to Improve the Human Condition Have Failed*. New Haven, CT: Yale University Press.

Shore, C. (2000) *Building Europe: The Cultural Politics of European Integration*. London: Routledge.

Stone Sweet, A. and Sandholtz, W. (1998) 'Integration, Supranational Governance and the Institutionalization of the European Polity', in Sandholtz, W. and Stone Sweet, A. (eds), *European Integration and Supranational Governance*. Oxford: Oxford University Press, 1–26.

Strange, S. (1998) 'Who are EU? Ambiguities in the Concept of Competitiveness', *Journal of Common Market Studies*, Vol. 36 (1), 101–14.

Thrift, N. (2005) *Knowing Capitalism*. London: Sage.

Torres, R. (2001) *Towards a Socially Sustainable World Economy: An Analysis of the Social Pillars of Globalisation*. Geneva: ILO.

Tsoukalis, L. (1997) *The New European Economy Revisited*. Oxford: Oxford University Press.

Walters, W. and Haahr, J. H. (2005) *Governing Europe: Discourse, Governmentality and European Integration*. London: Routledge.

Watson, M. (2005) *Foundations of International Political Economy*. Basingstoke and New York: Palgrave.

Weiler, J. H. H. (1991) 'The Transformation of Europe', *Yale Law Journal*, Vol. 100 (8), 2403–83.

Weiler, J. H. H. (2002) 'The Reformation of European Constitutionalism', *Journal of Common Market Studies*, Vol. 35 (1), 97–131.

Went, R. (2004) 'Globalisation: Can Europe Make a Difference?', *Review of International Political Economy*, Vol. 11 (5), 980–94.

Wincott. D. (2006) 'European Political Development, Regulatory Governance, and the European Social Model: The Challenge of Substantive Legitimacy', *European Law Journal*, Vol. 12 (6), 743–63.

3

The euro and open regionalism in the politics of 'permanent renegotiation' and the international political economy of monetary power: a critical engagement with 'new constitutionalism'

Gerard Strange

The history, meaning and future trajectory of EU's project of 'open regionalism' is contested in critical scholarship (Gamble and Payne, 1996). Defined principally by the construction of the internal single market, including monetary union, alongside an entrenched commitment to further developing trade and wider economic openness with the rest of the world, the EU's open regionalism has been broadly welcomed by many critical liberals and social democrats, albeit often guardedly. But it has also been the subject of sustained critique from many others on the Left (see, for example, the contrasting edited volumes by Notermans 2001 and Cafruny and Ryner, 2003).

An important strand of the Left's critique of open regionalism, with which this chapter engages, has developed out of the influential work of leading Marxist neo-Gramscian scholar, Stephen Gill. Gill has approached the study of globalisation and regionalism through the conceptual lens of global 'new constitutionalism' (Gill, 2008: Chapters 7 and 9). New constitutionalism envisages the EU's open regionalism as part of a broader neoliberal hegemonic project built around an institutionalised, disciplinary, meta-framework of binding and market-favouring transnational rules, laws and legally enforceable agreements. This operates at both the global level, through American-backed 'neoliberal' agency and America's dominance over the core institutions of global economic governance and, at the regional level, through treaty-based projects of economic integration such as the EU's. Such rule-based power, Gill argues, favours neoliberalism since it serves to 'lock in' the market, private property, sound finance and capital mobility as 'automatic' or constitutionalised constraints on the 'progressive' interventionist capacities of formally independent nation-states.

EMU, many of its Left critics claim, both contributes to and operates within this broad new constitutionalist frame, imposing and consolidating neoliberalism while *actively* stifling possibilities for social democratic alternatives at the EU level. The central argument that flows from Gill's framework contains both internal and external dimensions. Internally, the framework of EMU governance, underwritten in the EU's treaties, imposes 'self-limitation' on the social and economic purposes monetary union can serve (Cafruny and Ryner 2007: 141). First, the EU treaties formally grant goal-setting and operational independence to the ECB (Cafruny and Ryner, 2007: 148; Buller and Gamble 2008: 259–60). Alongside the grant of independence the treaties mandates that the prime objective of the ECB is the maintenance of price stability within the eurozone. The result, critics claim, has been to 'lock in' monetary 'orthodoxy' and anti-inflationary bias at the heart of EMU. Second, EMU has institutionalised 'macroeconomic asymmetry' in the eurozone creating a supranational monetary policy alongside decentralised, intergovernmental fiscal policy. Within this asymmetric framework, the SGP constrains the fiscal policies of eurozone member states through its famous 3 per cent budget deficit and 60 per cent national debt rules. Together, these treaty commitments to monetary orthodoxy and constrained fiscal decentralisation bias EMU towards neoliberalism, ensuring that 'policy making is "locked into" a monetarist framework to an unprecedented degree' (Cafruny and Ryner, 2007: 148; see also Chapters 1 by Ryner and 6 by Bieler in this volume).

New constitutionalists argue that EMU's internal self-limitation is reinforced by its subordination to external forms of 'neoliberal' power, specifically the monetary and financial power of the US and the 'disciplinary' rules of global economic governance institutions. It is generally conceded by new constitutionalists that US power is not what it once was. America no longer exercises 'integral hegemony' as it did until the early 1970s under the terms of the Bretton Woods agreement. This had underpinned an international 'social compromise' described by Ruggie (1982) as 'embedded liberalism'. Despite the collapse of integral hegemony, US monetary and financial power remains *structurally* dominant, as is evident in the dollar's continued global pre-eminence. Moreover, this structural power is underpinned by a transatlantic 'organic alliance' among strongly integrated, finance sector-based, US and European business elites, who share a commitment to neoliberalism (Cafruny and Ryner, 2007: 143–7). Cast subordinately within this broader hegemonic frame, the euro, despite its structural presence, has been unable to challenge neoliberalism and as such has been subject only to 'benign neglect' on the American side (Cafruny and Ryner, 2007: 149; Cohen, 2009).

According to new constitutionalists, EMU's internal and external 'self-limitation' has been the primary cause of a succession of crises that have afflicted the euro since its launch. It is claimed that with each crisis the attempt has been made to further consolidate neoliberalism through new market-favouring policy initiatives and policy change – for example, the Lisbon employment process and more recently the austerity measures associated with the current crisis. This crisis-based neoliberal path dependence in policy has increasingly marginalised social democracy, but the concomitant trajectory of eurozone crisis has not been resolved. Rather, the ideological legitimising bases for EMU have been eroded. This has brought into question the future of the euro amid calls from a range of ideological sources for the complete or partial renationalisation of Europe's money (Cafruny, 2003; Lapavitsas *et al.*, 2010).

The rest of this chapter critically interrogates the principal claims of the new constitutionalist thesis as applied to the evaluation of EMU. In doing so, it argues for the continued efficacy of the euro in terms of social democratic advance at both the EU and global levels. It is acknowledged that, in the context of globalisation and open regionalism, EMU provides few, if any, guarantees for social democratic regulation and that the nature, meaning and operational parameters of social democracy have to be substantively rethought (see, for example, Annesley and Gamble, 2003; Clift and Tomlinson, 2006). Nevertheless, it is argued that new constitutionalism's exclusive focus on the internal and external *constraints* that EMU imposes on social democracy is overdrawn. As a consequence, new constitutionalism has failed to recognise the importance of EMU as a political *response* to neoliberalism, globalisation and (declining) American power; and by the force of its own argument it has failed to give sufficient attention to wider global power shifts which, like the euro, have challenged both US and neoliberal dominance (Hettne, 2005; Henning, 2006; Cohen, 2008). First, the chapter critically examines the internal dimension of EMU's alleged 'self-limitation'. Drawing on evidence from the recent eurozone crises as well as the SGP crisis of the early to mid 2000s, it is argued that EMU's internal self-limitation has been consistently subject to successful challenge and reform, contradicting the notion of neoliberal lock-in through the EU's internal constitutionalism. Second, the chapter critically examines EMU's external dimension and the external limitations allegedly imposed on eurozone macroeconomic policy by American power and the wider structures of global governance. It is argued that new constitutionalism exaggerates American and neoliberal dominance, deflecting attention from fundamental changes in the *structure* and *politics* of global monetary power, not least the creation of the eurozone itself. These changes, alongside Lisbon Treaty provisions facilitative of exchange rate activism, pave the way for the political assertion of structural power by the eurozone, with *potentially* positive implications for social democratic advance at the EU level.

Permanent crisis or permanent renegotiation? Reform of EMU's internal domain and the French and German models of decision making

From the start, EMU's 'self-limitation' – a primary source of crisis, according to new constitutionalists – has been subject to constructive political challenge and reform, what has been termed a process of 'permanent renegotiation' (Henning, 2007: 336; see also *The Economist*, 23 October 2010: 58). Although crises heighten processes of policy change, the basis for permanent renegotiation also lies in the politically ambiguous demarcations of authority and competencies within the complex 'constellation' of EMU's governance, what Dyson (2008) refers to as EMU's built-in 'institutional fuzziness'.

As Dyson emphasises, institutional fuzziness partly reflects the still incomplete nature of EMU and ongoing debates about the wider strategic objectives EMU *might* serve in the future (Dyson, 2008: 3). Central to this debate has been alternative 'models' of *decision making* within EMU, described by Henning (2007: 316) as the 'German' and 'French' models (see also Barber, 2010; *The Economist*, 10 July 2010: 23–6). The German model gives emphasis to the efficacy of price stability and broadly endorses ECB independence, as granted under the treaties, as a means of securing this specific objective. More generally, the model favours rule-based decision making and as such has often been identified with neoliberalism (Burnham, 2001; Gill, 2008). The French model focuses on the broader strategic orientation of EMU and emphasises the efficacy of politicised governmental control over monetary and fiscal policy. It therefore favours decision making by the European Council – the erstwhile 'collective government' of the EU – as well as the strengthening of the policy authority of the Economic and Financial Affairs Council (Ecofin) *vis-à-vis* the ECB. Typically, advocates of a more social democratic EMU favour this model.

According to new constitutionalists, the German model, centred on ECB independence, has unambiguously dominated EMU. This, it is claimed, has favoured what Burnham (2001, 2010) refers to as the 'depoliticisation' of macroeconomic management and thereby radically constrained the development of social democratic policy initiatives within EMU. It is important to note, however, that EMU's emphases on price stability and rule-based governance do not in themselves rule out social democratic programmes, albeit that neither do such emphasises guarantee social democracy (Annesley and Gamble, 2003: 146). Indeed Germany's own post-Second World War political economy, based on an embedded form of 'social market' economy and featuring institution-alised commitments to social investment and industrial corporatism as well as export-led growth and sound finance, provides evidence that it is possible to successfully combine highly orthodox monetary and market favouring policies with broader and deeply entrenched commitments to social democracy. Moreover, while the *formal* dominance of monetary orthodoxy in EMU is acknowledged here, it is argued that contestation, renegotiation and reform away from this founding default position have been significant features in the evolution of EMU and policy change therein. Such policy change, often occurring in response to crisis, has typically favoured the French model of politicised decision making and revealed significant policy divisions within the ECB, the supposed axis of orthodoxy and neoliberalism within EMU. While policy conflict, openness to renegotiation and the ultimate dominance of the French model tends to contradict the new constitutionalist characterisation of EMU in terms of neoliberal lock-in, it supports Dyson's claim that EMU has been 'simultaneously depoliticising and *repoliticising*' (Dyson, 2008: 3, emphasis added). One case in point was the reform of the SGP in 2005 following a protracted period of policy crisis. It has been generally recognised that the reformed SGP marked a consid-erable formal relaxation of eurozone 'automatic' budgetary discipline in favour of political discretion. Indeed as new constitutionalist critics of 'Maastricht–EMU' have acknowledged, the 2005 reforms represented 'a radical retraction of the objectives initially set for the SGP ... a belated admission of the trade off between macroeconomic "balance" in the medium term and growth' (Cafruny and Ryner, 2007: 163, n. 66).

The 2010–11 euro crisis, fiscal activism and post-crisis EMU governance reform

A more recent case of 'repoliticisation' has been evident in the on-going reform of EMU governance following the euro crises of 2010–11. This has shifted EMU *towards* fiscal centralisation and activism. For EMU's Left critics this is problematic since a crucial contention has been that lack of fiscal centralisation reflects a deliberate 'neoliberal' bias in EMU's 'very design' towards 'negative' forms of integration. Hence, as new constitutionalists have pointed out, the EU's currently limited powers to tax and spend have been underpinned and compounded by legal provisions explicitly forbidding ECB fiscal activism (Cafruny and Ryner, 2007: 149).[1] Such formalised fiscal constraints suggest the dominance of a depoliticised model and, it is claimed, has ruled out 'positive' forms of coordinated macroeconomic activism central to social democracy and favoured in the French model (van Apeldoorn *et al.*, 2003: 29; Ryner, Chapter 1 in this volume).

Yet in responding to the eurozone's bond crisis of 2010, the EU utilised the French model of decision making (*vis-à-vis* an emergency meeting of the European Council and Ecofin between 7 and 10 May) to apparently sweep aside EMU's monetary orthodoxy in order to mobilise a massive stabilisation package – the European Financial Stabilisation Facility (EFSF) – in support of eurozone deficit countries threatened by the withdrawal of credit lines from global money markets. At €750 billion, the EFSF (as originally agreed in May 2010) represented over 8 per cent of eurozone gross domestic product (GDP), dwarfing the EU's pre-crisis permanent budget (approximately 1.5 per cent of eurozone GDP). As such, it provided the EU with a new and significant (in macroeconomic terms) collective fiscal capability. While initially agreed as a temporary measure to be withdrawn after three years, the announcement of the EFSF presaged, according to *The Economist* (15 May 2010: 78), a more permanent shift towards 'a kind of fiscal federalism' with lasting implications for both the macroeconomic management of the eurozone and for decision making processes within EMU (see also *Time*, 24 May 2010: 19).

Subsequent developments have arguably confirmed this view. Policy debate has been marked by the familiar tension and conflict between the German/ECB and French decision making models. For example, the ECB was initially strongly resistant to the idea of making the EFSF a permanent facility, despite the fact that Jean-Claude Trichet, the Bank's president, had played an instrumental role in prompting Ecofin to launch the EFSF as a temporary emergency fund. But once the fund was formally agreed, the ECB's defence of its narrow monetary mandate and the independence of its decision making became increasingly compromised. Initially this was caused by the need to quickly operationalise the EFSF, to stave off a Greek default. This required that the ECB act as 'lender of last resort' and buy up 'junk' bonds to underpin the solvency of the Greek government, the first eurozone country to be denied credit in global money markets. The ECB committed to undertake unlimited bond purchases despite the fact that such interventionist action was formally forbidden under a strict interpretation of the EU treaties and despite opposition from orthodox (read neoliberal) opinion within the ECB's Executive Board around Axel Weber (then head of the Bundesbank) and Jürgen Stark, Germany's other Board member.

In March 2010 the EU convened as special 'taskforce' on the future of economic governance in the EU, headed by the European Council's permanent president, Herman Van Rompuy. The six scheduled meetings of the taskforce were, not surprisingly, dominated by the euro crisis. Policy debate focused both on whether and how the EFSF should be entrenched and how budgetary discipline within the eurozone could be strengthened. The taskforce included the full Ecofin Council along with representatives from the European Commission and the ECB. During the deliberations of the taskforce the ECB continued to argue strongly against a further consolidation of the EFSF and specifically opposed plans to make it a permanent facility. Instead, the Bank focused attention on the importance of strengthening 'automatic' budgetary discipline within EMU. The Bank argued for the augmentation of existing SGP rules and sanctions on deficit member states alongside the strengthening of centralised budgetary surveillance by the European Commission. Recommendations included the imposition of punitive penalties, such as the withdrawal of voting rights and even suspension from the eurozone for countries persistently in breach of the SGP.

Yet, despite such arguments, the final report of the Van Rompuy taskforce, published on 21 October 2010 and agreed unanimously by finance ministers with support from the Commission, contained two core recommendations fundamentally at odds with both the ECB's policy preferences and more specifically with orthodox opinion within the ECB. Rather, both in terms of decision making procedure (focused on Ecofin consensus building) and substantive policy recommendations, the report reflected the counter-influence of the French model. First, the report recommended that the EFSF be replaced by a permanent facility (the European Stabilisation Mechanism or ESM) when the EFSF lapses in 2013. (Ecofin subsequently adopted the ESM as a permanent fund of €500 billion in May 2011.) Second, while the report favoured new proposals for strengthening budgetary surveillance and sanctions, it did not endorse the more extreme measures canvassed, such as expulsion from the eurozone for member states persistently breaching SPG rules. Specifically, the taskforce *rejected* the call for automaticity as advocated by the ECB (*FT. com*, 20 October 2010). Instead, drawing on a compromise reached by the French and German governments, the report recommended introducing a 'reverse majority rule' for the adoption of budgetary 'enforcement measures'. Contrary to ECB demands, this leaves the ultimate power over SGP sanctions with Ecofin and the political discretion of finance ministers acting under the qualified majority voting (QMV) procedure (European Union, 2010: 14).

Towards economic government

The subsequent trajectory of the eurozone crisis throughout 2011 has left governance reform on-going. In view of the continuation and deepening of the crisis it seems likely that further reforms, including measures requiring substantive treaty change and renegotiation, will have to be seriously entertained despite the protracted political uncertainty this would probably entail (Farrell and Quiggin, 2011). Against this backdrop, the French government, in particular, has been keen to press its long-standing demand for 'economic government' in the eurozone, focused on an enhanced and institutionalised role for the European Council as active 'overlord' of EMU, the proposed ESM and the ECB.

The proposal for economic government partly reflects a belief that EMU suffers from both an absolute and relative (by comparison to other monetary authorities) lack of democratic legitimacy and accountability, a deficiency highlighted by Left critics. But the widely held understanding among eurozone policy elites that the underlying causes of the euro's crises have been *structural* in nature has reinforced the broader policy efficacy of this view. The structural weakness of the euro has been evident in the long-running macroeconomic asymmetries between surplus earning competitive exporters, such as Germany, and less competitive member states running structural trade deficits. This has underscored the crisis and suggests that that the longer-term stabilisation of the eurozone will require a commitment from its authorities to a greater degree of fiscal centralisation. This would include some degree of formalised fiscal union, albeit not necessarily a fully developed or federalist transfer union. In turn, this would require greater political accountability, the most obvious and expedient route to which would be to enhance the existing power of the European Council within EMU, especially *vis-à-vis* the ECB. Given all this, the French proposal for economic government for the eurozone has gained greater policy credence and political purchase.

There is certainly growing support from within EMU's policy community for the further centralisation of fiscal power, if only to formalise and make permanent the *de facto* move towards ECB-based fiscal centralism that has occurred since 2010 as a result of the EFSF. This points to the future introduction of 'euro bonds', as does Ecofin's approval of the proposed ESM. Given on-going policy divisions within EMU's policy community, but also the imperative of political expediency in the face of crisis, a move towards a 'two-tier' system of 'blue' eurobonds introduced alongside 'red' national bonds has been discussed as a feasible policy compromise. But even such a limited euro bond issue would be of fundamental significance. First, it would introduce a fiscal stabilisation mechanism that permanently altered the policy role of the ECB. The introduction of eurobonds would, in effect, 'automatise' ECB fiscal activism and thereby require a significant change to and redrafting of the existing treaties, which formally forbid such activism. Despite opposition from 'orthodox' opinion within the ECB, others at the Bank, notably Trichet (its outgoing President), have favoured such a move as necessary in order to address the underlying reality of structural imbalances and as the only efficient way of achieving fiscal consolidation in the eurozone. Second, the introduction of euro bonds would require a new level of political union to legitimise and oversee automatised fiscal activism (Trichet himself has long lamented EMU's lack of federal support structures). Hence, policy-level discussions around the possible introduction of eurobonds have generally presupposed a concomitant move towards eurozone 'economic government'. As noted above, this has been favoured by a succession of French governments, both socialist and conservative, and has received strong support in recent years from important interests currently outside the eurozone but within the EU, notably, the British Labour Party and the British Treasury (Buller and Gamble, 2008). Van Rompuy, whose role as EU President would be enhanced by such a governance change, also favours 'economic government'.

Such further moves towards fiscal centralisation are regarded by many commentators as unavoidable on the assumption, first, that they are necessary to overcome the euro crisis and second, that policy makers will not allow the euro to fail (Farrell and Quiggin, 2011). However, divisions within EMU's policy community mean that they are by no means inevitable. As already indicated, orthodox opinion, focused on Germany and German representation in the ECB, has consistently argued against the EFSF and concomitant ECB emergency activism, not to mention the introduction of euro bonds. Orthodoxy has instead called for the consolidation of fiscal discipline at the national level to underpin a strengthened and automatised SGP. In line with this approach, a number of larger eurozone countries under bond market pressure have recently signalled a determination to tighten national fiscal policy in order to pre-empt contagion and shore up confidence. Critical here has been the introduction of permanent 'balanced budget' rules through national-level legislation – so-called 'debt brakes' (Farrell and Quiggin, 2011: 97–8). *Prima facie*, this would appear as evidence of the consolidation of neoliberal depoliticisation in the eurozone as well as the continuing strength of neoliberalism globally. This judgement is reinforced by the fact that similar moves to place strict limits on deficit financing have been widely canvassed in the US following the recent debt ceiling controversy (see Burnham, 2010).

Yet the prospect or a partial of complete break-up of the euro caused by such a singular emphasis on austerity and fiscal tightening, against a backdrop of continuing uncertainty regarding the future trajectory of the global economy, has put orthodox opinion on the back foot in recent months. Indeed not only has the continuation of the euro crisis served to mobilise the French model of decision making, it has also brought sharply into focus deep and long-standing divisions within the ECB, the supposed bulwark of the 'German model' within EMU. This reflects wider divisions within neoliberalism that have become evidence during the GFC.

The division within the ECB has crystallised around fiscal centralists (notably Trichet) and activists on the one hand, and orthodox monetarists and minimalists (notably Weber and Stark), on the other, with the latter forced on the defensive by the tide of events. From the beginning of the euro crisis in early 2010 the ECB struggled to contain these underlying divisions brought to the fore by the political necessity of its crisis management role, particularly bond market intervention. But by early 2011 fundamental conflict within the Bank over crisis management as well as the future of EMU governance, had become public. One early sign of division and weakness for the ECB was the Bank's failure to dominate the Van Rompuy taskforce on the future of EMU governance or to provide it with policy leadership. The result was that the Bank was left embarrassed by Van Rompuy's final report to the European Council. Following a reported row between Trichet and Weber, Trichet, as the ECB's chief representative in the taskforce, was forced to withdraw his earlier endorsement of the report. This did not prevent its unanimous adoption by the European Council, however. Instead, it lead ultimately to the resignations from the ECB's Executive Board of both Weber (who had been frontrunner to replace Trichet as President in October 2011) and Stark, whose positions were made untenable by their opposition to bond purchasing and the subordination of ECB independence to political control.

These developments represent important defeats for neoliberalism and the German model of decision making at the heart of EMU. But, as was argued above, they at least partly reflect the strength of the French model in the context of EMU's built-in 'institutional fuzziness'. The euro crisis has brought the French model to the fore to reveal a degree of internal political contestation within EMU that has been denied by EMU's new constitutionalist critics. As such, it points to weaknesses not only in neoliberalism but also its critical appraisal by many on the Left.

The Euro's external domain: world order change, the 'exchange rate weapon' and the diffusion of monetary power

Somewhat curiously, the euro's external dimension has not featured prominently in recent Left assessments of EMU and the crisis (see, for example, EuroMemo Group 2010; Lapavitsas *et al.* 2010). This is surprising, because, *prima facie*, the common exchange rate is *the* most important and powerful macroeconomic instrument made available to the eurozone as a *direct* consequence of currency union. Particularly in the absence of full fiscal union, deployment of the 'exchange rate weapon' (Henning, 2006), though controversial, could in principle underpin a sustainable expansion of demand in the eurozone, providing a macroeconomic platform for a social democratic programme of recovery.

Despite this potential, a key feature of macroeconomic management in EMU has been what Cohen and Subacchi (2008: 4) identify as a 'passive' exchange rate policy. For Left critics, this reflects the fact that the EU's monetary policy, despite the creation of a single currency, has, to date, functioned largely as a conduit for the projection of American monetary power and thence neoliberalism. But as the GFC has revealed, this hegemonic conceptualisation overstates the sustainability of America's dollar-based 'exceptionalism' and the unity of American-led policy around neoliberalism. It serves to deflect empirical and analytical attention from fundamental changes in the contemporary IPE which have challenged US dominance and in so doing have contributed to what others, including many critical scholars, regard as the broad unravelling of hegemony, neoliberal or otherwise (Henning, 2006; Arrighi, 2007; Beeson, 2009;

Strange, 2011). Moreover, the key changes have been at the structural level, the foundations of hegemonic dominance according to new constitutionalists.

One change has been the rise of developing economies as leading global exporters who, as a consequence of net earnings from international trade, have accumulated massive foreign reserve holdings. In China's case, for example, accumulated reserves are estimated at $2.7 trillion, 80 per cent of which are dollar-denominated assets. More generally, the core developing countries are estimated to have accumulated $12 trillion of sovereign wealth funds (SWFs) and export-based reserves (Taylor, 2011). The globalisation of the dollar and the growth of US debt dependence have given significant counter-leverage to developing countries when faced by US attempts to exercise monetary power unilaterally. This has been evident in the developing countries' growing influence and power in global economic governance organisations as well as in evidence of US hegemonic 'overstretch' (Arrighi, 2007) which has contributed to the US' $14 trillion national debt.

Another important structural change has been the direct impact of globalisation on the US economy. Over the past forty years the US has been transformed from a relatively closed to a relatively open economy. As Henning (2006) notes this, along with counter-power elsewhere, has weakened the net efficacy of the exchange rate weapon for the US. For example, the US is now more exposed to the inflationary impact of dollar depreciation as a consequence of its increased reliance on imports from Asia and Europe. Similarly, the global integration of US multinational corporations and their use of developing economies as highly profitable global production and export platforms may limit the efficacy of dollar depreciation as a tool of macroeconomic management by the US. For example, US multinational corporations (MNCs) operating in China but exporting back to the US benefit directly from the yuan peg against the dollar and have therefore opposed moves by the US Congressional trade lobby to secure a significant appreciation of the Chinese currency. Such structural changes are key dimensions of what Cohen (2008) has referred to as the 'diffusion' of international monetary power, a process that has undermined US dominance and in doing so heightened the prospects for global monetary conflict and policy change.

The euro's structural power
Monetary union in the EU represents a further dimension of structural change and the diffusion of international monetary power that has weakened US and neoliberal dominance in the IPE. Indeed, according

to Henning (2006) the arrival of the euro in 1999 represented the most important structural transformation in international monetary relations since the Bretton Woods Conference in 1944. In 'one fell swoop' it created a potential counter to the unilateral exercise of monetary power by the US, a core characteristic of the IPE in the post-Bretton Woods period evident, for example, in America's dominance over the Plaza and Louvre Accords of the 1980s. Moreover, the decision to create a monetary union in Europe was, Henning contends, the direct consequence of the overextension of monetary power by the US. It was the destabilising inflationary impact of this in the 1970s that underlined calls by European policy elites for a 'zone of monetary stability' in Europe and which led initially to the galvanisation of the European Monetary System in the 1980s around a coordinated policy of semi-fixed exchange rates *vis-à-vis* the deutschmark-centred Exchange Rate Mechanism (ERM).

Monetary union was thus the culmination of the European Community's strategic response to the perceived impact and threat of US economic unilateralism in the post-Bretton Woods era. Providing a new structural capability for a region roughly the equivalent in weight to the US in terms of GDP, the euro created a 'greater symmetry in the international monetary system – read less US dominance' that could contribute to better (i.e. growth orientated) macroeconomic policy outcomes for Europe and globally (Henning, 2006: 130). Indeed, such an outcome had been anticipated by the European Commission in a major report of 1990 and was explicitly used to support the case for economic and monetary union (European Commission, 1990; Henning, 2006: 130).

The projection of power

Enhancement of macroeconomic 'autonomy' (Cohen, 2006: 42–3), or what Gamble (2002: 6) refers to as 'the capacity to act', especially through the pooling of 'exchange rate risk', is widely acknowledged as a major structural benefit derived automatically from currency union in a globalised world (see also Dyson, 2008: 5–6; Cohen and Subacchi, 2008: 2–4; Henning 2010: 2). Yet, thus far, the EU has not been wholly successful in projecting structural power. Nowhere has this been more the case than in the monetary domain where policy has favoured a passive, but overvalued, euro. According to new constitutionalists, this is the result of the EU's combined subordination to American macroeconomic policy and the internal dominance of ECB monetary orthodoxy within EMU that, it is claimed, rule out a shift away from passivity. Others are less dismissive but have nevertheless highlighted governance incoherence and the lack of clear lines of policy authority and representation within

EMU's external dimension as an important limitation (Bretherton and Vogler, 2006: 72–4; Cohen, 2006: 46–8; Cohen and Subacchi, 2008: 4; Van Rompuy, 2010).

Yet, *contra* new constitutionalism, the EU treaties specifically allow for EMU authorities to politically determine the exchange rate policy orientation of the eurozone and, having done so, to defend such a policy through appropriate forms of foreign exchange market intervention and in relevant international policy fora, such as the G20 and IMF. The key legal provision is Article 219 of the Lisbon Treaty, which gives Ecofin (in its Eurogroup configuration) authority over formal exchange rate agreements with third parties. In the absence of a formal agreement it further allows the Council to issue 'general orientations' on the euro's exchange rate *to* the ECB.

Thus, the balance of authority enshrined in Article 219 gives ministers, *prima facie*, considerable power and discretion over the euro exchange rate (Henning 2007: 316). Formally speaking the French model of decision making dominates exchange rate policy. New constitutionalist critics have claimed that this power is largely nominal (Cafruny, 2003: 294) but evidence suggests otherwise. Prior to the 2010–11 crisis, the ECB had twice (September and November 2000) *actively* intervened in foreign exchange markets, albeit in an attempt to shore up the external value of the euro. Crucially, however, the Bank was able to act only *after* a political consensus had emerged in the eurozone on the need for and efficacy of a higher value for the euro (despite market valuation to the contrary) and only *after* lengthy negotiations conducted with the Eurogroup and the Economic and Finance Committee (EFC) had led to a formal agreement (the Turku Agreement) on policy action and its terms (Henning, 2007: 323–7). This suggests room for policy change.

One recommendation, favoured by the French government and broadly consistent with social democracy, is for a new and more active strategic orientation to EMU's external monetary policy focused on the projection of a 'weaker' euro. This would involve a decision by EMU authorities to signal a managed depreciation of the euro alongside a clear long-term policy commitment to defend the currency's value around its lower long-term equilibrium rate (see Cohen and Subacchi, 2008:5). This would operate as a default policy position in lieu of a wider multilateral agreement on future currency arrangements and global macroeconomic reform aimed at achieving balanced global growth. Any move towards such active exchange rate management would represent a decision by EMU authorities to deploy the exchange rate weapon and would mark a clear break with EMU's long-running exchange rate policy of *laissez-*

faire 'neutrality'. The difficulty for such a policy, one highlighted by new constitutionalist analyses, is that it would risk a confrontation with the EU's erstwhile hegemonic partner – the US – over global leadership and the future of global economic management.

Conclusions: the global economy, the future of the euro and the future of social democracy – the imperative of influence

In many respects the GFC and the euro crisis have revealed the dangers for the EU – social democratic or otherwise – of holding steadfast to an alliance with a declining hegemon, one with which it has enjoyed strong military, political and cultural as well as economic ties in recent decades. The downside to this relationship is that the EU has paid insufficient attention to structural power shifts (including the launch of the euro in 1999) that, more recently, have favoured both itself and the wider developing world relative to the US. The result, as Herman Van Rompuy has argued, has been declining political influence for the EU over global economic affairs. The EU's economic prosperity – to a large degree built on integration - will be imperilled, Van Rompuy warns, by its failure to project the political influence its economic status, as the richest integrated economic space in the world, warrants. But to project power, Van Rompuy argues, the EU must first cohere internally around clear strategic purposes and objectives and learn to 'speak with one voice' so as to promote and defend these objectives in international economic fora, including the G20 and IMF as well as the WTO. The second task is to strengthen relations with the emerging economic powers, especially China. But this, in turn, requires acknowledging that US power and the US–EU 'special' relationship, though still important, is not what it once was (Van Rompuy, 2010).

Van Rompuy's assessment of EU political weakness as a global actor parallels recent academic analyses highlighted in this chapter (e.g. Bretherton and Vogler, 2006; Cohen 2009) and its salience has been increased by the impact of the GFC on the EU. EMU's partial or complete failure might, on some accounts, ultimately strengthen economic performance in some of the competitively weaker countries currently in the eurozone by reinstating national exchange rates as competitive adjustment mechanisms (Lapavitsas *et al.*, 2010). But by the same token, it would expose those countries leaving the eurozone to the full force of international money markets; and it would damage the performance of and narrow the policy options available to other countries, particularly the economically strongest ones, such as Germany, whose competitiveness and policy autonomy has been enhanced by euro membership (Henning, 2010). More importantly, however, the collapse of the euro would greatly weaken the EU's *potential* for exercising global political influence, leverage and leadership in concert with others. Although the arrival of the euro has marked an important structural change in international economic relations that has favoured the consolidation of the EU's relative economic autonomy, eurozone policy has, in practice, been driven by the assumption of American economic dominance and a willingness of the eurozone authorities to subordinate the management of the euro to that dominance, a point well made by new constitutionalists (Cafruny and Ryner, 2007). But the GFC has brought American and dollar leadership, as well as its neoliberal *form*, sharply into question, thereby challenging the efficacy of EU policy assumptions and leaving the EU itself seriously exposed to loss of political influence, the new bulwark of economic prosperity and stability in a globalised world (Cohen and Subacchi, 2008; Van Rompuy, 2010).

From a social democratic viewpoint, the broader issue the crisis raises is how the major imbalances in the global economy, evident in the distinct impact it has had on China and the developing world, on the one hand, and the US and Europe, on the other, can be more effectively managed to secure a return to strong but sustainable (in both economic and ecological terms) global growth. Keynesian policies implemented at the regional and global levels would be one way forward (Skidelsky, 2009) although these would have to be more effectively reconciled with ecological imperatives.

At the EU level one move would be for EMU authorities to signal a decision to stabilise to the euro at a lower exchange rate reflecting long-term underlying competitiveness. As noted above, Ecofin could do this under existing treaty provisions. Commitment to bigger and harder political decisions would also need to be signalled and this would require a prior agreement around a macroeconomic strategy that recognised structural divisions between rich and poor eurozone countries and gave greater priority to sustainable growth. This requires a move towards a stronger degree of formalised fiscal centralisation (e.g. euro bonds) but underpinned at some point by a feasible and sustainable commitment to fiscal consolidation, what Farrell and Quiggin (2011) refer to as 'hard Keynesianism'. Here, the eurozone authorities can learn much from China and other leading developing countries that have used accumulated sovereign wealth and reserves from export earnings strategically as 'rainy-day' funds (Taylor, 2011).

Global Keynesianism, itself a form of 'regulatory liberalism', enjoys widespread support from reform-minded global policy elites and has made some impact at the level of global economic governance. For example, it has informed the joint G20–IMF initiative (originally proposed by the Obama administration) aimed at long-term global recovery – the so-called Pittsburgh Framework for Sustainable and Balanced Global Growth (FSBG) (Gamble, 2009: 153–6; Strange, 2012). This framework has yet to live up to earlier expectations and its failure to make more decisive progress is indicative of the fact that regulatory liberalism is only one of a number of powerful and competing post-GFC projects that might, in principle, be mobilised in an uncertain world prone to economic conflict and political fragmentation (Gamble, 2009: 141–67). Neoliberalism has been put on the defensive by the GFC and its aftermath, which has revealed internal policy divisions within the neoliberal camp, especially over deficit financing and liquidity management. But broader forms of conservative market fundamentalism, alongside regulatory liberalism and protectionism (the other potent policy alternative identified by Gamble) offer different visions for and understandings of the *form* to be taken by post-neoliberal capitalism as well as what the political community's role should be in constructing a new order both through the state and through wider governance and power structures and networks.

The diffusion of global economic and monetary power during the neoliberal era has meant that neither of the most feasible meta-alternatives currently dominate or enjoy decisive backing from a leading state in the way that neoliberalism gained general ascendency on the back of American pre-eminence (Harvey, 2005). Indeed the vacuum created by the diffusion of power, coupled to continuing uncertainty about the future of the global economy, points to the politically expedient default of diverse protectionisms as the logical extension of the absence of state leadership. In particular, this points to a weakness for social democracy, since social democracy has itself long been divided between openness and protectionism and this division has been exacerbated by the GFC and the euro crisis. The break-up of the euro would remove a crucial structural barrier to the political articulation of protectionism.

Uncomfortable as it may be for many on the Left, some form of American leadership (in concert with others) is likely to be decisive in determining whether a turn towards widespread protectionism can be forestalled. A strong EU with the global leverage the single currency can bring can help manage this leadership in favour of social democracy but against protectionism. If protectionism and its negative economic and political consequences is to be avoided, leadership in defence of openness will have to be collective, acknowledging new centres of power and authority, including the EU and China, while seeking to frame these by common commitments to the renewal and strengthening of economic multilateralism, a core legacy of America's past dominance and one on which a European-sponsored open social democracy can build (Higgott, 2009; Ikenberry, 2011). A new 'Bretton Woods' cast more in terms of Keynes' original ideal and including a new form of IMF- centred global 'currency', is one 'out rider' possibility emerging out of regulatory liberal responses to the GFC, as is the FSBG. This might be combined with a more universal shift towards 'hard' Keynesianism at national and regional levels. In the emerging new order characterised by the diffusion of power, the state and the political are 'back in' but what forms the new politics takes is an open question. The argument of this chapter is that a strong EU – armed with the single currency – can help ensure social democratic outcomes although these are hardly guaranteed. But there are few, if any, feasible or attractive systemic alternatives currently available on the Left.

Note

1 The relevant provision is now Article 125 of the 2009 Lisbon Treaty.

References

Annesley, C. and Gamble, A. (2003) 'Economic and Welfare Policy', in Smith, M. J. and Ludlum, S. (eds), *Governing as New Labour*. Basingstoke: Palgrave, 144–60.

Van Apeldoorn, B., Overbeek, H. and Ryner, M. (2003) 'Theories of European Integration: A Critique', in Cafruny, A. and Ryner, M. (eds), *A Ruined Fortress? Neoliberal Hegemony and Transformation in Europe*. Lanham, MD: Rowman & Littlefield, 14–45.

Arrighi, G. (2007) *Adam Smith in Beijing: Lineages of the Twenty First Century*. Cambridge: Verso.

Barber, L. (2010) 'Can the Euro Survive?', FT.com, 29 October.

Beeson, M. (2009) 'Hegemonic Transition in East Asia? The Dynamics of Chinese and American Power', *Review of International Studies*, Vol. 35, 95–112.

Bretherton, C. and Vogler, J. (2006) *The European Union as a Global Actor*, 2nd edn. London: Routledge.

Buller, J. and Gamble, A. (2008) 'Britain and the Euro: The Political Economy of Retrenchment', in Dyson, K. (ed.), *The Euro at 10: Europeanization, Power and Convergence*. Oxford: Oxford University Press.

Burnham, P. (2001) 'New Labour and the Politics of Depoliticisation', *British Journal of Politics and International Relations*, 3 (1), 127–49.

Burnham, P. (2010) 'Class, Capital and Crisis: A Return to Fundamentals', *Political Studies Review*, 8, 27–39.

Cafruny, A. (2003) 'Europe, the United States and Neoliberal (Dis)Order: Is There a Coming Crisis of the Euro?', in Cafruny, A. and Ryner, M. (eds), *A Ruined Fortress? Neoliberal Hegemony and Transformation in Europe*. Lanham, MD: Rowman & Littlefield, 285–305.

Cafruny, A. and Ryner, M. (eds) (2003) *A Ruined Fortress? Neoliberal Hegemony and Transformation in Europe*. Lanham, MD: Rowman & Littlefield.

Cafruny, A. and Ryner, M. (2007) 'Monetary Union and the Transatlantic and Social Dimensions of Europe's Crisis', *New Political Economy*, Vol. 12 (2), 141–65.

Clift, B. and Tomlinson, J. (2006) '"Credible Keynesianism? New Labour Macroeconomic Policy and the Political Economy of Coarse Tuning', *British Journal of Political Science*, Vol. 37, 47–69.

Cohen, B. J. (2006) 'The Macrofoundations of Monetary Power', in Andrews, D. M., *International Monetary Power*. Ithaca, NY: Cornell University Press, 31–50.

Cohen, B. J. (2008) 'The International Monetary System: Diffusion and Ambiguity', *International Affairs*, Vol. 84 (3), 455–70.

Cohen, B. J. (2009) 'Dollar Dominance, Euro-Aspirations: Recipe for Discord?', *Journal of Common Market Studies*, Vol. 47 (4), 741–66.

Cohen, B. J. and Subacchi, P. (2008) 'Is the Euro Ready for Prime Time?', Chatham House Briefing Paper, www.chathamhouse.org.uk.

Dyson, K. (2008) 'The First Decade: Credibility, Identity, and Institutional "Fuzziness"', in Dyson, K. (ed.), *The Euro at 10: Europeanization, Power, and Convergence*. Oxford: Oxford University Press, 1–34.

Dyson, K. (ed.) (2008) *The Euro at 10: Europeanization, Power, and Convergence*. Oxford, Oxford University Press.

EuroMemo Group (2010) *Confronting the Crisis: Austerity or Solidarity?*, www.euromemo.eu.

European Commission (1990) 'One Market, One Money', *European Economy*, No. 44.

European Union (2010) 'Strengthening Economic Governance in the EU: Report of the Task Force to the European Council', 21 October.

Farrell, H. and Quiggin, J. (2011) 'How to Save the Euro – and the EU', *Foreign Affairs*, 90 (3), 96–103.

FT.com (2010) 'Trichet Opposes Deal on EU Budget Rules', 20 October.

Gamble, A. and Payne, A. (eds) (1996) *Regionalism and World Order*. Basingstoke: Macmillan.

Gamble, A. (2002) 'The Case for the Euro', in Bush, J., Elliot, L. and Gamble, A., *In or Out? Labour and the Euro*, Fabian Pamphlet, No. 601. London: Fabian Society.

Gamble, A. (2009) *The Spectre at the Feast: Capitalist Crisis and the Politics of Recession*. Basingstoke: Palgrave Macmillan.

Gill, S. (2008) *Power and Resistance in the New World Order*, 2nd edn. Basingstoke: Palgrave Macmillan.

Harvey, D. (2005) *A Brief History of Neoliberalism*. Oxford: Oxford University Press.

Henning, C. R. (2006) 'The Exchange Rate Weapon and Macroeconomic Conflict', in Andrews, D. (ed.), *International Monetary Power*. Ithaca, NY: Cornell University Press, 117–38.

Henning, C. R. (2007) 'Organizing Foreign Exchange Intervention in the Euro Area', *Journal of Common Market Studies*, Vol. 45 (2), 315–42.

Henning, C. R. (2010) 'The Euro Shields Germany from Consequences of Fiscal Consolidation', *Real Time Economic Issues Watch*, Peterson Institute for International Economics, 21 June.

Hettne, B. (2005) 'Beyond the New Regionalism', *New Political Economy*, Vol. 10 (4), 543–71.

Higgott, R. (2009) 'Governing the Global Economy: Multilateral Economic Institutions', in Beeson, M. and Bisley, N. (eds), *Issues in 21st Century World Politics*. Basingstoke: Palgrave Macmillan.

Ikenberry, G. J. (2011) 'The Future of the Liberal World Order', *Foreign Affairs*, Vol. 90 (3), 56–68.

Lapavitsas, C., Kalterbrunner, A., Lambridinis, G., Lindo, D., Meadway, J., Michell, J., Painceira, J. P., Pires, E., Powell, J., Stenfors, A. and Teles, N. (2010) 'The Eurozone Between Austerity and Default', Research on Money and Finance Occasional Report, September.

Notermans, T. (ed.) (2001) *Social Democracy and Monetary Union*. Oxford: Berghahn Books.

Van Rompuy, H. (2010) 'The Challenges for Europe in a Changing World', Address to the Collège d'Europe, Bruges, 25 February.

Ruggie, J. G. (1982) 'International Regimes, Transactions and Change: Embedded Liberalism in The Postwar Economic Order', *International Organization*, Vol. 52 (4), 379–415.

Skidelsky, R. (2009) *Keynes: The Return of the Master*. London: Allen Lane.

Strange, G. (2011) 'China's Post-Listian Rise: Beyond Radical Globalisation Theory and the Political Economy of Neoliberal Hegemony', *New Political Economy* 16 (5), 539–59 (also published on-line, NPE, January 2011).

Strange, G. (2012) 'The Euro, EU Social Democracy and International Monetary Power', *Globalizations*, 9 (2).

Taylor, A. (2011) 'The Financial Rebalancing Act', *Foreign Affairs*, Vol. 90 (4), 91–9.

PART II

Europe and the transformation of the Left

4

Europeanisation of the Left: cooperation or competition?

Michael Holmes and Simon Lightfoot

The process of European integration has inspired very mixed reactions from the left. For some the EU is a capitalist club that restricts the policy options of Left-orientated governments by binding them to neoliberal policies (see Gill, 1998; van Apeldoorn, 2002; Baimbridge *et al.*, 2007; Storey, 2006). However, others on the left see European integration, and especially the European social market, as the most appropriate means for realising their goals (see Wilde, 1994; Blackburn, 2005; Strange, 2006). This chapter explores the way that different party families of the Left have responded to European integration, and how their interrelationships have coloured their responses to integration. The chapter focuses on the three main Left-leaning groups in the European Parliament (EP), the social democrats, the Greens and the radical Left (see March and Mudde, 2005 for a discussion about the terminology used).

A key framework for the analysis is Europeanisation. This is a complex and contested term (see Featherstone, 2003 for a good discussion of its various usages). We take it to be 'a process in which Europe, and especially the European Union, becomes an increasingly more relevant and important part of political reference for the actors at the level of the member states' (Hanf and Soetendorp, 1998: 1). Clearly, political parties are among those actors influenced by the EU. Europeanisation has affected political parties in three important ways.

First of all, it has practical organisational implications. Parties have been faced with a new political arena to contest, and have adapted their internal structures to facilitate engagement with European institutions (Ladrech, 2002). They debate European issues in their national parliaments, participate in European elections and in virtually every instance take up any seats they win in the EP. Participation in European elections and the

EP has in turn meant that parties have become increasingly involved with Euro-parties and an emerging Euro-party system.

The second way in which Europeanisation affects political parties is that it has led to changes in policies. Partly, this has been simply in terms of EU membership placing new issues and demands on the political agenda. But there is also evidence of domestic programmes and policies being adapted to include an increased EU-related content. This policy dimension can be considered at three levels. First of all, there is the basic policy on integration, whether parties support the idea or not. Second, there is the policy towards the EU as a particular form of integration, which is often expressed in terms of support for or opposition to the EU's institutional structures. Third, there are the stances on particular policies.

But parties do not make policy decisions purely in isolation. Partly, their decisions will depend on the positions being adopted by rival parties. Therefore, the third aspect of Europeanisation relates to patterns of such competition. The EU has contributed to changing patterns of party competition, based around the policy choices outlined above. We examine the extent to which Left parties are either pro-EU or Euro-sceptic and evaluate whether these stances are for ideological reasons or to demarcate themselves from left-of-centre rivals. Patterns of party competition are also affected by the way in which the decision making structures of the EU place a very great emphasis on governmental participation. Thus, Europeanisation has added to the pressures of participation in government.

This chapter applies these three aspects of the Europeanisation to parties of the Left. The next section identifies three broad families that can be considered as forming the Left and elaborates how these are expressed at the EU level. It then sets out their responses to European integration, concentrating on the organisational adaptation that they have undertaken in relation to such integration. The following section explores in greater detail the policy adaptation that has occurred, placing the discussion in the context of an analysis of the EU's policy breadth from competing social market and neoliberal perspectives. Finally, the chapter examines current positions of the main Left party families, by outlining their visions for a new Europe and exploring the possibilities for greater Left-wing cooperation in relation to the integration project.

We are aware that by focusing on party alliances, we are moving away from the standard application of Europeanisation of parties, which emphasises 'domestic adaptation to European regional integration' (Vink and Graziano, 2008: 7). However, domestic adaptation feeds back into party behaviour at the European level. We evaluate the extent to which the three aspects of Europeanisation being considered – organisational adaptation, policy adaptation and competitive re-orientation – are evident in such collaboration at the European level.

A number of studies of the Europeanisation of political parties has reached similar conclusions: that while Europeanisation appears to have significant superficial effects upon parties, it has not significantly altered the underlying patterns of party success and failure. In particular, although Mair suggests that 'the Europeanisation dimension is finally beginning to force itself with greater weight into the various national electoral arenas' (2008: 165), he argues that in general 'party systems appear to remain relatively impervious to the direct impact of Europeanization' (2000: 47). In applying Europeanisation to Left-wing party alliances at the European level, we come to the same conclusion: while there is an identifiable impact, it has not greatly altered party performances, particularly in terms of Left-wing collaboration.

The practical adaptation of the Left

The Left is very far from being an homogeneous group. This was evident even in the loose transnational federations that existed prior to the start of European integration, such as the Socialist International. This chapter concentrates on the party alliances that have emerged in the EU, and focuses on the three such alliances that lay claim to a Left or socialist identity. First, it is necessary to distinguish between two forms of transnational party alliance in the EU (Poguntke *et al.*, 2007). On the one hand, there are the 'party groups' in the EP. On the other hand, there are the extra-European parliamentary party federations, which we term 'Euro-parties'. Although there are links between the groups and the Euro-parties, there are also important distinctions between them.

The development of party alliances at the EU level has been influenced by a number of key events. The initial impetus for party cooperation came right at the outset, with the first party groups emerging in 1953 with the establishment of the European Assembly. This soon evolved into the EP, and in 1979 a further development took place with the introduction of direct elections to the EP. This encouraged the emergence of party cooperation outside the EP, since there was now a rationale for parties to work together to organise joint manifestos and campaigns, even if they did not hold EP seats. The inclusion of the 'party article' in the Treaty on European Union (TEU) that acknowledged explicitly the role of parties in the EU provided further incentive for collaboration. Recent developments in the funding of Euro-parties required them to institutionalise their contact more formally (see Lightfoot, 2006; Hanley, 2008). Finally, the various enlargements have also had an impact, as the rules laying down the numbers of parties required to form a group in the EP have been modified with the arrival of each new member state.

The social democrats are the Left-wing alliance with the longest history in the EU (see Lightfoot, 2005). Collaboration among parties affiliated with the Socialist International began as soon as the European Assembly was up and running, and a Socialist Group has existed in the EP ever since. In parallel, a social democratic Euro-party slowly emerged alongside the EP group. The Socialist International set up a special Liaison Bureau for its EP members in 1957, and following the first enlargement, a Confederation of Socialist Parties in the EP was established. By 1992 this had become the Party of European Socialists (PES). For a period, the PES came close to eliding the party group/Euro-party divide. But following the 2009 election, the PES group in the EP was altered by inclusion of the Italian Democrats, becoming the Progressive Alliance of Socialists and Democrats.

It took longer for another Left-wing alliance to emerge. Communist parties from the six original member states had met in 1959 to try to agree a common response to the emerging process, but it was not until 1973 that a Communist and Allies Group was formed in the Parliament. However, there were 'glaring and increasing policy divergences' (Dunphy, 2004: 65) which meant that 'the Group hardly ever held common meetings, and seldom agreed on a common line (Jacobs and Corbett, 1990: 68). The Group limped on until the 1989 EP elections, when it split in two, a more reformist Group of the United European Left (GUE) and a more hard-line Left Unity. The GUE group disappeared in 1993, when its very large Italian contingent left to join the PES. But following the 1994 election the remnants of GUE and Left Unity were able to put aside enough of their remaining differences to form a single Confederation of the United European Left. In 1995, this group was joined by various Nordic Green–Left parties, including the Swedish Left Party and the Finnish Left Alliance (GUE/NGL, 2007). The group operated 'more as an umbrella for various Communist and left parties than as a unitary group' (Raunio, 2001: 232). The tensions among the parties are evident when we consider the formation in 2004 of a Euro-party, the Party of the European Left (PEL). The PEL comprises eighteen member parties drawn from sixteen countries (including some non-EU states such as Moldova and Switzerland) and a further nine observer parties, but not the Nordic parties.

This is still not the full story of Left-wing participation in the EP. From the outset a small handful of MEPs chose to remain outside both the social democrat and the Communist groups, preferring instead to sit with the loose Technical Group. In 1984, this group developed into a slightly more coherent Rainbow Group. Alongside Greens, region-alists and Danish anti-marketeers, the group featured some Left-wing socialists, including the Dutch Green Progressive Accord and the Italian Proletarian Democracy Party (Jacobs and Corbett, 1990: 57). By 1989, the Greens were sufficiently numerous to form their own Green Group for the first time, but it retained the Left-socialist members from its earlier incarnation. This Green–Left cooperation in the EP continues, with a member from the Danish Socialist People's Party sitting with the Greens. Despite tensions, the Greens formed a Euro-party in 1993, and in 2004 this became the European Green Party (EGP).

This discussion reveals two important factors. First of all, it shows the extent to which political parties are subject to one of the measures of Europeanisation. In organisational terms, parties at the European level exhibit a strong degree of adaptation to the exigencies of participation in the EU. They have gone beyond merely participating in the EP to the formation of EP party groups that attempt to coordinate their member parties' activities; and they have gone further by establishing Euro-parties, trying to develop cooperation beyond the aegis of the EP.

But despite such organisational contacts, the problems of developing common Left-wing positions in the EU can also be seen. There are significant problems within the various alliances – fluctuations in membership, changes of name and identity, splits and mergers, discon-tinuities between the party groups and the euro-parties of what are ostensibly the same party family. The result is quite loose cooperation rather than tightly disciplined cohesion. And that is before any consid-eration is made of the possibility of greater cooperation between these disparate alliances. The organisational dimension shows the growing extent of Europeanisation, but it also reveals the plethora of organisational obstacles that exist to stymie closer Left-wing cooperation.

The policy adaptation of the Left

The second aspect of the Europeanisation of parties is policy adaptation. At a basic level, participation in the EU has brought new issues and demands to the political agenda. But Europeanisation has had a greater impact than that. As already indicated, this needs to be considered at a number of levels: in terms of individual EU policies; the normative ideal of integration; and EU institutions. There is clear evidence of policy adaptation on the part of many Left-wing parties in Europe. There is a very clear pattern of initial suspicion and hostility giving way to acceptance, support and, in the cases of some parties, even outright enthusiasm and leadership.

The majority of social democratic parties, even those who are now enthusiastic supporters of the EU, went through either an ambivalent phase or indeed even outright opposition to integration. However, the positions of the parties have shifted to a more pro-European position over time. For example, French, German and Italian socialists had already adopted a much more pro-integration position by the time of the Treaty of Rome, while the Irish Labour Party, which led the 'No' campaign in that country's membership referendum in 1972, dropped its opposition immediately after the vote (Holmes, 2010). Even parties from Scandinavia and the UK have gradually shifted to a more pro-EU position. Thus, there has been a clear tendency of social democratic parties to 'leap later but further than competitors to embrace Community solutions' (Butler, 1995: 115). This Euro-enthusiasm extends to many of the social democratic parties from Central and Eastern Europe (see Enyedi and Lewis, 2006: 239–43).

A similar pattern is evident in parties further to the Left, although the initial Euro-scepticism was stronger and they have not travelled as far towards a more pro-EU position. From early on, Communist parties were 'violently hostile' to a European integration project which was identified as 'capitalist, Atlanticist, reformist and a rampart against the Revolution' (Bell, 1996: 222). But already by the time the GUE was established in 1989, its founding declaration stated that it was 'firmly committed to European integration' (GUE/NGL, 1994), while their rivals in the Left Unity group 'avoided the anti-European integration language so frequently used by the constituent parties' (Dunphy, 2004: 70). By the time the PEL was being launched in 2004, its manifesto recognised that 'the European Union as well as the whole European continent are becoming an increasing important space for alternative politics' and announced that 'we want to build a project for another Europe and to give another content to the EU' (PEL, 2004). The Left Party in Germany is an example of how far some parties have travelled in this direction (see Roder, 2012).

For Left–Green parties, attitudes about European integration partly relate to the broader Green debates about party strategy between realists and fundamentalists. As Bomberg argues, 'Europeanization has accelerated both trends of professionalization of Green strategy and the mellowing of their ideological edge' (2002: 34–8). Those parties who have gone furthest down the realist road, embracing traditional forms of party organisation and coalition government, have also been the parties that have embraced European integration with greatest enthusiasm. But, generally, there has been recognition that certain core Green objectives demand international cooperation, and that therefore the EU offers an unparalleled opportunity to influence decisions – particularly given that Green parties are at best in the minority and at worst entirely absent in most countries. Therefore, the Greens have come to regard the EU as 'a historical success story' (European Greens, 2006: 2), even if they criticise some aspects of it.

Therefore, we can see a steady move towards support for the idea of integration and for the EU as the institutional expression of integration. This is evident across all three party alliances, with the social democrats having moved furthest, the Greens being more recent converts to the cause and the socialists retaining the greatest reservations. But when we move to look at stances on individual policies, the differences begin to mount up.

Up to the SEA, it was possible to argue that the 'European social model' of the EU accommodated free market principles alongside a commitment to social cohesion. Policies in the social, environmental and employment spheres formed an integral part of the vision of a 'European social space' put forward by former Commission President Jacques Delors (Grant, 1994: 67). However, after the Act a more orthodox neoliberal stance took hold. For example, EU competition policy and the Lisbon Strategy for growth institutionalised what Gill calls 'disciplinary neo-liberalism' (1998), while others argue that enlargement to Central and Eastern Europe (CEE) 'makes demands of candidate states which coincide with the aims of parties at the pro-market libertarian end of the axis' (Marks *et al.*, 2006: 168). This is especially noticeable among social democratic parties in these states, which are strong supporters of the EU and also favour strongly market-based programmes (Holmes and Lightfoot, 2011). The EU's policy direction since the 1980s shows an 'underlying liberal bias', and once policy directions have become institutionalised in the EU, they are far harder to reverse than in national political systems (McGowan, 2001: 75).

For many on the Left, the main focus for criticism was EMU. Delors aimed to create an 'organised space' within which to regulate capitalism at a European level. This could be seen as being in keeping with national social democratic traditions, and also created a new framework of policy opportunity through which social democratic parties could engage with the European project (Marks and Wilson, 1999: 120). But EMU also created problems for Left-wing governments, as the convergence criteria 'forced all countries to adopt deflationary rather than expansionary fiscal strategies' (Scharpf, 1999: 116). Scharpf argues that 'European integration has so far not helped to overcome the constraints imposed upon Keynesian full-employment policies at the national level, and the rules adopted for EMU are not designed to change that situation' (1999: 116). Basically, social democratic leaders 'had to accept a neoliberal economic constitution' (Aust, 2004: 186). The EMU project has therefore been caricatured as 'binding Leviathan', as it limited the scope for Left-wing governments to pursue their traditional economic policies (Dyson, 1999).

The process of 'binding Leviathan' involves more knots than EMU alone. The debate over the Bolkestein Directive on Services in the Internal Market provides a further example of the free market orientation of the EU. The Directive was designed to enable service industries to benefit from the Single Market. Its most controversial aspect was the 'country of origin' principle, allowing companies to comply with regulations in their country of origin even if they were operating elsewhere. Again, the fear was that this would lead to a 'race to the bottom' (McGiffen, 2005: 87). The Directive is particularly interesting because an extensive campaign resulted in some of its most controversial clauses being omitted or watered down. While some hailed this as a victory for social Europe, the deal to salvage the directive was brokered between the PES, the Liberals and Christian Democrats, with the Greens and Radical Left marginalised. This suggests there are some significant differences of emphasis on individual policies among the three different Left-wing groups, and we shall examine these further in the next section.

Evidence of the increasingly pro-management industrial relations line being taken in the EU emerged from a series of ECJ rulings in the late 2000s. First, there was the *Laval* case. Laval was a Latvian construction company which undertook a school refurbishment in the Swedish town of Växholm, but refused to abide by Swedish wage agreements. The case came to the ECJ in 2008, and the court ruled in favour of Laval. This led the European Trade Union Confederation (ETUC) to declare 'the ruling amounts to a licence for social dumping' (ETUC, 2008). The *Laval* case was reinforced by similar rulings in the *Rüffert* case, where a company contracted by a regional government in Germany had sub-contracted to a Polish company paying lower wages than set by collective agreements, and in the *Viking* case, where Finnish trade unions had sought to prevent the Viking Line shipping company from employing Estonian workers at lower wage rates.

By the end of the decade, however, the context had changed significantly. The financial crisis of 2008 and the ensuing recession produced demands for re-regulation of the financial and economic sectors, for far greater wage equality and for a leading state role in managing economies. This is evident in the tone of the EU's Europe 2020 Strategy, introduced to take over from the Lisbon Strategy. The new strategy aimed for 'smart, sustainable and inclusive' growth with 'high levels of employment, productivity and social cohesion' (European Commission, 2010: 3). However, reaction to the new strategy was mixed, with an obvious tension between those who wanted a strong shift towards greater social regulation and those who argued that the globalised world economy meant that Europe still needed extensive market-based reform.

New Left visions and the problem of party competition

For Left-wing parties, the financial crisis raised the possibility of a revived enthusiasm for regulation of markets and for Keynesian strategies, though it also created serious problems of recession and unemployment. Parties have responded in different ways, which brings us to the third aspect of Europeanisation – party competition. Left-wing parties might agree on many policies, but they are also in competition with each other for votes, seats and influence. This was particularly obvious during the debates over the draft European Constitutional Treaty (ECT) in France, where there was a serious internal division in the French Socialist Party (Marthaler, 2011), and in the Netherlands, where the Labour Party and the Socialist Party were in opposite camps (Harmsen, 2012). And it has carried through into debates about the subsequent Treaty of Lisbon and the party responses to the financial crisis.

The PES vision for the EU at this time focused on the need for the creation of a 'social Europe'. This was evident in their position on the ECT (Lightfoot, 2012), and in 2006 the party launched its 'New Social Europe' programme. This talked of full employment, universal child care, social partnership and sustainability, and asserted that the PES's aim 'is to renew and strengthen Europe's welfare states' (PES, 2006). It specifically rejected the ideas that Europe could no longer afford its welfare states, and that the primary purpose of the EU should be to promote free trade and competition. Of course, the financial crisis challenged these aspirations (see Moschonas, 2009). Nonetheless, 'New Social Europe' remained a cornerstone of the Party's manifesto for the 2009 EP elections, as part of a wider commitment to a 'progressive reform agenda' based on a proactive investment policy for growth (PES, 2009). But despite criticism of unregulated markets and growing inequalities, the crisis was interpreted as a failure of national financial systems, rather than a failure of the EU. Indeed, the PES was still prepared to state that the main problem with the Lisbon Strategy was that it had 'been difficult to implement' (PES, n.d.).

Because the PES document gave a high priority to tackling climate change and to investing in the 'green economy', it is not too difficult to see connections with the European Greens. Their manifesto was titled a 'A Green New Deal for Europe' (European Greens, 2009), a suitably social democratic phrase to borrow. Some of their criticisms of 'fierce and unfettered competition' and the neoliberal 'mantra of competitiveness and growth' might have sat a little uneasily with the PES, but the manifesto concluded with a commitment to building alliances and seeking out allies. This had also been evident in the European Greens' position on the Constitutional Treaty and the Treaty of Lisbon, which had been supported as flawed but nonetheless generally progressive documents (Saylan, 2006).

However, the stance of the PEL was far less accommodatory. Its 2009 manifesto started out by identifying 'an opportunity to change the foundations of the European Union', and accused the EU of 'interfering in the lives of people' while criticising a broad swath of EU policies. Even more, the manifesto argued that the neoliberal shift of the EU was only possible 'because of a kind of great coalition between the parties of the European conservative forces and the European socialists'. The group had dismissed the ECT as 'the constitutionalisation of the liberal model' (GUE/NGL, 2004), and the PEL clearly continued its opposition to both the Lisbon Treaty and Lisbon Strategy in the 2009 manifesto. There were commitments to pacifism and to the redistribution of wealth and an opposition to capitalism and globalisation which would be hard to imagine from the PES.

It is thus clear that the Europeanisation of the Left has come least far in relation to patterns of party competition. While there are clear and extensive areas of overlap in terms of how all the major strands of Left-wing opinion view the EU and the integration project, nonetheless a common Left-wing platform or programme is very far away indeed. This is partly because these parties are in competition with each other for votes and seats, and often use EU issues as a way of marking their separate identities, and a means of demarcating their political space. This competition can be seen in both the EP and national political arenas. In relation to the EP, we have already identified the vote on the Bolkestein Directive as an example of where Left unity was conspicuous by its absence. There is unity between the three groups on a whole variety of political issues and we do see relatively cohesive voting patterns when their policy preferences converge (see Hix *et al.*, 2007). This (partial) unity has remained relatively constant despite the enlargement of the EU, although the divisions clearly hamper the development of strong Red–Green leadership from the EP.

Possibly the main factor influencing the persistence of competition on the Left, apart from ideology, is governmental participation. Parties that have participated in government have had to engage far more extensively with the EU than those that have been restricted to a parliamentary presence. One example can be found in Ireland, where 'the experience of being in government [had] a major impact on attitudes' in the Labour Party (Holmes, 2006: 168), and encouraged the party's move to a much more pro-EU position. These pressures are not confined to social democratic parties. Howarth notes the adoption of a more conciliatory tone towards the EU by the French Communists in 1999 and links this to PCF participation in the Plural Left government of Lionel Jospin (2001: 120).

One reason why participation in national government is so important is because it opens the door to involvement in the Council of Ministers, the EU's primary decision making body. Participation in Council meetings made participants aware that policy goals might be more readily realisable through the EU than at a national level. This has been a particularly strong influence on shifts in Green Party policies. For example, between 1998 and 2002 Green ministers held twenty-eight votes in the Environment Council and exerted considerable influence over policy direction. The opportunity to participate in this Council gave them leverage over policy decisions on core Green objectives that they would have struggled to duplicate in their national settings.

There is evidence that the political space is not as 'stretched' as it once was, and that there are prospects for closer cooperation in the future. But before reaching that point, it is important to bear in mind the multiple pressures created by Europeanisation. Individual parties now have to engage in a multi-level game, involving multiple arenas. The very evident difficulties in creating binding common positions *within* the party families and federations of the Left in Europe show that any ambitions to construct *wider* collaboration will be very difficult indeed.

Changing Left, changing Europe?

Two of the strongest political features of the post-Second World War landscape in Europe have been the success of Left-wing parties and the rise of European integration. Both of these are now subject to considerable challenge and change. Socialism has been jolted by the end of the era of sustained growth and redistribution, the abandonment of Keynesian models and the collapse of Communism, and since the 1980s has been struggling to find a new agenda. Meanwhile, the EU has continued to grow, but the problems over the ratification of successive treaties (the TEU in 1992, the Treaty of Nice in 2000, the Draft Constitutional Treaty in 2005 and the Treaty of Lisbon 2010) and the problems of low turnout in EP elections (Lightfoot, 2010) show that it, too, has struggled to engage and excite people.

This chapter has demonstrated that the future of Left-wing politics is closely bound up with the future of European integration. Left-wing parties have clearly become much more extensively involved and engaged with the EU. In many cases, particularly among social democrats and Greens, they have even become strong supporters and advocates of the EU, perhaps paralleling the growth in Right-wing Euro-scepticism (see Taggart and Szczerbiak, 2004). But such Europeanisation is not complete, and in particular there are still important policy differences between the parties of the Left, and these parties still compete with one another on EU issues. But a more cohesive Left-wing response to the EU, and a more coherent Left-wing agenda for the future of integration, could be vital not just for the Left-wing parties themselves. The EU has an evident difficulty in creating engagement with its citizens.

A Left-wing agenda could contribute to a stronger Europe and a reinvigorated left. Scharpf argues that most European citizens regard the achievements of the post-war welfare state 'as constructive elements of a legitimizing social contract' and that if the contract should be revoked due to EU policies there is a danger that 'the rising political dissatisfaction will again undermine either the political legitimacy of democratic governments or their political commitment to economic integration' (1999: 122). But a strong vision for the future of the EU can be constructed, and it can be argued that 'a strong European state with a red–green political leadership' is the only plausible future for the Left (Wilde, 1994: 182).

Even without that political leadership, many progressive features and policies can be ascribed to the EU. The Union has contributed to the democratisation in CEE states and has promoted respect for human rights there. It has also been a positive force in environmental policy, both within the EU and globally. The EU is taking a lead on poverty reduction, and is the world's biggest donor of overseas aid. And it has adopted social and employment policies which have provided some degree of social protection. What is clear is that the parties of the Left, as Strange (2006) argues, need to embrace the opportunities offered for a new form of political mobilisation offered by the EU in an attempt to develop a governance regime capable of institutionally embedding a progressive regime to replace the embedded neoliberalism.

References

Van Apeldoorn, B. (2002) *Transnational Capitalism and the Struggle over European Integration.* London and New York: Routledge.

Aust, A. (2004) 'From "Eurokeynesianism" to the "Third Way": The Party of European Socialists (PES) and European Employment Policies', in Bonoli, G. and Powell, M. (eds), *Social Democratic Party Policies in Contemporary Europe.* London and New York: Routledge.

Baimbridge, M., Whyman, P. and Burkitt, B. (2007) 'Beyond EU Neoliberalism: A Progressive Strategy for the British Left', *Capital and Class*, Vol. 93, 67–91.

Bell, D. (1996) 'Western Communist Parties and the European Union', in Gaffney, J. (ed.), *Political Parties and the European Union.* London and New York: Routledge.

Blackburn, R. (2005) 'Capital and Social Europe', *New Left Review*, Vol. 34.

Bomberg, E. (2002) *Green Parties and the EU.* London and New York: Routledge.

Butler, A. (1995) *Transformative Politics: The Future of Socialism in Western Europe.* Basingstoke and New York: Macmillan and St Martin's Press.

Dunphy, R. (2004) *Contesting Capitalism? Left Parties and European Integration.* Manchester: Manchester University Press.

Dyson, K. (1999) 'Benign or Malevolent Leviathan? Social Democratic Governments in a Neo-liberal Euro Area', *The Political Quarterly*, Vol. 70 (2), 195–209.

Enyedi, Z. and Lewis, P. G. (2006) 'The Impact of the European Union on Party Politics in Central and Eastern Europe', in Lewis, P. G. and Mansfeldova, Z. (eds), *The European Union and Party Politics in Central and Eastern Europe.* Basingstoke: Palgrave Macmillan.

ETUC (2008) *Laval case (Vaxholm)*, www.etuc.org/r/847 (accessed 29 September 2010).

European Commission (2010) *Europe 2020: A European Strategy for Smart, Sustainable and Inclusive Growth.* Brussels: European Commission.

European Greens (2006) *A Green Future for Europe*, http://europeangreens. eu/fileadmin/logos/pdf/policy_documents/Future_for_Europe.English.pdf (accessed 30 September 2010).

European Greens (2009) *A Green New Deal for Europe: Manifesto for the European Election Campaign 2009.* Brussels: European Greens, http:// europeangreens.eu/fileadmin/logos/pdf/manifesto_EUROPEAN_GREENS. pdf (accessed 27 September 2010).

Featherstone, K. (2003) 'Introduction: In the Name of "Europe"', in Featherstone, K. and Radaelli, C. M. (eds), *The Politics of Europeanization.* Oxford: Oxford University Press.

Gill, S. (1998) 'European Governance and New Constitutionalism: Economic and Monetary Union and Alternatives to Disciplinary Neoliberalism in Europe', *New Political Economy*, Vol. 3 (1), 5–26.

Grant, C. (1994) *Delors: Inside the House that Jacques Built.* London: Nicholas Brealey.

GUE/NGL (1994) *Constituent Declaration*, www.europarl.eu.int/gue/tre/en/declar.htm (accessed 30 September 2010).

GUE/NGL (2004) *History.* European United Left/Nordic Green Left European Parliamentary Group, www.guengl.eu/showPage.jsp?ID=39 (accessed 30 September 2010).

Hanf, K. and Soetendorp, B. (1998) 'Small States and the Europeanization of Public Policy', in Hanf, K. and Soetendorp, B. (eds), *Adapting to European Integration: Small States and the European Union.* Harlow: Longman, 1–13.

Hanley, D. (2008) *Beyond the Nation State: Parties in the Era of European Integration.* Basingstoke: Palgrave Macmillan.

Harmsen, R. (2012) 'The Dutch Left and European Integration: Framing the Constitutional Debate', in Holmes, M. and Roder, K. (eds), *The Left and the European Constitution: From Laeken to Lisbon.* Manchester: Manchester University Press.

Hix, S., Noury, A. and Roland, G. (2007) *Democratic Politics in the European Parliament.* Cambridge: Cambridge University Press.

Holmes, M. (2006) *The Development of the Irish Labour Party's European Policy: From Opposition to Support.* Lewiston, NY: Edwin Mellen Press.

Holmes, M. (2010) 'The Irish Labour Party: The Advantages, Disadvantages and Irrelevance of Europeanization?', in Hayward, K. and Murphy, M. C. (eds), *The Europeanization of Party Politics in Ireland, North and South.* London and New York: Routledge.

Holmes, M. and Lightfoot, S. (2011) 'Limited Influence? The Role of the PES in Shaping Social Democracy in Central and Eastern Europe', *Government and Opposition*, Vol. 46 (1), 32–55.

Howarth, D. (2001) 'France', in Lodge, J. (ed.), *The 1999 Elections to the European Parliament.* Basingstoke: Palgrave

Jacobs, F. and Corbett, R. (1990) *The European Parliament.* Harlow: Longman.

Ladrech, R. (2002) 'Europeanization and Political Parties', *Party Politics*, Vol. 8 (4), 389–403.

Lightfoot, S. (2005) *Europeanizing Social Democracy? The Rise of the Party of European Socialists.* London and New York: Routledge.

Lightfoot, S. (2006) 'The Consolidation of Europarties? The "Party Regulation" and the Development of Political Parties in the European Union', *Representation*, Vol. 42 (4), 303–14.

Lightfoot, S. (2010) 'The 2009 European Parliamentary Elections and the Party Groups', in Lodge, J. (ed.), *The 2009 European Parliamentary Elections.* Basingstoke: Palgrave.

Lightfoot, S. (2012) 'Left Parties at an EU level from Laeken to Lisbon', in Holmes, M. and Roder, K. (eds), *The Left and the European Constitution: From Laeken to Lisbon*. Manchester: Manchester University Press.

Mair, P. (2000) 'The Limited Impact of Europe on National Party Systems', *West European Politics*, Vol. 23 (4), 27–51.

Mair, P. (2008) 'Political Parties and Party Systems', in Graziano, P. and Vink, M. P. (eds), *Europeanization: New Research Agendas*. Basingstoke: Palgrave Macmillan.

March, L. and Mudde, C. (2005) 'What's Left of the Radical Left? The European Left After 1989. Decline and Mutation', *Comparative European Politics*, Vol. 3 (1), 23–49.

Marks, G. and Wilson, C. (1999) 'National Parties and the Contestation of Europe', in Banchoff, T. and Smith, M. (eds), *Legitimacy and the EU: The Contested Polity*. London and New York: Routledge.

Marks, G., Hooghe, L., Nelson, M. and Edwards, E. (2006) 'Party Competition and European Integration in the East and West: Different Structure, Same Causality', *Comparative Political Studies* Vol. 39 (2), 155–75.

Marthaler, S. (2012) 'The Yes–No Dichotomy of the French Left', in Holmes, M. and Roder, K. (eds), *The Left and the European Constitution: From Laeken to Lisbon*. Manchester: Manchester University Press.

McGiffen, S. (2005) *The European Union: A Critical Guide*. London: Pluto.

McGowan, F. (2001) 'Social Democracy and the European Union: Who's Changing Whom?', in Van Den Anker, C. and Martell, L.(eds), *Social Democracy: Global and National Perspectives*. Basingstoke: Palgrave Macmillan.

Moschonas, G. (2009) 'Reformism in a "Conservative" System: The European Union and Social Democratic Identity', in Callaghan, J. *et al.* (eds.), *In Search of Social Democracy: Responses to Crisis and Modernisation*. Manchester: Manchester University Press.

PEL (2004) *Manifesto of the Party of the European Left*, www.european-left.org/about/docus/doc/manifesto (accessed 29 September 2010).

PES (2006) *New Social Europe – Ten Principles for Our Common Future*. Brussels: Party of European Socialists.

PES (2009) *People First: A New Direction for Europe. PES Manifesto, European Elections June 2009*. Brussels, Party of European Socialists, www.pes.org/system/files/images/ManifestoBook-EN_Online.pdf (accessed 27 September 2010).

PES (n.d.) *Lisbon Strategy*, www.pes.org/en/pes-action/political-initiatives/lisbon-strategy (accessed 29 September 2010).

Poguntke, T., Aylott, N., Ladrech, R. and Luther, K. R. (2007) 'The Europeanization of National Party Organisations: A Conceptual Analysis', *European Journal of Political Research*, Vol. 46, 747–71.

Raunio, T. (2001) 'The Party System of the European Parliament after the 1999 Elections', in Lodge, J. (ed.), *The 1999 Elections to the European Parliament*. Basingstoke: Palgrave.

Roder, K. (2012) 'The German Left from Laeken to Lisbon', in Holmes. M. and Roder, K. (eds), *The Left and the European Constitution: From Laeken to Lisbon*. Manchester: Manchester University Press.

Saylan, O. (2006) 'The Greens/Free Alliance', in Eschke, N. and Malick, T. (eds), *The European Constitution and its Ratification Crisis: Constitutional Debates in The EU Member States*. Bonn: Zentrum für Europäische Integrationsforschung.

Scharpf, F. (1999) *Governing in Europe: Effective and Democratic?* Oxford: Oxford University Press.

Strange, G. (2006) 'The Left Against Europe? A Critical Engagement With New Constitutionalism and Structural Dependence Theory', *Government and Opposition*, Vol. 41 (2), 197–229.

Storey, A. (2006) 'The European Project: Dismantling the Social Model, Globalising Neoliberalism', *Irish Review*, Vol. 34, 20–33.

Taggart, P. and Szczerbiak, A. (2004) 'Contemporary Euroscepticism in the Party Systems of the European Union Candidate States of Central and Eastern Europe', *European Journal of Political Research*, Vol. 43 (1), 1–27.

Vink, M. P. and Graziano, P. (2008) 'Challenges of a New Research Agenda', in Graziano, P. and Vink, M. P. (eds), *Europeanization: New Research Agendas*. Basingstoke: Palgrave Macmillan.

Wilde, L. (1994) *Modern European Socialism*. Aldershot: Dartmouth.

5

The impossibility of social democracy: from unfailing optimism to enlightened pessimism in the 're-social democratisation' debate

David J. Bailey

On the question of what defines social democratic parties – i.e. when should parties be considered social democratic, and when they should not – scholars face the problem that throughout their history parties typically referred to as 'social democratic' have themselves undergone a number of significant revisions. Indeed, for some observers, it is the tendency for (programmatic, organisational or ideological) revision, in the light of changing economic or political circumstances, that characterises social democracy itself (Callaghan *et al.*, 2009: 1). Despite this tendency for revisionism, this chapter argues that there have nonetheless been three core commitments that have historically signified the 'social democratic' aspect of social democratic parties (on this definition, see Bailey, 2009b: Chapter 2): (1) social democratic parties are, and have historically been, committed to the reform (rather than the (immediate) replacement) of capitalist relations of production; (2) social democratic parties have historically been committed to seeking these reforms through an electoral and parliamentary political strategy; finally, and more substantively, (3) social democratic parties are committed to achieving policy outcomes that have a redistributive, levelling, or egalitarian effect that favours their core electoral constituency (which comprises a broad subaltern group including (but extending beyond) organised labour), *subject to the constraints arising from commitments (1) and (2)*. This social democratic model originated, and has arguably been most prevalent and successful, within western Europe. The analysis in this chapter therefore focuses on west European social democratic parties, in order that we might draw some more general lessons regarding the potential and/or probable direction that social democratic parties might take in the future.

The 'de-social democratisation' of social democratic parties

The changes undertaken by social democratic parties since the early 1980s might be described as a process of 'de-social democratisation' (Moschonas, 2002: 244). Thus, while not denying that social democratic parties retain the broad defining commitments outlined above, the extent to which these commitments form a distinctive 'social democratic' model – in terms of organisation, party programme, or ideology – has arguably declined since the 1980s, as social democratic party elites have responded to a tightening of both economic and political constraints by arguing for (and attaining) a downscaling of redistributive reformist ambitions within their parties (Kitschelt, 1994; Bailey, 2009a). Since the mid 1970s social democratic parties have seemed increasingly unable and/or unwilling to assert their 'traditional' social democratic programme (including macroeconomic regulation, fiscal redistribution and/or widening democratic participation). In its place, social democratic parties have moved towards what many have described as 'Third Way' social democracy (Giddens, 1998). This new form of social democracy includes: a move away from class as the basis for electoral mobilisation (Kitschelt, 1994); the centralisation of internal party decision making (Moschonas, 2002: 123–5); an acceptance of the neoliberal view that private markets are more efficient than the public sector at allocating resources (Thomson, 2000: 156–7; Przeworski, 2001); a move towards minimal, or more means-tested and 'prioritarian', welfare provisions and a focus on pro-employment, or 'productivist', support for those disadvantaged in the labour market (Huo, 2009). Given the downscaling of redistributive goals, and the reduction in the attempt to ensure the decommodification of their working-class orientated constituency, a number of commentators have viewed this process as a 'de-social democratisation' of social democratic parties (Moschonas, 2002; Motta and Bailey, 2007). The question, therefore, particularly for those disappointed by these developments, has become one of whether social democratic parties can be expected to return to a more redistributive agenda. It is the contending positions within this 're-social democratisation' debate that the present chapter sets out to explore.

The 're-social democratisation' debate

Three broad positions exist within the 're-social democratisation' debate. First, there are those who reject a necessitarian view of de-social democratisation and therefore view or anticipate a process of 'contingent divergence', whereby the decision to 're-social democratise' (or, for that matter, 'de-social democratise') is contingent upon decisions taken within social democratic parties (rather than a result of necessary adaptations to social, political, or economic change). Second, there are those who seek a cosmopolitan reincarnation of social democracy, particularly through the pursuit of 'Social Europe'. Finally, there are those who view empirical developments to date as an indication of the impossibility of social democracy. Each of these positions is set out in more detail below.

Contingent divergence

The most optimistic position within the 're-social democratisation' debate focuses on the continued, and empirically evident, scope for autonomous social democratic party agency. In contrast to those who perceive a common trajectory towards 'Third Way' social democracy, a number of scholars have highlighted divergent responses by social democratic parties to the socio-economic changes those parties have faced since the 1970s. Thus, a number of important contributions to the comparative political economy literature illustrate both the way that social democratic parties' responses to post-1970s developments differ from those of their centre-right rivals (Boix, 1998; Garrett, 1998; Allan and Scruggs, 2004; Amable *et al.*, 2006), alongside the also divergent responses undertaken by different parties within the social democratic party family (Hall, 2002; Huo, 2009; Kwon and Pontusson, 2010). For such scholars, these trends evince the contingent nature of social democratic responses to external pressures (Hay and Rosamond, 2002; Watson and Hay, 2003; Hay, 2004, 2006), thereby providing grounds for optimism for those seeking a 're-social democratisation' of social democratic parties.

'Social Europe' and the cosmopolitan reincarnation of social democracy

Rather than place their hope in the prospects for contingent divergence, a second group of scholars within the 're-social democratisation debate' proclaim the possibility of a more redistributive social democratic agenda, *provided it be sought through coordinated supranational activity* (Held and McGrew, 2002; Held, 2003) and particularly through the EU (Lightfoot, 2005; Strange, 2006). According to this view, the scale of the EU (in terms of both population and economic activity) provides an opportunity to circumvent the constraints imposed upon social democracy (as pursued at the national level), thereby providing the opportunity for its cosmopolitan reincarnation in the form of a 'Social Europe' agenda pursued and realised at the EU level. The optimism of cosmopolitan social democrats within the 're-social democratisation' debate, therefore, is *conditional upon* the ability of social democratic parties to promote a coordinated approach towards the EU.

The impossibility of social democracy

The third and final position within the 're-social democratisation' debate, as outlined here, highlights the (insurmountable) obstacles facing social democratic parties in the pursuit of their central aims. For those adopting this view, the pursuit of redistributive outcomes sits uncomfortably alongside the inequality inherent in both parliamentary democracy and the capitalist relations of production (both of which social democratic parties are committed to utilising in their pursuit of egalitarian reforms). Thus, policies that aim to reduce the economic inequality faced by the core constituents of social democratic parties risk undermining the scope for profit making within the economy, and thereby destabilising capitalist relations of production, the continuation of which social democratic parties are committed to overseeing (Panitch, 1976; Coates, 2003). Similarly, any attempts at political redistribution, whereby participation within decision making processes is broadened to incorporate members of the social democratic constituency (thereby having a politically redistributive effect) is potentially incompatible with the elitist model of decision making inherent in parliamentary democracy (whereby decision making capacity is confined to those with an electoral mandate) (Bailey, 2009b: 36–40). Thus, faced with a crisis of profitability and/or an overpoliticised working class, social democratic parties confront a dilemmatic choice between the three defining commitments outlined at the beginning of the chapter. In such a situation, those arguing for the impossibility of social democracy expect social democratic party elites to seek to de-prioritise the commitment to (and reduce constituents' demands for) redistribution, in an attempt to ease the tensions between the conflicting commitments that threaten to destabilise social democratic parties (Bailey, 2009a). Social democratic parties' commitment to redistribution is therefore incompatible with their commitment to working within the confines of capitalism and parliamentarianism. This incompatibility explains the failure, the post-1970s 'de-social democratisation', and the unsuccessful re-social democratisation, of social democratic parties (Bailey, 2009a; Lavelle, 2009). Furthermore, in contrast to those anticipating a move towards cosmopolitan social democracy, those who proclaim the impossibility of social democracy tend also to be sceptical about the opportunities for re-social democratisation at the supranational level (cf. Storey, 2008). Indeed, while some observers have noted that the EU is itself a source of neoliberalisation (Scharpf, 2002, 2010; Moschonas, 2009), others have viewed the much-heralded cosmopolitan opportunities existent at the EU level as little more than obfuscatory and empty promises promulgated by party elites and held on to by only the most optimistic members of the party constituency (Bailey, 2005).

Case studies: re-social democratisation under crisis?

The experience of crisis destabilises the programmes, ideas and practices that would otherwise be accepted as 'normal' within political parties, thereby creating an opportunity for revision or change. A study of the different responses by social democratic parties to the economic and financial crisis that began in 2007 therefore provides an ideal opportunity through which to re-assess the relative merits of each of the positions within the 're-social democratisation' debate, and the expectations regarding social democratic party behaviour that each position elicits. As such, what follows is an attempt to outline responses to the economic crisis by three parties: the British Labour Party, the German Social Democratic Party (SPD) and the Swedish Social Democratic Party (SAP). As is common with such comparisons, the cases are chosen so as to represent one from each of Esping-Andersen's (1990) welfare regimes. They also vary in terms of the position in office of each social democratic party during the crisis: the SAP was out of office from 2006 (and therefore for the duration of the crisis); the SPD left office in October 2009 (and therefore provides an opportunity for us to contrast their record, both while in office and once they left office); and the British Labour Party was in office up until May 2010 (and therefore for almost the entirety of the crisis to the time of writing (September 2010)) (Table 5.1).

Table 5.1 outlines the alternative positions within the 're-social democratisation' debate and the respective expectations that each elicits regarding the prospect of 're-social democratisation'. Thus, those adopting a 'contingent divergence' position continue to be optimistic that 're-social democratisation' might occur at either the national or supranational level, irrespective of the move towards 'Third Way' social democracy in most European countries. From this perspective, the post-2007 crisis of

Table 5.1 Alternative positions within the 're-social democratisation' debate

	Contingent divergence	Cosmopolitan social democracy	Impossibility of social democracy
National level	Contingent re-social democratisation	Third Way convergence	Third Way convergence and a 'best alternative' discourse of legitimation
EU level	Contingent re-social democratisation	Pursuit and realisation of a 'social Europe' agenda	(Rhetorical) pursuit (and non-realisation) of a 'social Europe' agenda
Prospects for 're-social democratisation'	*Unfailing optimism*	*Qualified optimism*	*Enlightened pessimism*

overly liberalised financial markets might be expected to provide an ideal opportunity for social democratic parties to replace their 'Third Way' programme with a more traditional social democratic one. In contrast, while cosmopolitan social democrats might continue to anticipate obstacles to a national-level 're-social democratisation', we could expect a concerted attempt to advance (and implement) a coordinated European-level response to a crisis which has arguably exposed the importance of harnessing an otherwise untrammelled free market. Finally, those arguing for the impossibility of social democracy would expect the non-realisation of social democratic goals at both the national and supranational level. Moreover, given the focus of this approach on the incentives driving social democratic party elites to contain their constituents' demands, we might expect those elites to present a restrained commitment to redistribution as the best alternative available to their constituents at the national level, but also to seek to offset any potential disappointment arising from this restraint through the promise of a renewed commitment to 'Social Europe' at the supranational level (a commitment that should not be expected to be realised).

What follows is an attempt to ascertain which (if any) of the foregoing positions within the 're-social democratisation' debate provides the most plausible account of the actual responses produced by the three social democratic parties studied here to the post-2007 crisis.

British Labour Party

In responding to the post-2007 economic crisis, the Labour Government showed little sign of moving away from 'Third Way' social democracy. Thus, while we can witness a move away from outright support for liberal markets as the means through which best to allocate resources, the policies adopted as a result nevertheless showed little sign of a move in the direction of redistributive measures that would constitute a process of 're-social democratisation'. Indeed, the Government's key objective throughout the period was to stabilise the financial system in order to avert a more severe financial market crisis. To ensure continued borrowing and bolster confidence in the market, therefore, the Bank of England lowered the base rate to 0.5 per cent from March 2009 and purchased large amounts of government debt[1] in a process of quantitative easing that sought to inject financial liquidity into the market. The banking industry was stabilised through a combination of full and partial nationalisation of a number of banks, a fund to assist bank recapitalisation and a number of banking guarantee schemes (OECD, 2009; Thain, 2009). In terms of economic policy, New Labour introduced a moderate stimulus package in November 2008 (amounting to around 1.6 per cent of GDP over two years), which included the temporary reduction of VAT from 17.5 per cent to 15 per cent (December 2008–December 2009) and the bringing forward of planned capital expenditure. Further, in a self-proclaimed act of 're-social democratisation', Chancellor Alistair Darling heralded these initiatives as 'Keynesian policies' which would help the economy deal with the recession (Thain, 2009). However, there were few signs that these measures would have a redistributive effect, or even that they would directly raise household income (Hodson and Mabbett, 2009: 1053). Thus, the measures to stabilise the banking system were both costly and largely to the benefit of the banking sector, and maintained much of the bonus and pension regime that benefited the highest paid within the sector (Hill and Lucas, 2010; Parker and Goff, 2010). Similarly, the costs involved in achieving these measures led to a sharp rise in public debt, which the government quickly moved to place under control. As a result, VAT returned to 17.5 per cent after just one year, national insurance contributions (for both employees and employers) were raised in two 0.5 per cent instalments over the 2008–9 period, and it was announced that public sector pay would be capped at 1 per cent for two years from 2011. A number of new measures were introduced that sought to increase the tax incidence on those on higher incomes (most notably, a new 50 per cent tax bracket and a 50 per cent tax on bankers bonuses). However, alongside these initiatives, the Labour Government indicated its commitment to austerity politics by announcing in late 2009/early 2010 that it would cut government spending by around 7 per cent if it were to remain in office after the election. Further, given that this was a promise made during the run up to a general election, we might view this as a conservative estimate of likely spending cuts that would have been implemented had the Labour Party won the 2010 election.

In terms of welfare policy, in December 2008 the government published its White Paper, *Raising Expectations and Increasing Support*, which re-affirmed a commitment to a 'productivist' welfare policy. Thus, the White Paper advocated 'personalised conditionality', which included the promise that welfare benefit payments would be increasingly dependent upon applicants being visibly willing to seek and take up employment, including (most controversially) parents with young children. Thus, the White Paper announced, 'we will also start by exploring what the regime might look like for parents with three to six year-old children' (Department for Work and Pensions, 2008: 14). There was, therefore, no visible shift towards the re-social democratisation of welfare policy in response to the crisis. Indeed, the government stated, 'The current economic climate means we must step up both the support we offer to people on benefits and the expectations of them to get themselves prepared for work. To do otherwise would be to repeat the mistakes of the past, writing people off and encouraging ... long-term benefit dependency' (Department for Work and Pensions, 2008: 10). Thus, the Labour Government both retained its Third Way agenda and continued to argue that this represented the best alternative available to its constituents (particularly in comparison with the risks of either sustained economic crisis in the absence of austerity measures, or of inculcating a dependence culture in the absence of a productivist welfare policy).

On the EU, the Labour Government's position changed little as a result of the crisis. Following its initial Euro-enthusiasm during the 1997 election, upon gaining access to office the Labour Party chose increasingly to downplay its support for the EU for fear that a pro-EU position risked criticism from a typically Euro-sceptic media and electorate (Opperman, 2008). Further, while in response to the economic crisis the Labour Government was quietly supportive of a coordinated supranational policy, the content of what was being sought differed little from the 'Third Way' economic policy being promoted at the national level, much as had been the case prior to the crisis (Bulmer, 2008). Nevertheless, the opportunity for supranational cooperation was viewed (albeit in somewhat muted terms) as a potential vehicle through which to tackle the post-2007 crisis. Thus, although the Labour Government initially refused to consider a

European coordinated response to the crisis in the first week of October 2009, by March 2009 Prime Minister Gordon Brown could proclaim, 'Instead of heading for the rocks of isolation, let us together chart the course of cooperation. That is in all our national interests. That is why I propose that Europe take the lead in a bold plan to ensure that every continent now makes the changes in its banking system that will open the path to shared prosperity' (Brown, 2009). While the EU was identified as a potential means to respond to the economic crisis, therefore, the promise of EU-level 're-social democratisation' was espoused in a characteristically timid manner (on which, see Bailey, 2009b: 163).

SPD

In its initial response to the post-2007 crisis, the SPD, and the policies of the Grand Coalition of which it was a part, showed little sign of producing the kind of 're-social democratisation' that those adopting the 'contingent divergence' perspective might anticipate. Indeed, SPD Finance Minister, Peer Steinbrück, was at the forefront of opposition to any return to 'traditional' social democratic policy tools, accusing the British Government of adopting a 'crass Keynesianism' that would take a generation to pay off (quoted in Watt *et al.*, 2008). Despite this, the Grand Coalition did ultimately find it necessary to adopt a fiscal stimulus plan. This was initially (November 2008) a relatively cautious increase in spending, amounting to roughly 0.5 per cent of Germany's GDP, but was subsequently expanded in January 2009 to around 2.1 per cent of GDP. The measures introduced were typical of those adopted across the developed world (including investment in public infrastructure, tax deductions, incentives to stimulate car purchases, child allowance increases and a reduction in unemployment and health insurance contribution rates), and in part reflected partisan divisions within the coalition, with the CDU/Christian Social Union (CSU) securing a small tax cut and the SPD achieving increased spending on infrastructure and education. However, rather than represent a return to traditional Keynesian counter-cyclical measures, the Grand Coalition was keen to avoid any commitment to long-term deficit spending or the creation of significant public debt. As a result, and reflecting Steinbrück's earlier concerns, the Coalition agreed in 2009 to a new fiscal rule which would restrict the cyclically adjusted budget deficit of the federal government to 0.35 per cent GDP max (by 2016) and to balanced budgets for Länder (by 2020). Thus, short-term (and relatively small-scale) stimulus measures were linked to a long-term commitment to fiscal discipline, itself legitimated in terms of the economic risks of adopting an alternative course. The Grand Coalition also introduced a short-term worker scheme which, in a move consistent with the 'Third Way' prioritisation of employment over 'passive' welfare support, compensated workers by up to 67 per cent of lost income if they were forced to reduce their hours of employment (OECD, 2010).

The most notable period during which the SPD appeared to be moving away from its 'Third Way' agenda occurred during the run up to the 2009 elections. Thus, in the first half of 2009 the SPD attacked Chancellor Merkel for refusing to provide government support to carmaker Opel and to Arcandor (both of which were, according to the SPD, missed opportunities to avoid job losses). The Party's 2009 manifesto also promised tax breaks for low-earners, a plan for a €7.50 minimum wage, an increase in the top income tax rate by two points to 47 per cent (with a commitment to invest the revenue in education) and a promise to create 4 million jobs in the following decade (mainly through 'green industries' such as making electric cars and service jobs in health and geriatric care). Despite these attempts to re-appeal to core social democratic voters, however, the SPD lost considerable support to *Die Linke*, achieving one of the worst electoral performances in its history and being replaced in office by a new CDU/CSU–Free Democratic Party (FPD) coalition government. Once out of office, the SPD elected new leader Sigmar Gabriel, who in his first speech pledged both more grassroots party democracy and a wealth tax, but at the same time announced that he would oppose any leftward move for the Party. As a result, since leaving office the SPD has failed to establish a clear alternative programme. For instance, the SPD leadership called on Merkel's new government to insist on a strict austerity budget for Greece (in exchange for German financial assistance), while also arguing that the banking industry should contribute to the rescue package. In contrast to the view elicited from the 'contingent divergence' position, therefore, the experience of the SPD during the post-2007 crisis suggests that it was only once implementation became less of an issue (i.e. during an electoral campaign and therefore when the opportunity to actually realise such an agenda had ceased to be available) that one witnessed a 're-social democratisation' of the SPD's policy agenda.

The global economic crisis also sparked renewed interest by German social democrats in the prospects for supranational coordination. Thus, in March 2009 a number of key SPD actors made statements noting that EU aid to eurozone countries could be used as a means of achieving Party goals on a European level (Scally, 2009). Further, the following month SPD Vice-President Andrea Nahles co-wrote an article with Labour Party MP Jon Cruddas, in which they argued for a coordinated European programme that would see a return to a more traditional social democratic agenda, including a coordinated European fiscal stimulus, the prevention of unemployment, a more social Europe, public ownership/control of industry, a European minimum wage and a return to collective bargaining and a stronger right to strike (Cruddas and Nahles, 2009).

The assessment of the SPD's domestic agenda provided herein seems more in keeping with the view of the 'impossibility of social democracy' account than others, in that demands for redistribution have been both limited and any moves towards 're-social democratisation' have thus far gone un-implemented. Further, as anticipated by both the cosmopolitan social democrats and those proclaiming the impossibility of social democracy, the SPD did witness a turn towards the EU level in response to the economic crisis, although the question of whether this was realised will be the subject of further discussion below.

SAP

As a result of its 2006 electoral defeat, the SAP was out of office for the entirety of the post-2007 economic crisis. The SAP's response to the crisis, therefore, was particularly shaped by the need to appeal to the Swedish electorate ahead of the 2010 election. In contrast to the 2006 election, moreover, the SAP formed a coalition agreement with the Left Party and Greens, upon which it contested the 2010 elections. In agreeing to form a coalition with the Left Party, therefore, the SAP signalled its willingness to move towards a more traditionally social democratic agenda. The SAP and the Left–Green coalition have both criticised the centre-right Alliance for Sweden coalition government for failing to offer sufficient support for Swedish business. For instance, SAP spokespeople were quick to criticise the government for failing to support Saab in March 2009. Similarly, in unveiling its shadow budget in May 2010, the Left–Green coalition announced that it would cut payroll taxes for small businesses in an attempt to stimulate job creation. In a further sign of its willingness to adopt a more traditionally social democratic agenda, the Left–Green coalition announced a number of expansionary measures in response to the post-2007 crisis. Thus, the SAP agreed in October 2009 that it would reduce taxes paid by pensioners in order to ensure parity with wage earners. Other initiatives include a Left–Green coalition commitment to increase allowances and childcare services for single parents (in order to improve access to employment), and to raise the replacement rate of unemployment insurance. The SAP therefore adopted a more redistributive agenda, seeking to reduce differentials between those in work and those not in work (such as pensioners and the unemployed). The shadow budget also included defence cuts, a new wealth tax and investments in environmental initiatives. Similarly, the SAP's Party Programme adopted in 2009 included a commitment to full employment (rather than welfare cuts). The most pressing question, however, is whether these intentions would have been implementable if the Left coalition had been successful in its attempt to gain election to office in 2010. Indeed, the role played by the SAP in introducing austerity measures to Sweden while in office in the 1990s (on which, see Merkel *et al.*, 2008: 162–5) suggests that the pressures of governing a capitalist economy proved greater than the demands of their traditional constituents. Out of our three case studies, therefore, the SAP's record during the economic crisis is the one that most suggests the possibility of 're-social democratisation'. However, it is also notable that the SAP is the Party that has been out of office for the entirety of the crisis period.

The SAP also stands out from the other two case studies in this chapter in terms of its European policy. Whereas both the British Labour Party and the SPD appeared to look towards the European level in response to the crisis (albeit with varying levels of enthusiasm), in the case of the SAP this rhetoric has been much more muted. This is perhaps unsurprising as the SAP has been considerably more Euro-sceptic than a number of other social democratic parties within Europe, largely on the grounds that the EU is viewed by both social democratic voters and party members as *undermining* the scope for more traditional social democratic policy provisions. This is particularly the case since the ECJ's *Laval* ruling highlighted the liberalising effect that EU membership might have upon the Swedish model (Bailey, 2009b: 109–10). On the one hand, therefore, the SAP could agree in its Party programme to the rather anodyne statement that 'The EU must continue to develop in areas where the EU can best create common solutions to common problems. We want the EU to be a union of sustainable growth and full employment' (SAP, 2009: 94). Yet policy towards the European Union was almost entirely absent from the 2010 election campaign, with not one of more than one hundred press releases produced by the Party in the month prior to the general election being dedicated to the Party's European policy.[2]

EU: crisis as a spur to social Europe?

Lastly, in order to decide between the alternative expectations of the cosmopolitan social democrats and those arguing for the impossibility of social democracy, a final empirical consideration of the present chapter relates to the question of whether the EU has moved in a more 'Social Europe' direction as a result of the post-2007 economic crisis. Thus, while much existing literature remains sceptical about the possibilities of achieving substantive social democratic policies at the European level (Bailey, 2008; Scharpf, 2010), it is possible that the experience of economic crisis has prompted changes to EU-level decision making. While it is clearly beyond the scope of the present chapter to provide a full evaluation of the EU's response to the post-2007 crisis, we can nevertheless identify some key trends observed during the period.

As with a number of national responses, the EU-level response to the economic crisis has been more concerned with ensuring economic stability than it has with identifying an opportunity for more redistributive policy measures. Thus, in response to the collapse of Lehman Brothers in September 2008 the EU member states agreed the following month (albeit following a period of damaging unilateral policy announcements by member states) to a €2 trillion pledge to, in the words of Hodson and Quaglia, 'recapitalize and, if necessary, take shares in European banks'. This was therefore a policy that particularly favoured savers (Hodson and Quaglia, 2009: 942). Similarly, in 2010 the Eurozone member states created the EFSF that sought to secure member governments against potential sovereign debt crises. In contrast, the stimulus measure that was agreed in late 2008 (and might arguably have presented greater opportunities to introduce measures targeted specifically at lower-income groups) was small (c.1.5 per cent of EU GDP) in comparison to national-level responses, contained little opportunity for intermember state redistribution (Hodson and Quaglia, 2009: 943), and was anyway predominantly an aggregate of already existing spending pledges by member states (Barber, 2008). Further, attempts to move towards EU-level financial regulation and greater fiscal capacity continued to be hampered by the national constraints highlighted by commentators prior to the economic crisis. For instance, the difficulties faced by those seeking to secure substantive policy commitments at the European level acted to ensure the absence of revenue-raising regulations, such as a Tobin tax, despite apparent consensus among key governments in support of such an initiative (Buckley and Howarth, 2010: 120, 133). Subsequent proposals for the coordination of bank levies also faced difficulties due to the inability of member states to agree on a common method of implementation. The EU did, however, adopt a new financial regulation system in September 2010, witnessing the creation of a European Systemic Risk Board (ESRB), although opposition from (particularly) the UK government ensured that the new 'European Supervisory Authorities' would not impinge too greatly upon domestic regulations (Phillips, 2010). Redistributive policy mechanisms already in place at the European level, particularly structural funds and the globalisation adjustment fund, have also been largely viewed as ineffective on the grounds that they are both too small to have an impact upon the effects of the post-2007 crisis, and that applicant member states and regions face excessively difficult technical barriers to accessing the funds (Pignal, 2010; Pop, 2010). Further still, following the experience of sovereign debt crises in the so-called 'PIGS' countries (Portugal, Italy, Greece, Spain; now also PIIGS, to include Ireland), the focus for EU-level fiscal policy has moved towards an attempt to secure *stricter* fiscal discipline. It is the claim of this brief analysis, therefore, that those obstacles to 'Social Europe' which were identified prior to 2007 have continued to hamper any attempts to move towards a more redistributive response following the onset of the economic crisis.

Conclusion

While economic crises may create opportunities for political change, the present chapter argues that it is the most pessimistic analysis of social democracy that most plausibly accounts for the responses by social democratic parties to that crisis, as witnessed herein. Only in Sweden – where the Social Democratic Party was out of office for the entirety of the crisis period – have we witnessed a concerted attempt to respond to crisis through the advocacy of a more redistributive, 'traditional social democratic', agenda. In the cases of both Germany and the UK, in contrast, the social democratic party in each country has largely continued to espouse a 'Third Way' version of social democracy. Similarly, while the opportunities for 're-social democratisation' at the European level have been heralded by social democrats (to varying extents) in each of the cases discussed, the timidity with which this has been espoused in most cases, and the continued absence of any significant realisation of this ambition, coheres most closely with the view that such rhetorical statements act more to obfuscate than redistribute. It is the claim of this chapter, therefore, that it is only in adopting a more pessimistic view of the prospects for 're-social democratisation' that we might move towards a more realistic attempt to achieve greater social equality. Indeed, the social democratic myth itself might be viewed as part of the obstacle to such egalitarian results, as the more quickly we abandon the (impossible) social democratic strategy, the more effectively that we can start to seek out alternative means through which to empower contemporary subaltern groups.

Notes

1 This included the creation of the Asset Purchase Facility, with a budget of up to £150 billion, in early 2009.
2 Indeed, of all of the press releases, only one mentioned the possibility for European cooperation to facilitate policy making (in the area of international development), and the other single mention of the EU being a critical reference to the impact of the *Laval* Ruling (see www.socialdemokraterna.se/Media/nyheter/).

References

Allan, J. P. and Scruggs, L. (2004) 'Political Partisanship and Welfare State Reform in Advanced Industrial Societies', *American Journal of Political Science*, Vol. 48 (3), 496–512.

Amable, B., Gatti, D. and Schumacher, J. (2006) 'Welfare-state Retrenchment: The Partisan Effect Revisited', *Oxford Review of Economic Policy*, Vol. 22 (3), 426–44.

Bailey, D. J. (2005) 'Obfuscation through Integration: Legitimating "New" Social Democracy in the European Union', *Journal of Common Market Studies*, Vol. 43 (1), 13–35.

Bailey, D. J. (2008) 'Explaining the Underdevelopment of "Social Europe" : A Critical Realization', *Journal of European Social Policy*, 18 (3), 232–45.

Bailey, D. J. (2009a) 'The Transition to "New" Social Democracy: The Role of Capitalism, Representation, and (Hampered) Contestation', *British Journal of Politics and International Relations*, Vol. 11 (4), 593–612.

Bailey, D. J. (2009b) *The Political Economy of European Social Democracy: A Critical Realist Approach.* London: Routledge.

Barber, T. (2008) 'Europe's Shrinking Stimulus Packages', *Financial Times*, 16 December.

Boix, C. (1998) *Political Parties, Growth and Equality: Conservative and Social Democratic Economic Strategies in the World Economy.* Cambridge: Cambridge University Press.

Brown, G. (2009) Speech to the EP, 24 March.

Buckley, J. and Howarth, D. (2010) 'Internal Market: Gesture Politics? Explaining the EU's Response to the Financial Crisis', *Journal of Common Market Studies*, Vol. 48 (special issue 1), 119–41.

Bulmer, S. (2008) 'New Labour, New European Policy? Blair, Brown and Utilitarian Supranationaliam', *Parliamentary Affairs*, 61 (4), 597–620.

Callaghan, J., Fishman, N., Jackson, B. and McIvor, M. (2009) 'Introduction', in Callaghan, J., Fishman, N., Jackson, B. and McIvor, M. (eds), *In Search of Social Democracy: Responses to Crisis and Modernisation.* Manchester: Manchester University Press.

Coates, D. (ed.) (2003) *Paving the Third Way: The Critique of Parliamentary Socialism. A Socialist Register Anthology*. London: Merlin Press.

Cruddas, J. and Nahles, A. (2009) 'A New Path For Europe: Society Led by Markets and Profits Has Failed: We are Offering an Alternative for the Democratic Left', *The Guardian*, 8 April.

Department for Work and Pensions (2008) *Raising Expectations and Increasing Support: Reforming Welfare For the Future*. London: The Stationery Office.

Esping-Andersen, G. (1990) *The Three Worlds of Welfare Capitalism*. Cambridge: Polity.

Garrett, G. (1998) *Partisan Politics in The Global Economy*. Cambridge: Cambridge University Press.

Giddens, A. (1998) *The Third Way: The Renewal of Social Democracy*. Cambridge: Polity.

Hall, P. A. (2002) 'The Comparative Political Economy of the "Third Way"', in Schmidtke, O. (ed.), *The Third Way Transformation of Social Democracy: Normative Claims and Policy Initiatives in The 21st Century*. Aldershot: Ashgate, 31–58.

Hay, C. (2004) 'Common Trajectories, Variable Paces, Divergent Outcomes? Models of European Capitalism under Conditions of Complex Economic Interdependence', *Review of International Political Economy*, Vol. 11 (2), 231–62.

Hay, C. (2006) 'What's Globalization Got to Do with It? Economic Interdependence and the Future of European Welfare States', *Government and Opposition*, Vol. 41 (1), 1–22.

Hay, C. and Rosamond, B. (2002) 'Globalization, European Integration and the Discursive Construction of Economic Imperatives', *Journal of European Public Policy*, Vol. 9 (2), 147–67.

Held, D. (2003) 'Global Social Democracy', in Giddens, A. (ed.), *The Progressive Manifesto: New Ideas for the Centre-Left*. Cambridge: Polity, 137–72.

Held, D. and McGrew, A. (2002) *Globalization/Anti-Globalization*. Cambridge: Polity.

Hill, A. and Lucas, L. (2010) 'Bank Bosses' Gesture Won't Take Bonuses Off the Table', *Financial Times*, 22 February.

Hodson, D. and Mabbett, D. (2009) 'UK Economic Policy and the Global Financial Crisis: Paradigm Lost?', *Journal of Common Market Studies*, Vol. 47 (5), 1041–61.

Hodson, D. and Quaglia, L. (2009) 'European Perspectives on the Global Financial Crisis: Introduction', *Journal of Common Market Studies*, Vol. 47 (5), 939–53.

Huo, J. (2009) *Third Way Reforms: Social Democracy after the Golden Age*. Cambridge: Cambridge University Press.

Kitschelt, H. (1994) *The Transformation of European Social Democracy*. Cambridge: Cambridge University Press.

Kwon, H. Y. and Pontusson, J. (2010) 'Globalization, Labour Power and Partisan Politics Revisited', *Socio-Economic Review*, Vol. 8 (2), 251–81.

Lavelle, A. (2009) 'Explanations for the Neo-liberal Direction of Social Democracy: Germany, Sweden and Australia Compared', in Callaghan, J., Fishman, N., Jackson, B. and McIvor, M. (eds), *In Search of Social Democracy: Responses to Crisis and Modernisation*. Manchester: Manchester University Press, 9–28.

Lightfoot, S. (2005) *Europeanizing Social Democracy?: The Rise of the Party of European Socialists*. London and New York: Routledge.

Merkel, W., Petring, A., Henkes, C. and Egle, C. (2008) *Social Democracy in Power: The Capacity to Reform*. London: Routledge.

Moschonas, G. (2002) *In the Name of Social Democracy: The Great Transformation – 1945 to the Present*. London: Verso.

Moschonas, G. (2009) 'Reformism in a "Conservative" System: The European Union and Social Democratic Identity', in Callaghan, J., Fishman, N., Jackson, B. and McIvor, M. (eds), *In Search of Social Democracy: Responses to Crisis and Modernisation*. Manchester: Manchester University Press, 168–92.

Motta, S. C. and Bailey, D. J. (2007) 'Neither Pragmatic Adaptation nor Misguided Accommodation: Modernization as Domination in the Chilean and British Left', *Capital and Class*, Vol. 92, 107–36.

OECD (2009) *OECD Economic Surveys: United Kingdom*. Paris: OECD.

OECD (2010) *OECD Economic Surveys: Germany, Paris*. Paris: OECD.

Oppermann, K. (2008) 'The Blair Government and Europe: The Politics of Containing the Salience of European Integration', *British Politics*, 3, 157–82.

Panitch, L. (1976) *Social Democracy and Industrial Militancy: The Labour Party, the Trade Unions and Incomes Policy, 1945–1974*. Cambridge: Cambridge University Press.

Parker, G. and Goff, S. (2010) 'Banks Win Respite Over Bonus Details', *Financial Times*, 12 September.

Phillips, L. (2010) 'Finance Ministers Give Green Light to EU Oversight of National Budgets', *EUObserver*, 7 September.

Pignal, S. (2010) 'EU Workers Aid Fund Failing to Pay Out', *Financial Times*, 6 September.

Pop, V. (2010) 'Cash-strapped States Slow at Tapping EU Funds', *EUObserver*, 1 April.

Przeworski, A. (2001) 'How Many Ways Can Be Third?', in Glyn, A. (ed.), *Social Democracy in Neoliberal Times*. Oxford: Oxford University Press, 312–33.

SAP (2000) *Congress Guidelines Extra Congress 2000: Swedish Social Democratic Party Guidelines for Development and Equality*. Adopted by the Extra Party Congress, Stockholm, 10–12 March.

SAP (2009) *Political Guidelines*. Adopted at the Congress for Jobs.

Scally, D. (2009) 'SPD Sees Bailout as a Way to Exert Influence', *The Irish Times*, 25 March.

Scharpf, F. W. (2010) 'The Asymmetry of European Integration, Or Why the EU Cannot be a "Social Market Economy"', *Socio-Economic Review*, Vol. 8 (2), 211–50.

Scharpf, F. W. (2002) 'The European Social Model: Coping with the Challenges of Diversity', *Journal of Common Market Studies*, Vol. 40 (4), 645–70.

Storey, A. (2008) 'The Ambiguity of Resistance: Opposition to Neoliberalism in Europe', *Capital and Class* 32, 55–85.

Strange, G. (2006) 'The Left Against Europe? A Critical Engagement with New Constitutionalism and Structural Dependence Theory', *Government and Opposition*, Vol. 41 (2), 197–229.

Thain, C. (2009) 'A Very Peculiar British Crisis? Institutions, Ideas and Policy Responses to the Credit Crunch', *British Politics*, Vol. 4 (4), 434–49.

Thomson, S. (2000) *The Social Democratic Dilemma: Ideology, Governance and Globalization*. London: Macmillan.

Watson, M. and Hay, C. (2003) 'The Discourse of Globalisation and the Logic of No Alternative: Rendering the Contingent Necessary in the Political Economy of New Labour', *Policy and Politics*, Vol. 31 (3), 289–305.

Watt, N., Seager, A. and Elliott, L. (2008) 'Deficit Spending: "Crass Keynesianism" – German Finance Minister Scoffs at Brown's Stimulus Plan', *The Guardian*, 11 December.

6

Cooption or resistance? Trade unions and neoliberal restructuring in Europe[1]

Andreas Bieler

Since the mid 1980s, the EU has been restructured along neoliberal lines. This is expressed in the deregulation and liberalisation of national economies within the Internal Market programme as well as EMU, which instructs the ECB to make price stability its sole primary objective and constrains member states' fiscal policy through the neoliberal convergence criteria of the SGP. The flanking social measures of the Social Dimension do not change this fundamental neoliberal direction (Bieler, 2006b). Van Apeldoorn calls this arrangement 'embedded neoliberalism', which is mainly pushed by social class forces of transnational capital (van Apeldoorn, 2002). In its enlargement to Central and Eastern Europe, the EU exported an even more market-radical variant of neoliberalism to the new member states, which were not granted immediate labour mobility and full access to the EU's redistributive policies (Bohle, 2006). Restructuring of the European social relations of production has gone hand in hand with similar developments in the global political economy. Neoliberalism regained prominence in the 1970s as a political economy critique of Keynesianism, it was then implemented in the US and the UK as a programme of restructuring during the 1980s, before being accepted as a hegemonic creed at the global level during the 1990s and spread with the help of international organisations such as the IMF to every part of the world (Gamble, 2001). The exact way national social relations of production have been restructured differs from country to country and may include neoliberal policies such as privatisation, central bank independence, liberalisation, flexibilisation of the labour market, public sector restructuring, cutting-back of trade union rights, etc. Nevertheless, as Blyth makes clear, all neoliberal restructuring projects are based on the core assumptions that (1) inflation is a greater threat to economic development than unemployment and (2) state intervention causes unemployment and inflation in an otherwise efficiently functioning, free market economy (Blyth, 2002: 147).

The pressures resulting from neoliberal restructuring are unevenly distributed in the EU. While capital gained flexibility and new room for manoeuvre, states gave up the possibilities to stimulate the national economy via currency devaluations and lowering of interest rates. Moreover, the introduction of the single currency in combination with the deregulatory and monetarist bias of EMU as well as the lack of social re-regulation at the European level, facilitates the comparison of different national systems of industrial relations regulations. As a result, workers and trade unions as their institutional expression are most under pressure. Workers in regions with lower levels of productivity may be pressed to accept lower wages and a cut-back in working conditions, left as the only possible adjustment mechanism in the struggle for remaining a competitive location for industry and FDI. 'This may happen even without asymmetric shocks, insofar as employers (and governments) seek price advantages, no longer attainable by currency depreciation, through wage and benefit cuts instead' (Martin and Ross, 1999: 345). In short, due to the general deregulation and liberalisation within the Internal Market and EMU there are general pressures to lower conditions and to make labour markets more flexible. 'The logic of "regime competition" … has become a main feature and a driving force of current industrial adjustments within the European Union' (Bieling, 2001: 94, see also 103). Moreover, with economic decisions increasingly being taken at the supranational European level as well as within companies, trade unions' traditional position of influence on policy making at the national level has been undermined.

In response to further European integration around neoliberal restructuring, trade unions regularly responded with a 'yes, but' position (Dølvik, 1999). They supported further integration, but demanded the development of a related Social Dimension. This strategy has not led to significant changes to the predominant neoliberal rationale of integration. In fact, the EU frequently used employment and social policies to justify even further neoliberal restructuring (Schulten, 2006). Hence, it is often alleged that the 'yes, but' strategy by trade unions has resulted in some kind of symbolic Euro-corporatism, where unions can participate in discussions without having the chance of making a more significant impact on individual proposals (e.g. Ryner and Schulten, 2003). As Taylor and Mathers (2002: 54) have put it, '"the social partnership" approach that dominates the thinking of leading members of the European labour movement amount[s] to a strategy that not only further abandons the autonomy of the labour movement but confirms the logic of neoliberalism through "supply side corporatism" or "progressive competitiveness".' Thus, trade unions are accused of having been coopted into neoliberal restructuring and are, therefore, of no importance to anti-neoliberal movements. In this chapter, I will evaluate these claims and argue that trade unions are too quickly written off as possible actors of resistance. The next section will show that a whole range of trade unions in Europe, including those supporting EMU, have not accepted neoliberal restructuring. Strategies are then identified at the European level, which allow unions to resist neoliberal restructuring. The conclusion will provide some reflections on trade unions and the future of the EU.

Trade unions and neoliberal restructuring[2]

Considering the negative implications of neoliberal restructuring for trade unions, why have many trade unions supported the revival of European integration around neoliberal restructuring? Bieling (2001: 100) identifies three core reasons for why trade unions accepted the Internal Market. First, against the background of economic recession and the rise of the neoliberal discourse in the early 1980s, unions had already accepted that deregulation and privatisation were economically beneficial, or at least unavoidable, before the Internal Market programme was initiated in 1985. Secondly, there was an optimistic view that the Internal Market was a step towards political union including also a social union, comprising the necessary re-regulation at the European level. Thirdly, the presence of Jacques Delors as President of the Commission and his emphasis on the necessity of a social counterpart to economic integration including the participation of trade unions in European politics convinced unions to support the Internal Market. Acceptance of EMU and the institutionalisation of neoliberalism in the convergence criteria together with the establishment of the ECB, its focus on price stability and the lack of democratic control were more difficult for the unions. In the end, considering the unions' political weakness during the economic recession in Europe in the early 1990s and the small gains of the Social Chapter, trade unions accepted the Treaty of Maastricht (Bieling, 2001: 105). This support was not uncritical, but followed a 'yes, but' attitude. European integration was supported as such, but additional social policy measures were demanded. As indicated above, it is precisely this attitude that led to the accusations that trade unions had become coopted into neoliberal restructuring.

It is argued here that such assessments write off trade unions too quickly as possible actors in the resistance to neoliberal restructuring. The 'yes, but' attitude should not be regarded as acceptance of neoliberalism as such. European politics is class struggle and unions could simply not match the structural power of capital, nor challenge the dominant discourse of neoliberalism at the time. A detailed analysis of the Austrian, British, French, German and Swedish labour movements has demonstrated that the vast majority of unions, including those which have accepted EMU, continue to resist neoliberal restructuring (Bieler, 2006a). For example, German unions criticise the neoliberal implications of EMU as represented in the convergence criteria and the ECB's exclusive focus on price stability.

German Unions generally demand active employment policies at the national and European level and a more flexible interpretation of the convergence criteria, with some even wanting to add an unemployment criterion to demonstrate a stronger emphasis on employment and growth. Some unions also mention wage increases in line with inflation and productivity increases in order to ensure domestic demand as well as tax harmonisation to avoid regime competition within the EU as additional steps. This argument is based on the understanding that employment cannot only be achieved via structural measures, but also requires demand management. Public investment in European-wide infrastructure programmes is one possible way forward in this respect (Bieler, 2003a: 34–6).

In Britain, criticism of the neoliberal EMU is even more outspoken. Trade unions, which organise workers in export orientated and transnational manufacturing such as Amicus are in favour of EMU membership. Their industrial sector has suffered from the high sterling exchange rate with the Euro. EMU membership would remedy this problem. On the other hand, however, unions which organise workers in national production sectors, such as the public sector union UNISON, strongly oppose EMU. It is rejected, because it would limit national expenditure on public services and have a negative impact on growth and employment levels. The lack of democratic accountability of the ECB is also highlighted. These criticisms are echoed by general unions such as the GMB, that organise workers in the public and manufacturing sector and therefore understand the relevance of both positions (Bieler, 2003a: 31–4). The rejection of EMU membership due to its neoliberal bias clearly indicates the opposition to neoliberal restructuring by domestic labour in Britain. Transnational sector unions too, however, continue to oppose neoliberalism. As Strange outlines, British pro-EMU unions have always demanded an expansion of the EU's macroeconomic competence and a focus on high levels of employment as a precondition for their support (Strange, 1997: 21–3). To facilitate this, they have adopted Euro-Keynesian macroeconomic management as a new project, based on an ultimately centralised fiscal and monetary policy in a federal union and combined with EU social partnership industrial relations (Strange, 2002: 356–7).

In France, similarly, support for EMU did not automatically imply acceptance of neoliberal restructuring. On the one hand, the confederations CFDT, CFTC, CFE–CGC and UNSA supported EMU. Nevertheless, CFTC and UNSA combined this support with opposition to the underlying neoliberal structure of EMU. Only the CFE–CGC, organising predominantly cadres and managers in companies, i.e. privileged sections of the working class, endorsed the focus on price stability. The CFDT accepted neoliberal principles to some extent in that it did not reject the convergence criteria and the independent status of the ECB, but even this did not reflect a full endorsement of neoliberal restructuring. On the other hand, FO and G10–Solidaires strongly criticised EMU for its neoliberal rationale and especially the latter has intensified its co-operation with other social movements in the resistance to restructuring. The CGT was critical of the neoliberal rationale of EMU, but more hopeful that this could be changed within EMU rather than requiring its abandonment (Bieler, 2006a: 113–19).

The Austrian Trade Union Federation (ÖGB) set the tone of the general debate in Austria. It accepted that EMU and the single currency were beneficial in that they implied greater levels of economic stability. Nevertheless, it was argued, the underlying basis of EMU, its neoliberal rationale, needed to be changed. EMU should have full employment as its core focus and a related unemployment criterion was demanded in this respect. Moreover, the ECB should be asked to concentrate on growth and employment in addition to price stability, here following the US Federal Reserve Bank. This should also imply a redefinition of the inflation target. Finally, the ÖGB demanded that in order to ensure domestic demand within the EU, wage agreements should follow the formula of a productivity increase plus inflation (Bieler, 2006a: 107–8). This position was supported by the majority of unions, organising workers in domestic production sectors. Only the metalworkers' union and the chemical workers' union, organising workers in internationally orientated sectors, were less concerned about the neoliberal implications of EMU.

At the same time, while many European trade unions continued to criticise neoliberal restructuring, this was not an automatic position, as the Swedish case demonstrates. The Transport Workers' Union and the Commercial Workers' Union, both organising in a predominantly domestic production sector, linked their opposition to EMU to a clear rejection of neoliberal restructuring, perceived to be embodied in the convergence criteria and the role of an independent, undemocratic ECB. Nevertheless, several of the national sector unions, which had not adopted a position on EMU, e.g. the Municipal Workers' Union and the Construction Workers' Union, were less critical of neoliberal restructuring or, indeed, had adopted some neoliberal principles. For example, they accepted the low-inflation policy as well as the role of moderate wage development in maintaining economic stability. This acceptance of some neoliberal principles was even more visible in the positions of the transnational sector unions and of the blue-collar confederation LO (Bieler, 2003b).

In short, these brief examples indicate that a large number of trade unions continue to question neoliberal restructuring. At the same time, it has also become increasingly clear that the national level no longer suffices as the focus for opposition to neoliberalism. The next section will assess the possibilities available at the European level for trade unions to influence policy making within the EU.

Trade unions and the EU

At the European level most national union organisations are members of the ETUC, which claims to represent about 60 million workers in thirty-six countries. Furthermore, there are eleven European Industry Federations (EIF) representing national unions from certain industries, as, for example, the European Metalworkers Federation (EMF) or the European Federation of Public Service Unions (EPSU) (www.etuc. org/r/13). Within the institutional set-up of the EU, trade unions are clearly disadvantaged *vis-à-vis* interest groups of capital – for example, in their capacity to influence policy making. As briefly outlined on pp. 119–20, the EU has been characterised by neoliberal restructuring since the mid 1980s. The new, neoliberal form of state has been institutionally protected by removing monetary and economic policy making from the wider influence of actors.

First, in a move labelled 'new constitutionalism' by Gill (2001), monetary policy making with a focus on low inflation has been handed over to the ECB, made up of 'impartial' technocrats. Secondly, the core macroeconomic decisions are taken by the European Council, the meeting of heads of government and heads of state within the EU, which is largely outside lobbying pressure. In June of each year, the European Council passes the so-called 'broad economic policy guidelines', which must support the low-inflation policy of the ECB, therefore regularly re-confirming neoliberal restructuring. The European Commission, on the other hand, does provide trade unions with access to policy making. Its 'role in drafting legislation, together with its interdependencies with outside interests, make it the foremost venue for outside interests' (Greenwood, 2003: 30). Trade unions have a particularly close contact with the DG for Employment and Social Affairs, formerly DG V. Overall, however, the Commission has twenty-three DGs, and not all DGs are equally important. The DG for Competition and the DG for Economic and Financial Affairs are more decisive within the EU. Together with the DG Internal Market and the DG Trade they are the hard core of the Commission, driving the neoliberal project through the discourse of competitiveness (Rosamond, 2002). Trade unions' focus on the DG for Employment and Social Affairs has often marginalised them within the Commission's internal decision making process.

Multi-sector social dialogue is one of the core avenues for the ETUC to influence policy making in the EU since the Treaty of Maastricht in 1992. Should the ETUC and their employers' counterpart the Industrial and Employers' Confederations of Europe (UNICE) agree on a particular issue, this agreement is then passed to the Council of Ministers, which transfers it into a Directive without further discussion. First successes include the Parental Leave Directive in 1996 (Falkner, 1998). Overall, however, the significance of the social dialogue should not be exaggerated. To date, it has concluded only few agreements establishing minimum standards (Greenwood, 2003: 68). Moreover, the areas covered by the social dialogue are compartmentalised and do not include issues concerning the general macroeconomic direction of the EU. More fundamental issues such as the right to strike, the right to association and wage bargaining have been excluded from European competencies (Greenwood, 2003: 150). Sectoral social dialogue is hardly developed (for an overview, see Keller, 2003: 418–23) and European Works Councils could prove divisive for trade unions (Martin and Ross, 1999: 343–4). In short, trade unions are clearly structurally disadvantaged in the EU institutional set-up, which confirms those who are sceptical of the benefits of a social partnership strategy at EU level. Nevertheless, there are also some examples, where trade unions have successfully managed to develop strategies, which have the potential to overcome this situation.

The EMF organises workers in one of the most transnationalised sectors in Europe, including many TNCs in consumer electronics, car manufacturing and machinery production. In response to transnationalisation, it is argued that the EMF had to follow and internationalise its structure and activities (Bieler, 2005: 471–3). The crucial turning-point was the early 1990s. 'Under the influence of the opening-up of the European borders, growing international competition, complete Europeanisation of the economy and massive unemployment in Europe, [the EMF] had noticed a distinct tendency towards a competition-driven collective bargaining policy' (EMF, 2001: 1).

Plans for EMU further implied the danger of social dumping through the undercutting of wage and working conditions between several national collective bargaining rounds (EMF, 1998: 1–2). The EMF realised that wage bargaining was no longer a national issue in its sector, characterised by an increasingly transnationalised production structure. In response, the EMF started restructuring itself and began to discuss the potential of coordinating wage bargaining. The EMF coordination strategy has three main pillars (EMF 2001: 1): (1) an information exchange system about national collective bargaining rounds, the so-called European Collective Bargaining Information Network (EUCOB@); (2) the establishment of cross-border collective bargaining networks, including the exchange of observers for collective bargaining rounds (Gollbach and Schulten, 2000: 166–76); and (3) the adoption of common minimum standards and guidelines, of which wage bargaining coordination is not the only but arguably the most important aspect.

The coordination of national wage bargaining was approved in 1998 and the EMF tries to ensure that national unions pursue a common strategy of asking for wage increases along the formula of a productivity increase plus inflation rate (EMF, 1998: 3; Schulten, 2005: 274–89). As far as data is concerned, although national negotiators did not refer to the EMF guidelines, the actual bargaining results were pretty much within the formula until 2001. From then onwards the results of bargaining have been more out of line with the formula, but importantly the guidelines have been increasingly used as a political bargaining tool. The main goal of the coordination of collective bargaining is to avoid the downward competition between different national bargaining rounds and to protect workers against the related reduction in wages and working conditions. Thus, 'a coordinated European collective bargaining policy will play a major role in intensifying and reinforcing the social dimension of European unity' (EMF, 1998: 1). This, in turn, indicates the EMF's continuing resistance to neoliberal restructuring.

Importantly, the institutional changes have gone hand in hand with an expansion of members of staff. In 1989, the EMF had four full-time staff; by 2003 it employed nineteen. At the second EMF congress in Prague on 13 and 14 June 2003, internal decision making was further facilitated by permitting the Executive Committee to adopt recommendations from the policy committees by a two-thirds majority. This introduction of majority voting clearly indicates that the EMF has developed into an independent actor at the European level. The example of the EMF highlights the fact that despite structural disadvantages within the EU form of state, the coordination of bargaining provided a good, alternative way forward, characterised by the following three advantages: (1) it does not rely on an employers' counterpart, which has not been willing to engage in meaningful social dialogue; (2) the disadvantaged position within the EU institutional framework is of no consequence, since interunion coordination does not rely on the compliance of EU or national institutions; and (3) this strategy allows us to take national differences into account, often cited as the core reason of why European-wide union cooperation is impossible. If productivity is lower in one country than another, then the wage increase demands in the former country will accordingly be lower than in the latter.

A second example of European activity is the EPSU (Bieler, 2005: 475–7). It organises workers in the civil service from local to European government as well as in the health sector and general utilities such as energy and water. Thus, it organises workers in all those sectors that were traditionally part of the public sector with a clear national production structure. Nonetheless, the EPSU has become increasingly active as an independent actor at the European level since the 1990s, because the deregulation and liberalisation of traditionally domestic production sectors such as energy and public procurement has been driven by EU Directives. Moreover, the Commission is the EU's main representative in the negotiations of a General Agreement on Trade in Services (GATS). The international, European level has, therefore, become more relevant for trade union activity. In a letter to EPSU's affiliated unions, the General Secretary Carola Fischbach-Pyttel in 2003 pointed to the decisions in relation to public services to be taken at the European level. This included the Commission's position on GATS negotiations, the report by the working group on Social Europe within the Convention on the Future of Europe, the discussion by the EP of draft Directives on public procurement and a further opening of the electricity and gas markets, a Green Paper by the Commission on Services of General Interest as well as a general push by the DG Internal Market towards more deregulation of services of general economic interest (EPSU, 2003a). According to EPSU, the 'liberalisation policies of the European Commission with the majority support of the European Council are undermining public services' (EPSU, 2002).

In resistance to neoliberal restructuring, the EPSU has engaged to some extent in sectoral social dialogue in the electricity industry, now the most transnationalised sector within the EPSU's remit (Eironline, 2002, 2004b). Moreover, a new social dialogue committee in the local and regional government sector was established in January 2004, adopting a joint statement on telework as its first measure (Eironline, 2004a). In 2002, the executive committee of the EPSU adopted a bargaining information exchange system similar to the EMF and appropriately called it EPSUCOB@ and there is now an annual collective bargaining conference. A third strategy employed by the EPSU has been the lobbying of EU institutions. In relation to GATS, the EPSU is concerned that EU public services have become bargaining chips for the Commission in its attempt to open up other countries for European services exporters (EPSU, 2003a). Reservations were expressed by the EPSU in a meeting with the Commissioner Pascal Lamy of DG Trade on 17 February 2003 in relation to the tightness of GATS safety clauses, allowing countries to maintain their own regulations, the secrecy of the current negotiations, the pressure applied by institutions such as the World Bank on developing countries to move towards liberalisation in these areas, as well as the rights of foreign citizens carrying out contract work within the EU (EPSU, 2003b).

The EPSU's most innovative strategy is, however, its increasing cooperation with other social movements. In relation to GATS, in addition to its direct lobbying of the Commission, the EPSU has participated in demonstrations organised by Belgian unions and the Association for the Taxation of Financial Transactions for the Aid of Citizens (ATTAC) on 9 February 2003 to keep public services out of GATS. Furthermore, it took part in the European day of national action on GATS and public services organised by the European Social Forum (ESF) on 13 March 2003 as well as the ETUC European day of national action for a Social Europe on 21 March (EPSU, 2003a). The link with other social movements is also visible in relation to public procurement. In 2002 and 2003, EPSU and several other EIFs cooperated with a range of environmental and other social movements such as Greenpeace Europe and the Social Platform, itself a network of European non-governmental organisations (NGOs) promoting the Social Dimension of the EU, in lobbying the EU Council of Ministers and especially the EP to amend the Draft Directives on Public Procurement towards the inclusion of social, ecological and fair trade criteria in the award of public procurement contracts (Coalition for Green and Social Procurement, 2002). Ultimately, the Coalition was not very successful in influencing the decision making process, partly because it relied too much on lobbying within the institutional set-up of the EU (Bieler, 2011). Nevertheless, the focus on increasing cooperation with other social movements is a possible way forward of enlarging the social basis of resistance.

Two other examples of broad coalitions to influence EU policy making indicate that a combination of mass mobilisation together with lobbying can lead to more successful campaigns. In 2006, a broad coalition of trade unions and social movements, combining lobbying in Brussels with large demonstrations, campaigned against the Services Directive, which intended to liberalise the provision of services across borders in the EU. The campaign culminated in two large European demonstrations in Brussels and Strasburg in 2005 and early 2006 including trade unions and other social movements from all over Europe (ETUC, 2006). In the end it was at least successful in preventing the adoption of the initial draft of the Directive. Second, in 2001 and 2004 the EU Commission attempted twice to liberalise services in European ports. On both occasions, transport workers' unions were able to prevent restructuring through a combination of lobbying with internal information and mobilisation campaigns, international strikes and large demonstrations. As Turnbull states, 'by adding the argument of force to the force of argument, port unions have been able to play the information-gathering, report-writing, lobby resolution-passing game to much greater effect' (Turnbull, 2007: 133). These examples of European trade union activities demonstrate that unions continue to resist neoliberal restructuring. Although they are structurally disadvantaged within the EU institutional set-up, strategies which also incorporate wider mobilisations and include large demonstrations and/or strikes help to overcome these disadvantages.

Trade unions and the future of the EU

Of course, neither social movements nor trade unions are by default part of counter-neoliberal movements, nor are they automatically inclined to cooperate with each other. As Silver pointed out, contemporary capitalist restructuring has not resulted in a homogenisation of workers' conditions. Instead, 'while spatial fixes tended to erode the North–South divide, technological fixes, product fixes and protectionism tended to reconstitute the divide continually' (Silver, 2003: 170). Hence, workers in different regions of the world are in very different situations and transnational solidarity is often rather difficult, if not impossible. For example, eastward enlargement of the EU has led to tensions between eastern and western trade unions over the issue of free movement of labour. It was west European trade unions, which through the Economic and Social Committee of the EU, in research by the ETUC, as well as through pressure by the Confederation of German Trade Unions (DGB) and Austrian ÖGB on their respective governments, pushed successfully for a transition period of up to seven years in relation to the free movement of labour to protect jobs in their countries. As Bohle and Husz make clear, this political victory based on a lack of transnational solidarity may turn out to have disastrous consequences for labour in general in that it may result in long-term divisions between the eastern and western labour movements and thereby weaken European labour overall (Bohle and Husz, 2005: 108–9). Within eastern Europe itself, trade unions, often associated with the old communist regimes, have lost influence. Where they have been active recently, this was often not in support of solidarity but in defence of privileged workers. In a comparative analysis, Ost describes how unions first supported the restructuring of inefficient companies and remained passive in view of the related job losses and then, more active again, emerged 'as small unions of skilled, elite workers, a kind of unionism for the new labour aristocracy' (Ost, 2006: 327). In short, it is not clear whether CEE trade unions are in a position to resist restructuring.

On the positive side, however, the ESF process may provide the space for eastern and western European labour to overcome their tensions and move towards more intensive cooperation with other social movements in order to enlarge the social basis of resistance (Bieler and Morton, 2004, 2006). From 6 to 10 November 2002, European 'anti-globalisation' movements including trade unions, NGOs and other social movements gathered in Florence, Italy for the first ESF. During 400 meetings around 32,000–40,000 delegates from all over Europe, plus eighty further countries, debated issues related to the three key themes of the Forum: 'Globalisation and [neo]liberalism', 'War and Peace', as well as 'Rights–Citizenship–Democracy'.

The ESF culminated in one of the largest anti-war demonstrations ever on the afternoon of 9 November, when 500,000 protestors according to police estimates – almost 1 million according to the organisers – marched peacefully through the streets of Florence against the impending war on Iraq. Clearly, there were differences between the various social movements, established trade unions and new, radical unions. While established trade unions continue to focus on 'social partnership' with employers and state representatives in order to assert the demands of their members, radical trade unions emphasise the importance of bottom-up organisation with a focus on strikes, demonstrations and cooperation with other social movements to broaden the social basis of resistance. Moreover, tensions also exist between trade unions and social movements. While the latter are rather sceptical of trade unions' hierarchical internal organisation and their willingness to confront neoliberal restructuring, the former question the representativeness and internal accountability of social movements.

These differences, however, should not make us overlook the commonalities and resulting possible joint activities. Despite different structures and strategies, all movements present at the ESF identified neoliberal globalisation, in its economic, deregulatory form as well as its militaristic version (as embodied in the war on Iraq) as the main target for resistance. Hence a convergence of opinions emerged around several areas for joint activities, including the call to hold world-wide demonstrations against the impending war on Iraq on 15 February 2003 as well as joint activities in defence of the public sector against neoliberal restructuring (Bieler and Morton, 2004: 312–19). Since Florence, the ESF process has moved on, with the sixth forum taking place in Istanbul in July 2010. This process, together with the fact that there are successful case studies of transnational solidarity (see, for example, Bieler and Lindberg, 2010) indicates that transnational solidarity in resistance to neoliberal restructuring is feasible. In short, while cooperation between trade unions across borders and between trade unions and other social movements is not automatic, there are also clear possibilities of successful resistance to neoliberal restructuring. The EU offers one level on which such strategies can be put usefully into effect.

To conclude, many trade unions continue to contest neoliberalism and are, therefore, potential participants in the wider movement of resistance against restructuring. This is, however, not automatic but needs to be fought for. Ultimately, it will be crucial that trade unions, transformed into more inclusive organisations (Panitch, 2001: 368–70), work together with social movements in order to stem the neoliberal Anglo-American model and to re-establish a European social model of capitalism. This would provide a combination of traditional organisational structures with developments from below, creating a very powerful movement in size and numbers for the challenge of neoliberal restructuring at the national, European and global level.

Notes

1 This is an expanded version of an earlier article with the same title in *Capital and Class*, Vol. 93, 111–24.

2 The empirical part of this chapter is informed by a neo-Gramscian perspective. For an outline and critical engagement with this perspective, see Bieler *et al.* (2006).

References

Van Apeldoorn, B. (2002) *Transnational Capitalism and the Struggle over European Integration*. London and New York: Routledge.

Bieler, A. (2003a) 'Labour, Neoliberalism and the Conflict over Economic and Monetary Union: A Comparative Analysis of British and German Trade Unions', *German Politics*, Vol. 12 (2), 24–44.

Bieler, A. (2003b) 'Swedish Trade Unions and Economic and Monetary Union: The European Union Membership Debate Revisited?', *Cooperation and Conflict*, Vol. 38 (4), 385–407.

Bieler, A. (2005) 'European Integration and the Transnational Restructuring of Social Relations: The Emergence of Labour as a Regional Actor?', *Journal of Common Market Studies*, Vol. 43 (3), 461–84.

Bieler, A. (2006a) *The Struggle for a Social Europe: Trade Unions and EMU in Times of Global Restructuring*. Manchester: Manchester University Press.

Bieler, A. (2006b) 'European Integration and Eastward Enlargement: A Historical Materialist Understanding of Neoliberal Restructuring in Europe', in Bieler, A., Bonefeld, W., Burnham, P. and Morton, A. D. (eds), *Global Restructuring, State, Capital and Labour: Contesting Neo-Gramscian Perspectives*. Basingstoke: Palgrave, 71–90.

Bieler, A. (2011) 'Labour, New Social Movements and the Resistance to Neo-Liberal Restructuring In Europe', *New Political Economy*, Vol. 16 (2), 163–83; available in 2010: DOI 10.1080/13563461003789779.

Bieler, A. and Morton, A. D. (2004) '"Another Europe is Possible"? Labour and Social Movements at the European Social Forum', *Globalizations*, Vol. 1 (2), 303–25.

Bieler, A. and Morton, A. D. (2006) 'Canalising Resistance: Historical Continuities and Contrasts of "Alter-Globalist" Movements at the European Social Forums', in Gamble, A. *et al.* (eds), *Labour, the State, Social Movements and the Challenge of Neoliberal Globalisation*. Manchester: Manchester University Press.

Bieler, A, Bonefeld, W., Burnham, P. and Morton, A. D. (2006) *Global Restructuring, State, Capital and Labour: Contesting Neo-Gramscian Perspectives*. Basingstoke: Palgrave.

Bieler, A. and Lindberg, I. (eds.) (2010) *Global Restructuring, Labour and the Challenges for Transnational Solidarity*. London: Routledge.

Bieling, H.-J. (2001) 'European Constitutionalism and Industrial Relations', in Bieler. A. and Morton, A. D. (eds), *Social Forces in the Making of the New Europe: The Restructuring of European Social Relations in the Global Political Economy*. Basingstoke: Palgrave, 93–114.

Blyth, M. (2002) *Great Transformations: Economic Ideas and Institutional Change in the Twentieth Century*. Cambridge: Cambridge University Press.

Bohle, D. (2006) 'Neoliberal Hegemony, Transnational Capital and the Terms of the EU's Eastward Expansion', *Capital and Class*, No. 8, 57–86.

Bohle, D. and Husz, D. (2005) 'Whose Europe Is It? Interest Group Action in Accession Negotiations: The Cases of Competition Policy and Labour Migration', *Politique Européenne*, Vol. 15, 85–112.

Coalition for Green and Social Procurement (2002) 'Proposal for a Directive on the Co-ordination of Procedures for the Award of Public Supply Contracts, Public Service Contracts and Public Works Contracts', www.epsu.org/ projects/procure/CoalEN.pdf (accessed 30 January 2003).

Dølvik, J.-E. (1999) *An Emerging Island? ETUC, Social Dialogue and the Europeanisation of Trade Unions in the 1990s.* Brussels: ETUI.

Eironline (8 November 2002), www.eiro.eurofound.ie/2002/11/inbrief/ eu0211203n.html (accessed 11 July 2007).

Eironline (23 March 2004a), www.eiro.eurofound.eu.int/2004/03/feature/ eu0403203f.html (accessed 11 July 2007).

Eironline (6 July 2004b), www.eiro.eurofound.eu.int/2004/07/inbrief/ eu0407201n.html (accessed 11 July 2007).

EMF (1998) 'Collective Bargaining with the Euro'. 3rd EMF Collective Bargaining Conference, Frankfurt, 9–10 December, www.emf fem.org/ index.cfm?target=/default.cfm (accessed 26 October 2004).

EMF (2001) 'EMF Position on the European Industrial Relation System'. Adopted by the EMF Executive Committee, Luxembourg, 3 and 4 December, www. emf-fem.org/index.cfm?target=/default.cfm (accessed 26 October 2004).

EPSU (2002) 'Services of General Interest and the Convention on the Future of Europe – You Can Shape the Future of Europe! EPSU General Circular No. 13 (1712/2002)', www.epsu.org/Campaigns/sgi/gen13.cfm (accessed 17 June 2003).

EPSU (2003a) '2003: A Crucial Year for Public Services in Europe. Letter by the EPSU General Secretary Carola Fischbach-Pyttel to All Affiliated Unions', www.epsu.org/gen1.cfm (accessed 30 January 2003).

EPSU (2003b) 'GATS, PSI-EPSU and Pascal Lamy', www.epsu.org/Campaigns/ GATS/Lamy.cfm (accessed 17 June 2003).

ETUC (2006) 'Euro-demonstration. Strasbourg 14/02/2006', ww.etuc.org/a/1581 (last accessed 21 June 2007).

Falkner, G. (1998) *EU Social Policy in The 1990's: Towards a Corporatist Policy Community.* London: Routledge.

Gamble, A. (2001), 'Neoliberalism', *Capital and Class*, No. 75, 127–34.

Gill, S. (2001) 'Constitutionalising Capital: EMU and Disciplinary Neoliberalism', in Bieler, A. and Morton, A. D. (eds), *Social Forces in the Making of the New Europe: The Restructuring of European Social Relations in the Global Political Economy.* Basingstoke: Palgrave, 47–69.

Gollbach, J. and Schulten, T. (2000) 'Cross-border Collective Bargaining Networks in Europe', *European Journal of Industrial Relations*, Vol. 6 (2), 161–79.

Greenwood, J. (2003) *Interest Representation in the European Union.* Basingstoke: Palgrave.

Keller, B. (2003) 'Social Dialogues – The State of the Art a Decade After Maastricht', *Industrial Relations Journal*, Vol. 34 (5), 411–29.

Martin, A. and G. Ross (1999) 'In the Line of Fire: The Europeanization of Labor Representation', in Martin, A. and Ross, G. (eds), *The Brave New World of European Labor: European Trade Unions at the Millennium*. New York and Oxford: Berghahn Books, 312–67.

Ost, D. (2006) 'After Postcommunism: Legacies and the Future of Unions in Eastern Europe', in Phelan, C. (ed.), *The Future of Organised Labour: Global Perspectives*. Oxford: Peter Lang, 305–32.

Panitch, L. (2001) 'Reflections on Strategy for Labour', in Panitch, L. and Leys, C. with Albo, G. and Coates, D. (eds), *The Socialist Register 2001: Working Classes, Global Realities*. London: Merlin Press, 367–92.

Rosamond, B. (2002) 'Imagining the European Economy: "Competitiveness" and the Social Construction of "Europe" as an Economic Space', *New Political Economy*, Vol. 7 (2), 157–77.

Ryner, M. and T. Schulten (2003) 'The Political Economy of Labour Market Restructuring and Trade Union Responses in the Social-democratic Heartland', in H. Overbeek (ed.), *The Political Economy of European Employment: European Integration and the Transnationalization of the (Un) employment question*. London and New York: Routledge, 176–98.

Schulten, T. (2005) 'Foundations and Perspectives of Trade Union Wage Policy', in Hein, E. *et al.* (eds), *Macroeconomic Policy Coordination in Europe and the Role of the Trade Unions*. Brussels: ETUI, 263–92.

Schulten, T. (2006) 'Problemi e Prospettive della Politica Sindacale Europea', in Associazione per il Rinnovamento della Sinistra (ed.), *Quale Futuro per il Sindacato*. Bologna: Futura Press, 99–123.

Silver, B. (2003) *Forces of Labor: Workers' Movements and Globalization Since 1870*. Cambridge and New York: Cambridge University Press.

Strange, G. (1997) 'The British Labour Movement and Economic and Monetary Union in Europe', *Capital and Class*, No. 63, 13–24.

Strange, G. (2002) 'Globalisation, Regionalism and Labour Interests in the New IPE', *New Political Economy*, Vol. 7 (4), 343–65.

Taylor, G. and Mathers, A. (2002) 'The Politics of European Integration: A European Labour Movement in the Making?', *Capital and Class*, No. 78, 39–60.

Turnbull, P. (2007) 'Dockers versus the Directives: Battling Port Policy on the European Waterfront', in Bronfenbrenner, K. (ed.), *Global Unions: Challenging Transnational Capital through Cross-Border Campaigns*. Ithaca, NY and London, 117–36.

7

Beyond the Third Way: regionalism and socialist renewal in Europe

Owen Worth

At the time of writing, the Left in Europe is in a state of crisis. After its revival in terms of parliamentary success in the late 1990s, the Left has suffered a series of electoral defeats resulting in its removal from power in many European states, and its success in others being greatly reduced. Even in the great social democratic power houses such as Sweden, the Left has seen its once-dominant position eroded to a shadow of what it once was. The failure of the Left has also been more noticeable since the financial crisis, in that despite there has been a backlash against social welfare cuts taken during the financial crisis in the form of protests and civil unrest and the recent electoral success of François Hollande in France, the Left has been unable to fashion a meaningful or coherent political response. Indeed, since the strategy of the 'Third Way', the Left in Europe has not managed to forge a fresh collective of ideas that can in any way be seen as a unified continental response to the crisis. Yet, it is exactly this type of project that is required to reignite the European Left and propel it firmly beyond the problems and frailties that were inherent in the Third Way.

The Third Way emerged as a way of reorientating social democratic principles in the light of the decline of the post-war model that became adopted in western Europe by centre-left parties. By the 1980s the future of this traditional social democratic Left in Europe was unclear. The general hegemonic position that incorporated a framework based upon Fordist production and on a firm class-based social partnership hit its crisis point as early as the 1960s, when the emergence of various civil groups indicated that the socialist project could no longer be grouped around the traditional paternalism of post-war social democracy. From here the Left suffered a variety of setbacks that might have included internal resistance to change, but ultimately became undermined by the increasing internationalisation of the state and the growing move towards neoliberal economics, perhaps best demonstrated by the failure of the French Socialist Party to ratify its radical agenda while in office in the 1980s. As a result, the Left embarked upon new projects, aimed at both addressing the new realities of 'globalisation' and restating the objectives of a socialist project. As such, emphasis was placed upon new visions of socialist renewal, proposed by writers such as André Gorz and Alain Lipietz and upon attempting to create some dialogue between Left-wing Parties across Europe, especially within the French–Germany–UK axis (Gorz, 1990; Lipietz, 1992).

It was from within this environment that the concept of the 'Third Way' was born. While often associated with the beginnings of the Blair leadership within the UK Labour Party and the last phase of the Clinton administration in the US, the Third Way became the lynch-pin of the centre-Left within Europe with Schröder and Jospin creating a united front alongside Blair in the EU. Ten years on and the whole concept of the Third Way appears dead and buried. Both Schröder and Blair dropped the concept when it appeared to have served its usefulness, while Jospin failed to maintain any political position to allow him the opportunity to advance its cause. The concept itself had been transformed to one based on the Left centrism of Anthony Giddens and Ulrich Beck, rather than of the more radical Left–Green orientation of Gorz and Lipietz.

This chapter will provide an overview of the Third Way and argue that while the results were negative and led to the pacification rather than a challenge to market ideology, its roots were more honourable and ones that the European Left need to re-engage with. It looks back at the post-Fordist visions that Lipietz developed and the work of the British cultural studies theorist Stuart Hall and the influence that inspired the journal *Marxism Today* and of the tradition of *New Times* in the 1980s. Entwined within this was Hall's own theoretical methodology of 'Marxism without Guarantees', which provides a useful reflexive framework more capable of benefiting the Left today than those that have either insisted upon a return to traditionalism (rejection of regionalism, national unionism, etc.) or those (such as Giddens) that argue that the left can not sustain itself unless it embraces elements of neoliberalism (Hall, 1988, 1996). It is by revisiting these traditions that we might find some ideas for socialist renewal at a European level that could provide us with fresh strategies needed in order to address the current crisis policies that are being pursued under the auspices of the new 'era of austerity'.

The rise and fall of the Third Way

If the foresight of Hall and the philosophies of Gorz and Lipietz allowed the Left a platform for change and transformation, then the praxis of rhetoric that followed significantly moved away from the objectives associated with socialism and social democracy. The move was towards a Durkheimian framework of action that effectively sidelined any concept of class and wealth redistribution in favour of a model of inclusion/exclusion, which proposed engagement with (rather than a challenge towards) global capitalism (Giddens, 1994; Beck, 1997). This was initially seen alongside Giddens' long-standing critique of historical materialism, which reached its conclusion with *Beyond Right and Left*. Giddens argued for a total dismantlement of Keynesian-inspired social democracy to allow for a centrist approach to politics that could realise the objectives of socialism far more realistically (Giddens, 1994). Ulrich Beck continued this theme in the early 1990s, when he called for a 'Third Way' of understanding political society. Here, the Left–Right political order, in which the first and second 'ways' were conceived, had to change in the wake of the transformation of modernity. This was not just a question of economics; rather, Beck argued, society had to move beyond traditional politics (Beck, 1997). His 'radical centralism' was thus one that moved beyond the traditional virtues of 'Right' and 'Left', towards one that engaged with the hybrid nature of 'reflexive modernity'. For Beck, post-Keynesian paternalism represented an era that had left the ideological constraints of the Cold War, and as socialism became the lynch-pin of critique in this period, it should accompany it to the historical dustbin in both theory and practice (Beck, 1997: 148–50). Similarly, Beck argued that the form of critique that Marxism embodied may have 'captivated the critical intelligentsia for a century' but was now inapplicable (Beck, 1997: 176).

If Beck was to turn the idea of a Third Way from one where the main objective was to re-engage with socialism to one which aimed to move beyond it, then this was underlined by Gidden' seminal *Third Way* (1998), which drew extensively from Beck. The impact of Giddens' text on the practical restructuring of social democracy should not be underestimated. Self-proclaimed as Tony Blair's 'guru', Giddens' accessible book often provided centrist practitioners with a manifesto on which to pursue policy reform, and it received praise not just from the core alliance of the German SDP–British Labour Party–US Democratic Party, but also from South America and East Asia. Giddens goes far further in his rejection of socialism, arguing that it simply failed to understand the dynamic of the relationship between society and capital. As he observes:

> For Marx, socialism stood or fell by its capability to deliver a society that
> would generate greater wealth than capitalism and spread that wealth in
> more equitable fashion. If socialism is now dead, it is precisely because
> these claims have collapsed. (Giddens, 1998: 4)

Giddens gave a rather narrative account of how global capitalism could
provide a social dimension around which the social democratic movements
needed to organise alongside a radical restructuring of civil society. If the
first part of the book is geared towards explaining that both the neoliberal
Right and the socialist Left have ultimately failed to come to grips with
the social reproduction of capitalism, then the second part outlines a
'radical' programme of 'new' social democracy. This is geared towards
directing market accessibility to the excluded, private/public partnership,
and a reconstruction of the paternalist family unit towards one based
upon legality rather than religious morality. Perhaps the most notable
addition here – and certainly one that became highly influential to Blair
and Schröder – was the maxim 'no rights without responsibility', which
argued that welfare provision and economic rights should be tied to a
version of the Weberian Protestant ethic whereby individuals must learn
and contribute towards the workings of twenty-first-century capitalism.
(Giddens, 1998; Blair and Schröder, 1999).

If *New Times* and *Marxism Today* had called for a Third Way to
invigorate the socialist critique in the face of the 'new' Right and the
internationalisation of neoliberalism, the 'radical centricism' of Giddens
and Beck sought to humanise the neoliberal project. In doing so it had
all the appearance of a hegemonic project, one formed in the traditional
Gramscian sense, that aimed to consolidate a prevailing order through
the societal pacification of class relations (Worth, 2000, 2005). It was the
public realisation of this that contributed to its demise as a European
doctrine. While the Blair–Schröder–Jospin partnership may have added
great impetus to the creation of such a programme within Europe, it
also relied upon both its success in other parts of the world and upon
public support. The defeat in the US by Bush's 'compassion conservatism'
coupled with growing scepticism in France and Germany forced many
on the centre-Left in Europe to drop the rhetoric behind the Third Way.
Any unity between national parties also became increasingly strained
due to Blair's support for the Bush administration's war in Iraq. As such
the 'Third Way' was already in decline before the systematic rejection
of the Socialists in France and the demise of the SPD in Germany. EU
enlargement had also reduced it as a sustainable strategy within the EU as
traditional western social democrats were not able to coordinate the core

ideas behind the Third Way with those in the expanding EU who had a different historical trajectory.

The main reason that the Third Way failed as a political strategy, however, was that it had served its purpose. While still relevant as an alternative to import substitution strategies in the semi-periphery (Worth, 2005), in Europe it largely took the form of a useful sound-bite. This was partly because, despite Giddens' continued insistence that the Third Way did offer a genuine and radical alternative to the status quo (Giddens, 2002), much of it actually offered the Left no such substantial break. As Cammack argued, much of the Third Way's attraction to politicians lay with Giddens' 'way with words' rather than its policy content (Cammack, 2004). Yet perhaps the most telling criticism of the Third Way agenda came from those associated with *Marxism Today* and from Hall, demonstrating again the need for his critical re-engagement. In a special one-off issue, *Marxism Today* criticised the interventions of both Blair and Giddens by arguing that their twin purpose was to create a mandate to reside and govern, rather than to transform politics and society (Hall and Jacques, 1998). In rephrasing a blistering attack on Thatcher earlier on in the journal's history,[1] Hall described the whole Third Way project as 'a great moving nowhere show' and one which had failed to provide anything more than window dressing for the sustained project of market economics, associated with Thatcherism (Hall, 1998). The question for the Left in Europe remains how can they respond to develop a strategy that does not merely return to the traditional domains of national social democracy but uses European integration as a tool for potential unity, rather than as a barrier to social equality.

Regionalism and the Left

One of the few achievements of the Third Way perspective was that it was coordinated along transnational grounds rather than through national forms. This has been accompanied by strategies that are beginning – albeit gradually – to attempt to imagine social democratic struggles at a transnational and consequently a European level (Bieler, 2006; Upchurch, Taylor and Mathers, 2009). However, as Bailey reminds us, this move has been constantly tempered by the neoliberal realities that have been evident through economic coordination within the EU (Bailey, 2009).

Outside the more specialist discipline of European Studies, European politics is thus increasingly being analysed through the lens of 'new regionalism'. Formed more as an approach than as a sub-discipline, studies in 'new regionalism' tend to look at how the end of the Cold War has produced new forms of governance that situate themselves within a regional format and are mutually cooperative (Gamble and Payne, 1996). In this way, political strategies are being perceived as being more supranational in essence. While this may have opened space for theorising on the left, it has also attracted greater degrees of systemic critique, due to the globalisation of the neoliberal project and the view that all forms of regionalism are articulated expressions of this move (Gamble and Payne, 1996).

In light of the Third Way's inability to capture the imagination of Socialist Parties and movements across Europe, critical studies in regionalism have argued that due to the overwhelming rise of the neoliberal hegemony a new form of social consciousness has been constructed within civil society that has coopted movements on the Left. As a result, debates on the Left towards European unity have tended to revert back to a standpoint position and moved to a position of neoliberal engagement versus neoliberal rejection. While the prominent centre-Left parties in Europe have increasingly moved to the post-Third Way position, of necessity, the responses from the Left to solutions at a regional level have either been orthodox or sceptical. However, as Strange has argued, regional integration should not merely be viewed as a structural or constitutional process, but as one which is formed through an open-ended dialectical struggle (Strange, 2006). Indeed, one of the more contradictory developments of EU-scepticism from the Left is that it feeds and supports the criticism from the neoliberal Right, who argue that regionalism in the European form overregulates the freedom of the market due to its commitment to social governance (see Minford *et al.*, 2005 for a standpoint neoliberal position). The traditional Left may have aspirations to be 'internationalist', but in reality are split between those that pursue internationalism and those that favour a strategy of national scepticism.[2]

This flaw was stressed by Lipietz in his book *Towards a New Economic Order* (1992), when he argued that the move from the national social democratic projects associated with Fordism represented as much an opportunity for the Left as it did a hindrance. For while neoliberal restructuring and global competitiveness may have become the central features of post-Fordist production this does not mean that the political Left should move to the defence of outmoded national models. Indeed, Lipietz's starting point is to take post-Fordism and the new *global* competitiveness as a *necessary* constraint faced by *both* Left and Right within the context of a general crisis of national political economy. For Lipietz, the crisis of Keynesian national political economy did not, in principle, signal the end of all progressive national 'modes of regulation'. Nevertheless, globalisation meant that national social democracy, if it was to survive, had to be fully integrated with the new world order, with its survival depending on its success as a *competition* state. This did not rule out welfarism but it did subordinate national welfare objectives, such as sustained economic growth and full employment, to economic success in global markets. From this view, the globalisation of competitiveness under post-Fordism necessitated universal *reform*, yet the imperative of the competition state did not altogether imply the universalisation of its dominant neoliberal *form*. For Lipietz, the extension of deep regionalism represented the best hope for an embedded social democracy or a successful, organic radicalisation of the Third Way. Lipietz thus argued against a compromise or re-evaluation of social democratic principles (as the Third Way argues), but for a reconfiguration of them at the regional level.

If Lipietz argued for a renewal of the Left in terms of regional strategy, then Hall's theoretical contributions allowed us to imagine the form it might take. Hall's maxim of 'Marxism without Guarantees' stems not just from the practical need to re-apply the principles of socialism and democracy to account for social transformation, but also from the theoretical problems associated with post-war western socialism. In the article 'Marxism without Guarantees', Hall seeks to demonstrate the weaknesses that are inherent within the Marxist understanding of ideology and determinism. For Hall, such weaknesses have stemmed from shortcomings that Marx himself (and then Lenin and Kautsky) had placed on the concept of ideology and class and on his assumption that ideas and ideology grow out of respective class structures. While Gramsci's observations of the Italian working class and the political experience of socialism in both 'eastern' and 'western' Europe may have showed this to be insufficient, Hall was equally unimpressed by the answers provided by French Structuralism. For Structuralists, ideology represents an important superstructural component of a system that is ultimately determined by its economic base. While this may offer greater flexibility than the traditional model, it nevertheless retains much of the simplistic understandings of reductionism of its predecessor and places even less emphasis on the importance of agency and on the nature of transformation. Hall was quite categorical that ideology, as with class and the definition of the market itself, was not a fixed entity but something that was continuously redefined and reshaped due to dialectical struggle (Hall, 1996: 36–45).

For the European Left, such observations provide a different approach to notions of regional unity and neoliberalism. While Hall, as he illustrates in his groundbreaking work on the nature of Thatcherism, would certainly agree with a number of 'new constitutionalists' in arguing that the EU is an expression of the modern form of neoliberal capitalism, he would also stress that this is not a permanent feature. Instead, the EU can be seen as a specific set of superstructures that may have emerged from the materialist base, and are defined through a set of competing social forces which are open to change. In terms of regionalism, this form of ontology appears more accessible to the Left in terms of strategic thought than those that are often associated with criticisms within IPE. For while such arguments may favour Hall's commitment towards theory, much of the scholarly analysis remains closed in its negativity, rather than 'open' on the question of Europe. Neo-Marxian accounts of regionalism are still often eyed through a structural deterministic lens – where Europe is seen primarily as the product of a transnational capitalist class, whose main intent is to expand and maintain its influence (van der Pijl, 1998; Bieler and Morton; 2001). What is appealing about Hall's mode of critique and his approach to Marx and Gramsci is that he remains consistently open in terms of his analysis of the subject and the potential of transformation and change, hence the wording behind 'Marxism without Guarantees'. The primary objective behind the working slogan is that it presents its method of understanding social relations as one that is shaped, but not determined or structured, by the forces of production. It is here that Hall is at his most profound in his criticisms on structuralism:

> The relative openness or relative indeterminancy is necessary to Marxism as a theory ... Understanding 'determinacy' in terms of setting the limits, the establishment of parameters, the defining space of operations, the concrete conditions of existence, the 'givenness' of social practices, rather than in terms of the absolute predictability of particular outcomes, is the only basis of a 'Marxism without final guarantees'. It establishes the *open horizon* of Marxist thinking – determinacy without guaranteed closures. (1996: 45)

This informs our approach to studies on European regionalism and social democratic renewal in two ways. First, it claims that the notion that European integration represents a structural and inevitable move towards neoliberalism is premature. While neo-Gramscians (particularly Gill) are correct in demonstrating that the EU articulates policies that have been shaped through the hegemonic neoliberal project, they are incorrect to assume that it has merely taken on the form of a NAFTA, where economic neoliberalism is constitutionally and formally enshrined (Gill, 1998; Rupert, 2000). European integration, as those from the Right will testify, has bought with it a social challenge, which may have been pacified and coopted through Delors' 'social Europe', but did demonstrate the open terrain that exists within the confines of European Politics and the diversities that exist within them

Secondly, this demonstrates to us that any form of European socialist renewal must both be consistent and flexible at the same time. This is perhaps where Stuart Hall's background in Cultural Studies is most prominent. As he was more prone to study factors such as race and ethnicity, identity, semiotics and resistance, he was equally aware of the fragmented nature of class politics and of the complexities involved at building a new form of social democracy. Thus, Hall's vision of such a movement would be one that both engaged with the current dominant features of the present order – as a point of necessity, and one with the historical understanding to transform it (Hall, 1988). Hall himself was commenting on the plight of socialism as a failed ideology in Britain at the time, but his arguments hold great relevance for contemporary Europe and in reflection of the movement since the 1980s. By criticising the traditional Left, he was often prone to attack from the Bennite and Trotskyist Left that were prevalent in Britain at the time for advocating a pluralist stance and supporting a moderate position. However, in line with the principles behind the 'Marxism without Guarantees' mandate, Hall was equally critical of the moderate Left within the British Labour Party that would eventually evolve into the clearer 'Third Way' mandate. While others that were politically associated with him at the time endorsed a more formal organised engagement with capital and the market (see pp. 144–5), Hall always maintained the Gramscian argument that a counter-hegemonic social project is one that needs to engage with civil society's common-sense in order to *transform* it, rather than merely reside within its sway (Hall, 1988).

The flexibility of 'Marxism without Guarantees' allows for a 'general' formula for European socialism, as it stresses the relevant division between the civil and the political and is not bounded through specific national forms of exceptionalism. In this manner both common civil aims, such as those which have been coordinated (albeit prematurely and through similar elitist formations to that of the political party) at the ESF, and the political ideas that unite European Socialism (equality, democracy, etc.) and which should not be compromised, are accounted for. However, it also stresses the need to accept and account for the processes of change, of which regionalism has been a significant part, during the global transformation of the last thirty or so years. One must also be aware of potential reform projects such as those that are associated with what we now define as the 'Third Way' and (perhaps more importantly) be less naive – or perhaps more critical – in analysing political 'inventions' that add up to nothing more than (neo)liberal orthodoxy.

The European Left: critique and renewal

I have argued here that while the 'Third Way' project associated primarily with centre-left parties in the UK and Germany in the late 1990s may have substituted social democratic aims and objectives in favour of liberal democracy continuity, the initial theoretical arguments were far more radical and poignant. Lipietz's vision saw that Europe was geared towards a distinct transformation of the basic unit-sum sovereignty of the traditional state system of nationhood. As he explicitly argues:

> Harmonized ecological regulations; united capital taxation and labour norms; Europe-wide social welfare insurance; more extensive inter-regional net transfers on the transnational European scale; maintenance of an 'air chamber' between regions or nations which want to keep a particular aspect of a satisfactory 'social compromise' – this simply means the building of a European 'grand compromise', to be negotiated between citizens residing in Europe. And this means no less than building a nation. (Lipietz, 1992: 140)

In doing this it is characteristic of Lipietz that while he identifies and critiques dominant neoliberal interventions within the process of EU integration, he nevertheless invites us to imagine the possibilities for and benefits of an alternative inherent in integration as such and that he insists that progressive interventions must start from the new reality and efficacy of the regional level where, by comparison to the national level, new *opportunity structures* have largely emerged. His point here is that as the state *is* being *transformed* and that regionalism is a fundamental aspect of that transformation, Europe appears as a new terrain on which the politics of contestation must develop post-globalisation and post-Fordism. For Hall, the purpose of *New Times* that was to emerge out of *Marxism Today* provided similar avenues in the area of cosmopolitanism.[3] This allowed pioneers such as David Held to pursue cosmopolitanism as a distinct form of radicalism. Held has maintained that cosmopolitanism remains the only viable mechanism for taming the effects of globalisation and that European socialism needs to build a transnational civil society in order that they can contest the communitarian nature of the national-state (Held, 2002).

These two areas of transformation and restructurisation ultimately became utilised by 'Third Way' theorists and became increasingly used by centre-left parties as strategies for reform. In addition, within the *New Times* project, Charles Leadbeater and David Marquand did much to pave the way for Giddens through their work on individualism and the realignment of politics, respectively (Leadbeater, 1989; Marquand, 1989), with the former also moving later to an advisory position with New Labour. Yet, as a response to this, Hall and Jacques themselves acknowledged the problems with Blairism and the Third Way in the later special issue and called for a drastic Europe-wide rethink from political and civil society (Hall and Jacques, 1998), despite the fact that many earlier contributors were now directly involved with the practical project of New Labour. The notion of cosmopolitanism has also been one that has attracted criticism for its rather naive and ambiguous method of imposing radical change. As Bailey rightly argues in Chapter 5 in this volume, cosmopolitanism has to date been used by party elites in a manner that reduces it to an empty concept in reality. Perhaps the best criticism of cosmopolitanism is seen through the work of David Chandler. For Chandler, cosmopolitanism is a utopian ideal which, without a formal structural framework within its mandate merely re-enforces elites (Chandler, 2004). In particular Chandler refers to the growth of NGOs that have emerged since the end of the Cold War which Held *et al.* feel are realising this cosmopolitan alternative. The reality is a configuration of NGOs that works to promote their own interests and their own objectives and does little to foster civil solidarity behind and beyond the nation-state (Chandler, 2004).

Chandler reminds us of the problems associated with attempting to embark upon a programme that aims to both radicalise society and engage with existing liberal forms of plurality. However, for European socialism to re-invent itself in its contemporary form it needs to stress both internationalism and the involvement in civil society. Within the confines of 'Marxism without Guarantees' these are stressed methods that can be employed to break the traditional socialist cul-de-sac that had emerged by the 1980s. The Cosmopolitan civil 'movement' in its present form does suffer both from a utopianism where unstructured 'visions' compete with structured 'pipe-dreams' within forums ranging from the UN to the WSF/ESF and from a problem with accountability.[4] Indeed, until the Left can adequately formulate a project that empowers citizenship throughout the various levels of civil society by means that go beyond the professional elitism that dominates the political economy of NGOs towards one which actually seeks to interact with everyday practices and struggles, cosmopolitanism will only be employed as a means of gaining electoral support for political parties.

If the post-Fordist ideas of Hall and Lipeitz appeared to ultimately slide into the orthodox (or even radical) centralism of the Third Way, how, then could any contemporary strategy be employed in a manner that retains its commitment towards democratic socialism and radicalism, without reverting back to forms of national isolationism? In realising this, the European Left needs to conclude that any form of strategic revivalism is based upon two agendas. The first is that it looks towards moving beyond the restricted forms of post-war social democracy, practised within the nation-state, while the second should be geared towards *challenging* and *transforming* global capitalism. The Third Way borrowed from the tradition of Hall and Lipietz in moving the Left beyond the nation-state but rather than challenge the nature of global capitalism, it sought to endorse it. What remains appealing about their respective positions is that they retain such radicalism. Hall's critique of the traditional left and of the bounded concept of European self-determinism still remains the most useful direction for European socialism to take. Lipietz himself might have moved to a position where this can be achieved through an ecological party, after his continued electoral success as a French Green Party MEP,[5] but his vision of the 'possible' contained within the realm of post-Fordist production give us fresh critical directions for understanding what form of radicalism the Left in Europe might pursue. For both remained adamant that socialism had to maintain its organic commitments that could only be realised through acknowledging the process of historical change. It is on this realisation that a European socialist project should be grounded.

Conclusion

The Left in Europe remains in a state of crisis and in light of the global financial crisis needs to re-establish a strategic vision. One the one hand the 'Third Way' rhetoric that dominated the 1990s has appeared to reach its sell-by date and has largely failed to deliver and on the other the traditional Left has maintained that the only way to achieve socialist objectives is through national individualism. This is further reflected by the respective interpretations of the growth of regionalism within global politics, with the dominant position insisting upon the need to engage with European integration and with marketisation and the latter favouring scepticism. Intellectually the response from the academic Left has recently supported this scepticism, with a large component arguing that the EU adds to a new form of 'constitutionalism', where regional bodies comprise an institutional component of neoliberal hegemony. Efforts to re-focus the Left have naturally been seen as revisionist with the result being to reformulate social agendas within the large framework of neoliberalism. It is here where Delors' 'social Europe' and Blair, Schröder and Jospin's different visions of the Third Way belong.

However, this chapter has argued that there remains another avenue for the Left that aims to re-establish the main ideals of democratic socialism within the context of historical change. It is here that Stuart Hall's frameworks of 'Marxism without Guarantees' and Alain Lipietz's 'vision of the possible' remain relevant. Written from a post-Fordist, post-nationalist, perspective they provide us with a way in which the Left can identify the meaning of change and rebuild accordingly. Both reject the modernisation programmes that the Third Way rested upon and both maintain a commitment towards confronting the inequalities inherent within neoliberal global capitalism. The Third Way managed to move social democracy towards a position that could imagine itself beyond the stagnancy of the nation-state, but failed to ensure that its key principles could challenge the expression of capital at this wider level. For the European Left to rebuild itself as a force capable of challenging the supremacy of neoliberalism it requires recognition of regional and global change and the re-statement – rather than re-assessment – of socialist principles and the re-evaluation of the concept of transnational civil society.

Notes

1 See Hall (1979).
2 The position associated with the European United Left and Nordic Green Left has tended to favour a protectionist/national model of welfarism and this has remained the traditional form of critique, although there are distinct differences between the more internationalist (German Left, Portuguese Left Bloc, Italian Communist Refoundation and Spanish United Left) and those that have favoured a national-first approach (Dunphy, 2004). There are currently fifteen political parties or blocs within the group and include many of the major Communist parties and all the major left-wing Nordic parties. In addition, they contain France's Left Front and left-leaning populist–Nationalist Parties such as *Sinn Fein* (Ireland) and *Folkebevægelsen mod EU* (Denmark) which was supported by the Danish Euro-sceptic Red–Green Alliance.
3 To clarify, *Marxism Today* was a journal, founded in 1957 as a theoretical forum for the Communist Party of Great Britain. When Martin Jacques took over the editorship in the late 1970s it became more and more associated with Euro-Communism and by the 1980s, Stuart Hall was very-much the journal's 'star academic'. The name *New Times* was given to

the groundbreaking special issue of the journal in October 1988 (and later a book) that mapped out the rebuilding of socialism in the 1990s.

4 By these I refer to the many NGOs and civil society groups that compete for funding within official bodies to promote their own 'unique' interests to groups that play a considerable role within the European and World Social Forums (WSFs) but promote 'projects' ranging from the ambiguity of 'unfettered open space' to 'world government' aspirations. See Worth and Buckley (2009).

5 Alain Lipietz has been an elected MEP for the French Green Party since 1999. He was also initially selected as their representative at the 2002 Presidential elections, before internal problems within the party saw the candidacy switch to Noël Mamère.

References

Bailey, D. J. (2009) *The Political Economy of European Social Democracy: A Critical Realist Approach.* London, Routledge.

Beck, U. (1997) *The Reinvention of Politics.* Cambridge: Polity.

Bieler, A. (2002) 'The Struggle over EU Enlargement: A Historical Materialist Analysis of European Integration', *Journal of European Public Policy*, Vol. 9, 575–98.

Bieler, A. (2006) *The Struggle for a Social Europe: Trade Unions and EMU in Times of Global Restructuring.* Manchester: Manchester University Press.

Bieler, A. and Morton, A. D. (eds.) (2001) *Social Forces in the Making of the New Europe: The Restructuring of European Social Relations in the Global Political Economy.* Basingstoke: Palgrave.

Blair, T. and Schröder, G. (1999) *Europe: The Third Way/Die Neue Mitte.* London and Berlin: Labour Party and SDP.

Cammack, P. (2004) 'Giddens' Way with Words', in Hale, S., Leggett, W. and Martell, L. (eds), *The Third Way and Beyond.* Manchester: Manchester University Press.

Chandler, D. (2004) *Constructing Global Civil Society.* Basingstoke: Palgrave.

Dunphy, R. (2004) *Contesting Capitalism? Left Parties and European Integration.* Manchester: Manchester University Press.

Gamble, A. and Payne, A. (1996), *Regionalism and World Order.* Basingstoke: Palgrave.

Giddens, A. (1984) *Beyond Right and Left: The Future of Radical Politics.* Cambridge: Polity.

Giddens, A. (2002) *Where Now for New Labour?* Cambridge: Polity.

Gill, S. (1998) 'European Governance and New Constitutionalism: Economic and Monetary Union and Alternatives to Disciplinary Neoliberalism in Europe', *New Political Economy*, Vol. 3 (1), 5–26.

Gorz, A. (1990) *Critique of Economic Reason.* London: Verso.

Hall, S. (1979) 'The Great Moving Right Show', *Marxism Today*, January.

Hall, S. (1988) *The Hard Road to Renewal.* London: Verso.

Hall, S. (1996) 'The Problem of Ideology: Marxism without Guarantees', in Morley, D. and Chen, K.-H. (eds), *Stuart Hall: Critical Dialogues in Cultural Studies.* London: Routledge.

Hall, S. (1998) 'The Great Moving Nowhere Show', *Marxism Today*, 9–14.

Hall, S. and Jacques, M. (eds) (1989) *New Times: Changing Face of Politics in the 1990s.* London: Lawrence & Wishart.

Hall, S. and Jacques, M. (1998) 'Blair Wrong', *Marxism Today*, 1–3.

Held, D. (2002) 'Cosmopolitanism: Ideas, Realities and Deficits', in Held, D. and McGrew, A. (eds), *Governing Globalisation.* Cambridge: Polity.

Leadbeater, C. 'Power to the Person', in Hall, S. and Jacques, M., *New Times: Changing Face of Politics in the 1990s.* London: Lawrence & Wishart, 137– 50.

Lipietz, A. (1992) *Towards a New Economic Order.* Cambridge: Polity.

Marquand, D. 'Beyond Right and Left: The Need for a New Politics', in Hall, S. and Jacques, M., *New Times: Changing Face of Politics in the 1990s.* London: Lawrence & Wishart, 371–9.

Minford, P., Mahambare, V. and Nowell, E. (2005) *Should Britain Leave the EU? An Economic Analysis of a Troubled Relationship.* Cheltenham: Edward Elgar.

Van der Pijl, K. (1998) *Transnational Class and International Relations.* London: Routledge.

Rupert. M. (2000) *Ideologies of Globalization.* London: Routledge.

Strange, G. (2006) 'The Left Against Europe? A Critical Engagement with New Constitutionalism and Structural Dependency Theory', *Government and Opposition*, Vol. 41 (2), 197–229.

Upchurch, M., Taylor, G. and Mathers, A. (2009) *The Crisis of Social Democratic Trade Unionism in Western Europe: Prospects for Alternatives.* Aldershot: Ashgate.

Worth, O. (2000) 'Consolidating Neoliberal Hegemony: A Critical Analysis of the Third Way', Paper Presented at the NTU seminar series, Nottingham Trent University.

Worth, O. (2005) *Hegemony, International Political Economy and Post-Communist Hegemony.* Aldershot: Ashgate.

Worth, O. and Buckley, K. (2009) 'The World Social Forum: Post-modern Prince or Court Jester?', *Third World Quarterly*, Vol. 30 (4), 649–61.

PART III

The limits and potentials of greater European regionalism

8

Habermas on Europe: a critique

Lawrence Wilde

The idea that a reformed and progressive EU could take the lead in the 're-regulation of the world society' was first raised by Jürgen Habermas in the conclusion to his 1998 essay on 'The Postnational Constellation' (Habermas, 2001: 58–112). This vision of the EU as a cosmopolitan alternative to rampant neoliberalism is shared in various forms by other left-leaning social and political theorists such as Hauke Brunkhorst (2005), Roberto Unger (2005) and Ulrich Beck (2006). Writing in 2005, Habermas claimed that politics cannot meet the need for the regulation of the global economy until the 'intermediate arena' between the state and world levels is populated by a manageable number of global players. The EU 'has at last reached the stage when it can plausibly claim to be a global player,' with an enhanced potential to wield influence as a regional model because it represents the harmonisation of the interests of formally independent nation states (Habermas, 2008: 324–6). However, Habermas argues that the failure of the EU to achieve full political integration greatly weakens its power and influence, as witnessed by its inability to act decisively in response to the GFC. Only full integration, if necessary led by a core group, can create a strong Social Europe capable of offering an alternative model to neoliberalism (Habermas, 2009: 78–105, 194–5). As things stand, Habermas complains that even the reforms adopted as a result of the Lisbon Treaty leave the EU with democratic deficits, intergovernmentalism, excessive bureaucracy and blatant elitism (Habermas, 2009: 79–81). In his view, Europe needs to complete the task of full political integration, and the social democratic parties need to 'break out of their national cages and make a new room for manoeuvre at the European level' (Habermas, 1999: 196).

The empirical problems impeding the realisation of this vision have been all too evident since the turn of the century. First, we saw the failure of the EU to speak with one voice against the invasion of Iraq, second, the abandonment of the projected Constitution following its democratic rejection in France and the Netherlands and, third, the disarray displayed in the aftermath of the 2008 financial crisis, particularly over Greece, which threatened the continued existence of the euro. But there are also theoretical problems in Habermas' vision, concerning his claims about the need for a unified European public sphere, extended civic solidarity, constitutional patriotism and a coherent European identity. Although these ideas are clearly important components of his cosmopolitanism, I will argue that they are not as cosmopolitan as he would like us to think. Rather his vision of a strong Europe is too closely modelled on an idealised view of the evolution of the liberal–constitutional nation-state, leaving us to question whether a strong European identity would really serve to promote the development of a cosmopolitan consciousness. Nevertheless, the normative vision of Social Europe contributing to global re-regulation may yet be preserved by developing some of the insights Habermas provides on the potential for socialist post-national politics, in Europe and beyond.

Habermas and post-national democracy

Habermas' cosmopolitanism seeks to develop the propositions set down by Immanuel Kant in the late eighteenth century (Habermas, 1998: 165–201, 2006b: 113–93; Kant, 1992: 41–53, 93–130). Although Kant favoured the ultimate goal of a world republic, he settled instead for the intermediate goal of a league of nations on the basis of voluntary agreements. Habermas argues that this idea was flawed, yet explicable in the historical circumstances. Now, however, it can be revived with the goal of a 'politically constituted world society without a world government' (Habermas, 2008: 316). This idea, whereby decisions are taken at a variety of levels – local, national, regional and global – on different issues, as appropriate to social need, is outlined in more detail by advocates of cosmopolitan democracy such as David Held (1995, 2004) and Daniele Archibugi (2008). For Habermas, the EU is of pivotal importance for this normative perspective, because it is the only entity where the nation-states have already pooled sovereignty in a significant way, and it has emerged in world politics as a unitary player. In his view, if we are to reach a situation in which we can talk of a 'future world domestic policy', then strong regional or continental regimes that have already moved politics on from the national level are vital (Habermas, 2008: 324–5). So, whereas in the 1980s the focus for the Left was on how the threat to egalitarian politics at the level of the nation-state might be resolved at the European level, the focus has now shifted to the importance of establishing a Social Europe to promote cosmopolitan democracy.

Habermas fully recognises that the EU is dominated by a bureaucratic mode of administration. Insofar as functionalist and path-dependency arguments explain the success of the EU as a rational way of managing economic life in the region, they also show how 'elite intergovernmentalism' is perpetuated at the cost of neglecting to develop the active support for the ideal of European unity or, in Habermas' words, the need for the 'normative integration of citizens' (Habermas, 2006b: 68). The *débâcle* over the European Constitution is a good example of this, with virtually no attempt made to popularise the project or mobilise support for it and, for that matter, scant attention paid to the social guarantees that might have made it attractive to ordinary citizens. Habermas wants the EU to play the role of a global re-regulatory alternative to neoliberalism, but he does not think this possible until a European public sphere, with a collective identity, is created. He framed this problem for the first time in a 1990 appendix to *Between Facts and Norms* (Habermas, 1996: 506–7) and developed the discussion in *The Postnational Constellation* (Habermas, 2001: 58–112). More recently, Habermas' treatment of the EU has been conducted against the background of an expanded European Union, the abortive attempt to adopt a European Constitution and the GFC. His thoughts in this period are found in three collections of essays, *Time of Transitions* (2006a), *The Divided West* (2006b) and *Europe: The Faltering Project* (2009).

In *The Postnational Constellation* Habermas recognises that the goal of a cosmopolitan social Europe will be a stalled project until such time as full federation is realised. He sets two preconditions for the emergence of a federal Europe capable of contributing to the creation of a more democratic and egalitarian world order. First, that the EU would be able to compensate for the lost competencies of the nation-state and, second, that within it there could develop a collective identity strong enough to legitimate a post-national democracy (Habermas, 2001: 90). A social Europe cannot be achieved 'without a basis of solidarity', and the civic solidarity originally developed at the level of the nation-state needs to be 'expanded' to the European level (Habermas, 2001: 99–100).

On the question of competencies, Habermas appears confident that the EU could overcome the institutional barriers to a viable federation, although he emphasises that a second chamber of a European federation representing the governments of nation states would have to be stronger than the directly elected parliament (Habermas, 2001: 99). The strength of the state tradition in Europe is such that they would have to 'retain a substantially stronger status than would normally be enjoyed by the constituent parts of a federal state' (Habermas, 2006a: 109). However, he recognises that, despite the developing powers of the ECJ and the ECB, for the most part states have retained their competencies (Habermas, 2006a: 97). In Weberian terms, the EU does not have a monopoly on the legitimate use of force, but it does assert the primacy of EU law over the law of its member states (Habermas, 2006b: 137). At various points Habermas talks in terms of the need for the EU to be able to levy taxes, harmonise tax policy and social policy, be represented by a foreign minister and a finance minister, and to create its own army (Habermas, 2006a: 90-106, 2006b: 49–56, 2009: 57–8). However, Habermas is unequivocal in his criticisms of the unreformed EU, considering it to be in a 'lamentable condition', propelled by bureaucratic decision making processes and suffering from a serious democratic deficit (Habermas, 2006a: 76–8, 2006b: 82). He characterises the EU's situation as a tacit coalition between 'market Europeans' and erstwhile Euro-sceptics, the latter being prepared to accept the *fait accompli* of the single market and the euro rather than embrace federalism (Habermas, 2006a: 85). This applies equally to Left Euro-sceptics.

The failure of the constitutional project reflects a failure to develop popular support for the European project, and this brings us to the second precondition for a cosmopolitan Europe, a European identity. Habermas considers that such a project requires popular support and a sense of solidarity, so that forms of civic solidarity previously limited to the nation-state would have to be expanded to the European level (Habermas, 2001: 99). He accepts that we cannot, at present, speak of the existence of a European identity, but the real question ought to be whether we can realistically conceive of the conditions whereby citizens are able to extend their civic solidarity beyond national borders 'with the goal of achieving mutual inclusion' (2006b: 76). At this point we should note Habermas' use of the words 'expansion' and 'extension' (Habermas, 2001: 99, 2006b: 77, 78), because he clearly wants to delineate a trajectory of solidarity building civic consciousness from the national level to some sort of equivalent at the European level. In order to do this he makes a conceptual distinction between national consciousness and civic solidarity.

National consciousness develops when the idea of the nation becomes the principal source of collective identity, but civic solidarity develops only in a democracy in which people recognise themselves as free and equal citizens. The former involves a fixation on the state and its superiority over others, while the latter emphasises the liberal order within the state that enables a structure of 'solidarity among strangers' and thereby opens the way to a transnational extension of solidarity. Civic solidarity's focus on our liberties and democratic processes displays a universalistic content beyond national boundaries, and this gradual 'uncoupling' of the constitution from the state is what Habermas terms 'constitutional patriotism' (Habermas, 2006b: 78–9). Like all liberal nationalists, Habermas needs to make a clear distinction between good and bad nationalism. He acknowledges the 'Janus face' of nationalism, but insists that it reflects not simply blind fealty to the state but also awareness of the value of political rights and civil liberties (Habermas, 2001: 101–2). I find this argument problematic and will return to it below, but for now let us look at the distinction Habermas makes between civic solidarity and global solidarity (Habermas, 2001: 110, 2006b: 80).

When considering the possibility of cosmopolitan solidarity, Habermas concludes that this idea 'has to support itself on the moral universalism of human rights alone', rather than being rooted in particular collective identities (Habermas, 2001: 108). Moral outrage over violations of human rights provides a sufficient basis for solidarity among activists engaged in global politics, but this is a 'weakly integrated' cosmopolitan society. What is lacking at the global level, according to Habermas, is a 'common ethical–political dimension' to sustain a collective identity. Within nation-states, he argues, there is a common political culture in which the various actors engaged in negotiations operate within 'common value orientations and shared conceptions of justice' that enable agreements to be made beyond the limits of instrumental rationality. In other words citizens can agree to make some sacrifice of their narrowly defined self-interest in order to strengthen society, as, for example, when assenting to economic redistribution through progressive taxation. However, at the international level this 'thick communicative embeddedness' is missing (Habermas, 2001: 108–9).

The question then is raised as to whether the EU can offer some sort of mediation between the state level and global level by developing a transnational extension of civic solidarity (Habermas, 2006b: 67). Solidarity within the EU would require something more than the strong negative duties displayed by global activists. It would require a widespread sense of belonging if Europe were to speak with one voice in foreign affairs and execute an active domestic policy (Habermas, 2006b: 80). However, whereas this sense of belonging at a national level could draw on notions of a shared national history and therefore appeared to be somehow 'natural', at the European level such an allegiance would have to rely on an *explicitly* constructed collective identity. Habermas considers the shared experiences that may be mobilised to foster such an identity. His outline of these building blocks for European identity appears in an essay entitled 'February 15 or: What Binds Europeans', which refers to the massive demonstrations against the impending invasion of Iraq in numerous European cities in 2003. Co-signed by Jacques Derrida, it invokes seven experiences (Habermas, 2006b: 46–8):

1. The secularisation of the state, or the privatisation of faith.

2. Following long periods of class conflict, the emergence of a confidence in the state to compensate for market failures.

3. Growing awareness of the paradoxes of progress, so that we are able to assess with care what might be lost in the process of modernisation and what might be gained.

4. Against the background of both the traditions of the labour movement and Christian social thought, a 'solidary' ethos of struggle for greater social justice.

5. As a result of the destructive history of the twentieth century, sensitivity has emerged for violations of personal and bodily integrity, reflected in the fact that the death penalty is outlawed in Europe.

6. In view of the history of wars between European states, a commitment to reciprocal restriction of the scope of sovereignty.

7. In view of the loss of empire, the experience of decline can lead to Europeans achieving 'a reflexive distance towards themselves,' learning to see themselves from the perspective of the defeated.

Here, then, is a list of positive points of collective identity from a shared European existence, but what is its function?

The list attempts to draw on and encourage an awareness of how the deep divisions of the past have been overcome, and is clearly designed to appeal to a broad progressive consensus. For example, although there is an endorsement of state intervention to offset market failures (1) and social justice (2), this could appeal as much to Europeans in the Christian Democratic tradition as the Social Democratic one, as the reference to the religious input to the idea of solidarity (4) indicates (cf. Habermas, 2006a: 94; see also Stjernø, 2004). There is also a clear rejection of aggressive nationalism (6) consistent with socialist internationalism. However, while the list is not wholly arbitrary, it is certainly tendentious. One might just as easily invoke Paul Kennedy's thesis about the factors that made Europe successful as the driving force of capitalism, with the emphasis on economic laissez-faire and political and military competition (Kennedy, 1989: 20–38). The 'lessons' drawn would be quite different from the Habermas/Derrida list, presumably emphasising the benefits of cut-throat competition and naked force. Certainly one would favour the more humane version of the lessons of history, but this is of relevance only to educational projects and, as Habermas himself admits, the development of a European civic identity cannot be controlled from above or produced by administrative decisions (Habermas, 2006b: 82). While Habermas has faith that such an identity will develop as a 'learning process' (Habermas, 2006a: 105), this seems to be based on the assumption of a 'neutral' state that encourages the negotiation of competing interests in an even-handed manner. This underestimates the continued centrality of class struggle that, as we note in the list (2), has been (wrongly) consigned to history.

The GFC exposes the flakiness of principle (2) of European identity. For sure, the states did intervene to save the banking system and avoid economic meltdown, but the compensation is to be paid, as ever, by the working class. Habermas himself recognised this instantly in his first reaction to the crisis:

> What worries me most is the scandalous social injustice that the most vulnerable social groups will have to bear the brunt of the socialized costs for the market failure. The mass of those, who are, in any case, not among the winners of globalization now have to pick up the tab for the impacts of a predictable dysfunction of the financial system on the real economy. (Habermas, 2009: 184)

This appeal against the social injustice meted out to wage earners in every economic crisis sits uneasily with the commitment to a consensual European identity and calls into question the idea that such an identity is a precondition for the cosmopolitan role that Habermas has in mind for Europe. This criticism will be developed in the next section. For now, though, it remains to be seen what social and political forces are identified by Habermas that might impel us towards a politics of re-regulation.

Habermas is hopeful that a European public sphere can develop through which a European identity might emerge. In a text based on an address to the cultural forum of the German socialists (SPD), he insists on the importance of this communicative network crossing boundaries, bringing discussions of European issues into existing national public spheres (Habermas, 2009, 87–8, 181–3). Once again, he sees the emergence of European citizenship as an extension of the kind of civic solidarity developed at the national level. I have already indicated my scepticism at this approach, but the important point to note is the significance attributed to European (or global) issues pushing into domestic agendas. We might look to demonstrations over the invasion of Iraq, lobbying in the build-up to the Copenhagen summit of 2009, or the demonstrations against the post-crash austerity measures as early examples of this. For the most part, the actors concerned are outside of the mainstream political parties. As Habermas notes, the impetus for the idea of the social regulation of world society has been supplied by citizens and citizens' movements, rather than governments or political parties (Habermas, 2001: 112).

The activities of these new non-governmental forces on a number of transnational issues leads to a process, identified by Habermas as 'normative framing' (Habermas, 2001: 109–10). Normative framing flows from the reality of a global discourse on a range of issues. So, for example, international NGOs can help to shape the agendas of UN summits by bringing key issues to the attention of citizens across the world, and by using institutionally established forms of lobbying. This in turn helps to produce agreements on concrete targets and action plans to achieve them. In this way apparently weak forms of legitimation 'appear in another light' as this ability of citizens to shape agendas is taken into account. Habermas suggests that the 'opening up' of national agendas might develop into a 'self-propelling process' of shared will formation on European issues (Habermas, 2006b: 81).

The 'new actors' called for by Habermas do not exclude political parties (Habermas, 2009: 88), but Habermas has been sharply critical of social democratic parties that remain within their 'national cages', urging instead greater cooperation at the European level (2009: 196). He emphasises the need to work for agreements on social and economic policy to avoid a 'race to the bottom' between the various systems of social policy within the EU (2006a: 6). On a wider scale, he points to the need to bring the 'Global Economic Multilaterals' – the WTO, IMF and World Bank – under some form of accountability, however difficult this may be (Habermas, 2008: 345–52). In this respect Habermas has tried to lend his voice to opposing what Roberto Unger describes as the wholesale surrender to the 'the dictatorship of no alternatives' (Unger, 2005: 1–11). Above all, he presses the urgent need for the coordinated global regulation of the financial markets, and bemoans the fact that the lip service paid to that at the London summit of the G20 in 2009 has not been followed up with decisive action. Habermas is rightly incensed by the short-termism of Europe's 'lame' political elites 'who prefer to read the headlines in the tabloids' (Habermas, 2010). The message for the established parties of the Left is to work out a coordinated approach to global re-regulation.

Critique

The conceptualisations I consider questionable are Habermas' distinction between national consciousness and civic solidarity, the idea of cosmopolitan patriotism, the need for a strong European identity and the idea of a single European public sphere. On the first issue, Habermas raises the possibility that Europe could evolve into a political entity that bridges the gap between the idea of civic solidarity embedded in national communities and the purely moral appeal to cosmopolitan solidarity operating at the global level, but he offers no clear indication of how this might emerge. The chief problem is the persistence of nationalism, as Habermas himself admits when commenting that 'the divisive force of divergent national histories and historical experiences that traverse European territory like geological fault lines remains potent' (Habermas, 2006b: 81). For a European identity to emerge, these allegiances must become 'historical' in the sense that they can no longer be called upon to place an emotional veto on the emergence of a wider solidarity. It seems to me that Habermas is setting an impossible task in seeking to 'expand' civic solidarity to the European sphere, because that form of solidarity is bound up with national consciousness too closely to permit the conceptual distinction that is so important to him.

By his own admission, 'civic solidarity' at the national level is 'relatively thin' (Habermas, 2006b: 55). It is paid for 'in small change', in the sense that citizens pay their taxes but are no longer prepared to die for their country, and he contends that neither the US nor Britain could have sustained the war in Iraq if they had had to rely on conscription (Habermas, 2006b: 77). But if civic solidarity is so 'thin', then how can Habermas impute a 'thick communicative embeddedness' to the 'common political culture' that is supposed to exist at the level of the nation-state? (Habermas, 2001: 109; cf. Habermas, 2009, 86–7). And if a strong civic solidarity involves a willingness to risk our lives for someone's interpretation of the common good, are we not better off without it and ill-advised to want to 'extend' it to the European polity? Habermas' conceptual distinction between national consciousness and civic solidarity simply does not work. Insofar as we can talk of solidarity in civil society it is normally not orientated to the state at all. The 'good citizen' may be socially active through involvement in trades unions, charitable work, community action, or in any number of causes, but this does not involve a conscious rallying around the constitutional achievements of the liberal democratic state. Indeed it is often the most politically astute citizens who are most critical of the democratic deficits of those liberal democratic states, such as unfair voting systems, unelected second chambers, patronage and corruption (to name some of the features most familiar to British readers).

Habermas' claim that we can gradually uncouple the constitution from the state to achieve 'constitutional patriotism' is misguided, and it is mystifying how cosmopolitans can be drawn to the idea that there can be anything progressive in any form of patriotism. As Jan-Werner Müller has noted, from its inception, constitutional patriotism has been 'a strategy of avoidance', seeking to preserve the progressive aspect of the establishment of democracy while denying the destructive narcissism inherent in nationalism. It is perfectly understandable that the concept of constitutional patriotism emerged as a response to the dilemma of German national identity in dealing with the Nazi past, but it is difficult to conceive of it being exported to the level of the EU. A number of scholars have enthusiastically embraced this idea as the basis for a form of solidaristic European identity (Lacroix, 2002; Cronin, 2003; Müller, 2007), but such a construct fails to grasp that the emotional attachment inherent in patriotism at national level is non-transferable. Patriotism is defined by this emotional attachment, which is deeply rooted in the economic and military rivalries of a era which cosmopolitans should be anxious to put behind us. If such a strong identity were to develop at the European level it would be more likely to manifest itself in a 'fortress Europe' mentality that would contribute to a new round of struggle for global hegemony rather than promote a post-hegemonic cosmopolitanism, which is what Habermas rightly desires.

Recent events in the history of the EU suggest that there is little enthusiasm for the creation of a more integrated polity resembling a federal state. Not only the rejection of the European Constitution by voters in France and the Netherlands in 2007, but the initial rejection of the fall-back position of the Lisbon Treaty by voters in Ireland (2008), perhaps the most successful beneficiary of EU membership, indicates a lack of enthusiasm for a strengthened European identity. Federalists may blame these displays of negativity on residual national parochialism (at worst), or disquiet at the elitist process that produced the Constitution without an extensive debate about the merits and extent of change (at best). However, it is at least as plausible to view this resistance to the 'deepening' of the Union as an objection to being pushed towards an identity when the need for such an identity is not evident. In this view, European citizens accept the Union for what it is, a functional arrangement that provides mutual benefit, without being persuaded of the need to create a new state accompanied by an *ersatz* identity. The absence of a strong European identity does not necessarily indicate a strong residual nationalism. The mostly successful assimilation of large numbers of workers from the new states of eastern Europe gives hope that aggressive nationalism is receding. For sure, where it exists it is loud and violent, but it cannot interrupt the everyday adjustment to the reality of cosmopolitanism or its positive espousal by growing numbers of global citizens. The development of a cosmopolitan consciousness precludes the sort of European identity prescribed by Habermas. Rather it requires a move away from all political identities based on territorial political units at all levels, opening the way for the emergence of multiple forums of political affiliation. As Beck has argued, 'to build the common European house according to the national–international logic is neither realistic nor desirable; on the contrary, it is counterproductive' (Beck, 2006: 173). In place of state-centred political identities, other forms of solidarity develop in movement politics that engage with an array of issues such as the environment, social exclusion and poverty, at multiple levels, from everyday life to the global.

It is therefore possible to view a weak European identity not as an arrested development but rather as a signal for the development of post-national consciousness that does not require a regional mediation but cuts straight to the cosmopolitan ideal that we are 'citizens of the world'. It also avoids the pitfall of constructing a European identity implicitly reinforcing the old imperialist myth of civilisational superiority. As Fine and Smith have pointed out, rather than turning Europe into a 'vehicle for cosmopolitan ideas and solidarity', the idea of a strong European identity risks turning it into a vehicle for a 'new form of transnational chauvinism', an outcome that would contradict everything Habermas is trying to do (Fine and Smith, 2003: 483). Volker Heins has warned against the damage to cosmopolitan thought engendered by this ideological elevation of Europe against the 'Other' (namely, the US), and accuses Habermas of contradicting his own philosophy in 'proclaiming spatially based identities against others' (Heins, 2005: 447). This may not have been Habermas' intention, but Heins is right to point out the real tension in theorising a trajectory from the nation-state to global democracy via a supposedly cosmopolitan Europe. If a cosmopolitan consciousness is to emerge it is better that the attachment of Europeans to Europe remains emotionally weak. To embrace the world at large we must put down the flags and silence the anthems, rather than create new ones; Habermas, in contrast, bemoans as 'bizarre' the rejection of the EU flag and anthem in the Lisbon Treaty (Habermas, 2009: 81). If civic solidarity in distinction from national consciousness is an illusion, as I suggest, then support for a European project has to be grounded in something new, not 'extended' or 'expanded' in any way, shape, or form.

As for the commitment to a European-wide public sphere, Habermas is correct when he argues that the undemocratic nature of the EU obstructs the development of open debates about EU positions on the range of issues that confront it as a global actor. The absence of serious debate prior to the Copenhagen summit on global warming in 2009 is an obvious case in point. However, to postulate the need for a single public sphere adjusted to constitutional processes is wedded to an outdated, statist view that reproduces already privileged interests and discourages the emergence of new issues and claims. As Nancy Fraser has argued, there are multiple publics striving to be included in the discussions around the structures and processes that frame our lives (Fraser, 1997: 69–98). Furthermore, issues such as global warming, migration and women's rights do not stop at national or regional borders, and activists involved in those issues may well not be part of the same political *demos* (Fraser, 2008: 76–9). The task of creating democratic processes through which we can confront the realities of global power goes far beyond the Habermasian goal of a single European public sphere.

Habermas' cluster of arguments around a European identity and a European public sphere are too closely tied to state-based thinking to be conducive to the development of a cosmopolitan consciousness. Overcoming the limitations and prejudices of national consciousness will not be achieving by wrapping ourselves round a European flag, but rather by becoming active global citizens. In theory, there is much to commend Habermas' argument that a social Europe could present an alternative model to global neoliberalism if the competencies still in the hands of the nation-states were shifted to a democratically constituted Europe. However, his idea that the GFC might act as a harbinger of a changed political climate in Europe (Habermas, 2009: 185), or trigger 'a cross-border awareness of a shared European destiny (Habermas, 2010), sounds like wishful thinking rather than a sober assessment of the prospects for 'deepening' Europe. At the present moment, with the balance of political forces firmly on the Right in most of the EU states, and with the GFC provoking a vicious attack on the public sector, we seem further from the idea of social Europe than when Jacques Delors inspired that idea during his spell as President of the Commission (1985–95) (Wilde, 1994: 179–86).

Conclusion

Because Habermas' post-nationalist vision is so reliant on the speedy completion of the project of a democratic European state, it appears to be marooned now that that project remains stalled. However, there are insights in his political writings that suggest that progress can be made around the idea of a cosmopolitan Social Europe without having to wait for the debate about a constitution to come round again. Habermas' plea for the Left to break out of its 'national cage' remains pertinent, for the struggle for global re-regulation and social protection goes on inexorably at national, regional and global levels. This requires a much higher level of coordination and cooperation among parties and social movements broadly on the Left to help to shape what Habermas calls a 'future global domestic politics' that involves debates and decision making at national, regional and global levels (Habermas, 2008, 345–52, 2009, 181–3). The task is both to expose neoliberalism as an ideology with predictably destructive consequences within states and across the globe, and to present alternatives through social protection guarantees, redistributive taxation and re-regulation of the global economy.

Habermas is right to claim that there is widespread opposition to the widening gap between rich and poor, and that 'not all western nations are prepared to accept the social and cultural costs at home and abroad of the unrectified global disparities in wealth that the neoliberals would foist upon them' (Habermas, 2008: 351). The important point here is the link between social and cultural damage 'at home and abroad'. The challenge is for parties and movements of the Left to focus on the linkages between global policies dictated by economic elites and their local applications across a broad range of issues. There is something in Habermas' list of the shared European experience that is important in this struggle, namely his observation that there is an expectation that states will intervene to compensate for market failure, and also that there is a 'solidary' ethos of struggle for social justice. These observations are more than speculative, as empirical work has revealed a far greater commitment to social welfare in the EU compared with the US that could provide a basis for the development of a European 'social' alternative to US-led global neoliberalism (Alesina and Glaeser, 2005; Pontusson, 2005). This difference in political culture was reflected in the enormous difficulty experienced in the US in pushing through the federal intervention package in 2008, compared with the speedy acknowledgement of the need for state rescue in Europe. It is also evident in a much stronger support in Europe for social responsibility for employment, welfare, crime and the environment. There is, in short, an existing tradition for the Left in Europe to work on in a renewal of egalitarian politics.

The other useful insight from Habermas' work on post-nationalism is the significance he gives to 'normative framing', a dynamic process of negotiating and lobbying at a variety of political levels through which activists operating primarily in social movements have achieved some remarkable successes (Habermas, 2001: 109–11). Much of the progress in environmental issues and women's rights has been achieved through normative framing from forces in civil society. The development of multiple public spheres cutting across boundaries and pushing for radical initiatives at all levels of politics is a work in progress. Initiatives can generate pressure that builds over time until policies that seem unlikely to succeed become more than gestures and contribute to a revived politics of the Left. One example of a policy capable of drawing attention to these linkages is the 'Tobin tax', a global tax on financial transactions supported by Habermas in his first interview after the crash (Habermas (2009: 192). Its radical potential can be judged by the fact that a tax rate of only 0.05 per cent on each transaction would yield over $400 billion dollars. If raised globally and distributed through the UN, it could be used to alleviate world poverty, as Fidel Castro recommended to a UN conference as early as 2001 (Castro, 2001). Besides having the merits of taxing those responsible for the financial crisis it would increase the funds independently available to the UN at a time when progress on the Millennium Development Goals (MDGs) is clearly faltering. Local variations could also be used to attack poverty within the affluent states, as proponents of the 'Robin Hood tax' have argued.

Habermas' linking of social and cultural problems at home and abroad suggests a new meaning to the 'make poverty history' slogan, previously applied only to the severe poverty in the less developed countries, suffered by over 2.5 billion people, or almost 40 per cent of the world's population (Pogge, 2008: 2). Neoliberal policies have also created a new poverty in the richest states, with levels of social exclusion and its attendant problems that need to be prioritised as an issue by the Left across Europe. At the European level, a recent example of a policy that could generate widespread support and at the same time question neoliberal orthodoxy is the European Youth Guarantee. Flowing from a report to the EP by Emilie Turunen of the Danish Socialist People's Party, it seeks to secure the right of all young people to be offered a job, training or education within four months of their unemployment. The need is clear, as 5.5 million (20 per cent) of under-25s in the EU were unemployed in the summer of 2010, but although it was approved by the EP it is unlikely to be enacted by the Commission without a coordinated and energetic political campaign. It is on issues like this, central to combating social exclusion, that Habermas' goal of a cosmopolitan Social Europe will be fought.

References

Alesina, A. and Glaeser, E. (2005) *Fighting Poverty in the US and Europe: A World of Difference*. Oxford: Oxford University Press.

Archibugi, D. (2008) *The Global Commonwealth of Citizens: Toward a Cosmopolitan Democracy*. Princeton, NJ: Princeton University Press.

Beck, U. (2006) *Cosmopolitan Vision*. Cambridge: Polity.

Brunkhorst, H. (2005) *Solidarity: From Civic Friendship To a Global Legal Community*. Cambridge, MA: MIT Press.

Castro, F. (2001), 'Address to the World Conference Against Racism, Racial Discrimination, Xenophobia and Related Intolerance'. Durban, South Africa, 1 September, www.un.org/WCAR/statements/0109cubaE.htm (accessed 9 September 2010).

Cronin, C (2003) 'Democracy and Collective Identity: In Defence of Constitutional Patriotism', *European Journal of Philosophy*, 11 (1), 1–28.

Fine, R. and Smith, W. (2003) 'Jürgen Habermas's Theory of Cosmopolitanism', *Constellations*, 10 (4), 469–87.

Fraser, N. (1997) *Justice Interruptus: Critical Reflections on the 'Postsocialist' Condition*. London: Routledge.

Habermas, J. (1996) *Between Facts and Norms*. Cambridge: Polity.

Habermas, J. (1999) *The Inclusion of the Other: Studies in Political Theory*. Cambridge: Polity.

Habermas, J. (2001) *The Postnational Constellation: Political Essays*. Cambridge: Polity.

Habermas, J. (2006a) *Time of Transitions*. Cambridge: Polity.

Habermas, J. (2006b) *The Divided West*. Cambridge: Polity.

Habermas, J. (2008) 'A Political Constitution for the Pluralist World Society?, in Habermas, J., *Between Naturalism and Religion*. Cambridge: Polity.

Habermas, J. (2009) *Europe: The Faltering Project*. Cambridge: Polity.

Habermas, J. (2010) 'Germany and the Euro-Crisis', *The Nation*, June, www.thenation.com/ (accessed 16 July 2010).

Heins, V. (2005) 'Orientalising America? Continental Intellectuals and the Search for Europe's Identity', *Millennium: Journal of International Studies*, 34 (2), 433–48.

Held, D. (1995) *Democracy and the Global Order*. Cambridge: Polity.

Held. D. (2004) *Global Covenant: The Social Democratic Alternative to the Washington Consensus*. Cambridge: Polity.

Kant, I. (1992) *Political Writings*. Cambridge: Cambridge University Press.

Kennedy, P. (1989), *The Rise and Fall of Great Powers*. London: Fontana Press.

Lacroix, J. (2002) 'For a European Constitutional Patriotism', *Political Studies*, 50 (5), 944–58.

Pogge, T. (2008) *World Poverty and Human Rights*, 2nd edn. Cambridge: Polity.

Pontusson, J. (2005) *Inequality and Prosperity: Social Europe vs Liberal America*. Ithaca, NY: Cornell University Press.

Stjernø, S. (2004) *Solidarity in Europe: The History of an Idea.* Cambridge: Cambridge University Press.
Unger, R. (2005) *What Should the Left Propose?* London: Verso.
Wilde, L. (1994) *Modern European Socialism.* Aldershot: Dartmouth.

9

The edges of Europe: the 'Eastern Marches' and the problematic nature of a 'wider Europe'

Neil Robinson

Studies of how a 'progressive social Europe' can evolve often ignore one overriding question which will hamper any such vision: how to solve the geographical divisions that have historically divided any such project. The inability to account for the historical and political diversities that have been a feature of the development of Europe will undermine any potential Europe-wide vision for change. This is especially the case when we consider that despite its initial promise the watershed of 1989 did not lead to homogenisation in Europe: it pushed existing divisions eastwards and might have made them sharper so that Europe has remained incomplete.

This chapter is about this 'incompleteness' of Europe. To suggest that Europe is incomplete is not a novel idea. Europe might be said to be naturally incomplete since it has no natural borders either geographically and ideationally. Yet despite this, for most of its history there has been a European identity of sorts. This identity, as one historian of its emergence has put it, is 'a cultural, economic and political phenomenon ... What gives Europe its real historical identity is the generation of societies that were all interacting with one another in political, economic and cultural terms on a large enough scale to have certain significant similarities in common' (Heather, 2010: xv). Contrasted to this identity incompleteness can therefore have specific, analysable properties, namely the division between 'European' social orders, the failure to create and maintain the means to interaction and the production of similarities between them. This division has been in place since in the late 1940s. European expansion – the creation of a 'wider Europe' – was supposed to overcome this division, but did not do so completely. The result of this has been that European integration reached its limits in the east with the accession of

Romania and Bulgaria. Further EU expansion and its attendant processes, particularly NATO-cum-US expansion, have been a source of tension, both for the states in the east and for the EU, rather than a means of recreating a common, progressive European identity anew.

The origins of the European divide: natural states and open access orders after 1945

The onset of the Cold War in the late 1940s saw the creation of a much more fundamental divide in Europe than had ever been known before. There had been divisions before in Europe, but these had never before been formalised and constructed as completely as they were after 1945. Post-1945 both West and East in Europe went further than ever before in consolidating the social orders that their dominant military powers respectively promoted and based that social order on sub-regional economic and security systems, the EU (and its predecessors) and the North Atlantic Treaty Organisation (NATO) in the West, the Council for Mutual Economic Assistance (Comecon) and the Warsaw Pact in the East. The effect of this was to merge geography and social orders within Europe so that they became fully concomitant for the first time. This has made the end of one of these social orders and the expansion of the other that much the harder so that elements of the divide and its geographic nature endure.

The social orders that were created and consolidated at the onset of the Cold War fit into the analytical framework proposed by North *et al.* (2009a).[1] The states of what post-1945 was to become the Soviet bloc and its ideological affiliates in the Balkans were modern versions of what North *et al.* (2009a: 32–49) call 'limited access orders' or, because of their numerical preponderance historically, 'natural' states. In Western Europe, on the other hand, open access orders were revived or created (although this took some time in the case of Spain, Greece and Portugal). All social orders are institutional arrangements that manage violence and resource distribution. Natural states do so by distributing rent between a small set of elites so as to control competition between them. In turn these elites distribute resources to clients in order both to consolidate their position and to enforce some social control on non-elite members. The 'natural state' is thus marked by a high degree of personalism and personalised exchange – between elite members, and between elite members and their clients – and by the fact that access to resources is through the state, control of which is contested by elites, and which is the main vehicle for the redistribution of rent. Natural states are 'limited access orders' since they limit access to organisational forms – it is difficult, if not impossible, to develop associational forms that might place demands upon the state, or that have a life beyond the state – in order to limit demands to share rents collected by the state and distributed through the elite networks that inhabit it. Natural states are thus marked by a weakness of private and impersonal organisation. They tend to limit economic activity since the state tends towards economic control in order to manage the collection and distribution of rent.

Open access orders, on the other hand are, as their name suggests less controlling. They allow organisations to both generate resources that are not controlled by the state and to make claims upon the state. Consequently, the formation of organisations is less controlled; it is managed by impersonal public law, which is also institutionalised, and which allows for the of setting up of more durable organisations – what North *et al.* (2009a: 23) call 'perpetually lived organisations', institutions that have a legal identity separate from individuals and not vehicles for the satisfaction of their personal interests. This is true both in the political and economic spheres, and open access and wider organisational formation in each of these spheres promotes openness in the other. Open access orders develop out of limited access orders for the most part.[2] This development is dependent on elites; when it suits their interests they impose constraints upon themselves that are the basis (eventually) for open access orders. The imposition and growth of such constraints have to be consistent with their interests or they would not be created or endure (North *et al.*, 2009a: 150). Constraints are in the first place legal; competition over rent becomes regularised and managed through rule development to create stability and lower the costs of competition. These rules form the basis of legal systems, which then develop as durable institutions independent of particular elite members, and which come to protect other emergent durable and impersonal organisations (such as economic corporations) and create mechanisms for the spread of impersonal economic activity through creating markets.

The development of such features of an emergent open access order was limited in the natural states of the Soviet bloc. Soviet-type systems were particular kinds of 'natural state' in that they were founded with constraints upon elites built into them. These constraints were ideologically inspired: first, Leninist ideology created the vanguard party, and second it deemed it necessary to develop economically and provide some share of production to the wider population for consumption, primarily through welfare. Vanguard partyism meant that Soviet-type systems had an impersonal perpetually lived organisation that gave the (party)-state a corporate identity independent of powerful personages. The party could not be reduced to elite interests, not least because it had to ensure economic development and some improvement in living conditions through the appropriation of economic surplus and its allocation to goals necessary to 'build communism'. Sometimes (often) the improvement of living standards was more rhetorical than actual but even this rhetoric signalled that the party could not become a simple vessel for the satisfaction of elite interests. The position of the party made the development of a rule of law for elites, a necessary condition for the development of an open access order, impossible. Law was weak since the party fulfilled its function of managing disputes about rent allocation and because the party could not itself be subject to law since its character could only be defined at a 'historiosophic level' (Staniszkis, 1992: 85): it was the organisation that determined ideology because of its command of history and so was above temporal definition through law. All public activity and regulation, so the law or any form of organisation, could not have an identity that was not created by the party since its command of ideology gave it a 'linguistic monopoly over active agency' (Walker, 1992: 7). This did not stop private interests from existing and from seeking material advantage. The system compelled such interests to develop since there was a gap between the identity defined for you by the party and the actions that this identity demanded of you, and reality. Heroic workers and their stalwart leaders could not be overfulfilling the plan all the time given that plan fulfilment was impossible; the gap between party-assigned roles and reality had to be papered over by mutual protection (Urban, 1985). The weakness of law facilitated this protection and where this protection took forms that were economically corrupt (i.e. seeking material advantage) as well as politically corrupt (i.e. not living up to party-designated roles) the subordination of the law to the party insured that legal sanction could not be brought to bear without political consent.[3]

The status of law and its capacity to act as a constraint was thus low in Soviet-type systems until very late in their existence. This, however, did not mean that there were no constituencies within some Soviet-type systems desirous of seeing such constraints created; it is just that these constituencies were not primarily the result of within-system interest formation. Their peculiarities meant that the natural states of post-Second World War Eastern Europe did not as a matter of course possess effective means of internally generating pressure that would create movement towards the open access orders that existed in Western Europe. Such pressure as there was – revolt and dissent – was incompatible with elite interests and was therefore suppressed. There was thus no natural development of constraints on elites such as law through endogenous socio-political development. The generation of pressure for the types of organisation that sustain openness and constituencies for change and constraint on elite behaviours were built up indirectly, as a side-effect of the official response to the increased density of demands to share rent that developed over time in Soviet-type societies, and the problems that this created for sustaining economic growth and maintaining welfare as demanded by ideology. This official response to an increasing demand to share rent and the strains that this put on economic development was not uniform across the Soviet bloc. In Eastern Europe it took the form of securing sources of external resource transfers, earnings from trade and from foreign borrowings. The USSR also borrowed, but on a smaller scale since it was cushioned by the high oil prices of the 1970s (for figures see Robinson, 2004).

The differences in borrowing and reliance on trade between states within Eastern Europe and between Eastern Europe and the Union of Soviet Socialist Republics (USSR) created different levels of demand for constraints on elites. Trade and borrowing were a system of resource transfer to elites. The greater the extent of these, the more elites were dependent on them to satisfy their own desires and to maintain social peace. As the USSR's economy dried up as a source of rents due to impending collapse, and as Moscow tried to force reform in Eastern Europe to lower the costs of empire, alternative ways had to be found to preserve resource flows from the 'West'. These flows could only be insured if there was a credible commitment to economic reform; this was necessary to roll debt over and secure fresh lines of credit. Reform was also demanded where there was a significant amount of foreign trade diversity; the more diverse trade was the more there was interest in the creation of a level playing field so that preference could not be given to one sector at the cost to another and so that there could be a growth of domestic demand through reform. This was necessary to reduce the risks of reform, which in removing subsidies created by the planned economy, both implicit and explicit, might reveal that foreign trade was not profitable. What this meant was that there were greater demands for reform, and hence for constraints on political authorities, in Poland and Hungary (high levels of debt, high levels of trade and diverse trade), Czechoslovakia (high level of trade diversity), lower demands for change in Bulgaria and Romania (both of which had lower debt levels and less diversified trade with the West) and very low levels of demand for change in the USSR, which had low debt and a trade structure dominated by hydrocarbons and raw materials (Robinson, 2004: 111–12, 117–18).

The new contours of the European divide

Demands for change in the USSR were thus not as socially grounded as such demands were in Eastern Europe, and did not connect in the same way with elite interests. Natural states were thus able to endure in the states that succeeded the USSR since that they did not have the same constituencies within them demanding reform as the countries that were to become the accession states. Reform involved reorganising the state in order that it could support marketisation and commercial economic activity, which were necessary both to create open access orders and to have the creation of such orders supported by the EU. Reform was thus a form of state building, albeit one that was not a wholly national affair given that it involved support from international agencies, such as international financial institutions (IFIs), as well as foreign governments and the EU. State building-cum-reform in post-Communist states was a necessary condition for consolidating democracy since it helped to cement in place such features of democracy as the rule of law and economic societies.[4] It was not necessary to engage in state building, however, where there was no demand for it and where state building could be deferred in favour of regime consolidation. Constellations of elites ended state building (if they ever begin it) at the level of a natural state if they could achieve a stable political regime as a result. The presence of constituencies for reform in Eastern Europe meant that elites could not compromise on state building.

This was not the case further east. Instead of being forced to secure state development as a means of securing reform political leaders in the former Soviet Union, and to a large degree in the East European states that were laggards initially in reform, focused on regime consolidation. They did this because they were faced with the 'politician's dilemma': to reform/state building would bring uncertain benefits while incurring the opposition of vested interests (Geddes, 1994). Political leaders therefore paid lip service to reform for the most part (as was largely the case in Ukraine, Moldova Azerbaijan, Armenia and Kazakhstan), did not reform at all (as was largely the case in Belarus, Turkmenistan and Uzbekistan), or embarked upon reform but were rapidly diverted from reform (as was largely the case in Russia, Georgia and Kyrgyzstan). With hindsight, the decision to reform at all can be described as a sign of weakness in the face of powerful elites, rather than as an effort that had a serious chance of resolving both the regime and state question in favour of creating an open access order. Russia illustrates the problem perfectly. Yeltsin's choice to go with reform seemed to fit the times – the end of Communism, the end of history and all that – but it was also a sign of his weakness: Yeltsin had little authority and power to bargain with for support. Launching reform altered the balance of power and gave Yeltsin something to bargain with: the content of reform itself, which could be traded away. Yeltsin duly traded reform away for support, compromising reform to stabilise his relations with economic elites (brought into government) and regional elites (allowed to run their own economic policies and develop their own interests). The result was the recreation of a form of natural state, one in which elites competed for resources under the eye of the Russian President, and in which access to resources was through the state and the political system (Robinson, 2002). The only places in the USSR that managed to break this pattern fully were the Baltic states, where nationalism overrode other considerations and generated high levels of popular mobilisation for change, and change was facilitated by geographic proximity to Scandinavia.[5]

Differing levels of demand and support for change meant that the European divide created post-1945 could not be fully overcome. The dividing line between the open access orders of Western Europe and the limited access orders in the East just shifted eastward a little bit. The persistence of the divide is illustrated in Figure 9.1, based on World Bank (2010) Governance Indicator scores. These Governance Indicators are measured on a scale from −2.5 to 2.5 and individually measure Voice and Accountability, Political Stability and Absence of Violence, Government Effectiveness, Rule of Law, Control of Corruption, and Regulatory Quality. Together these Indicators measure both a range of constraints on elites (accountability, law, regulation, corruption control, limits to violence) and – sometimes at the same time – outputs of constraints on elites, such as government effectiveness and limits to corruption. They are therefore good proxy measures of the existence of limited and open access orders. In Figure 9.1 these measures have been combined into a single governance score: the higher the positive score the closer a state is to being an open access order, the lower the negative score of a state is the more it is a limited access order and the more basic its natural state.

Figure 9.1 shows the aggregated scores, first, of the 'Old EU' states – that is, the states of the EU that were members pre-2004 and have a democratic heritage dating back to the 1970s at least (Austria, Belgium, Denmark, Finland, France, Germany, Greece, Ireland, Italy, Luxembourg, Netherlands, Portugal, Spain, Sweden and UK). These are the states that were open access post-1945 and on one side of the European divide. The scores of the states that were limited access orders post-1945 and on the other side of the divide are recorded in four ways. First, there are scores for the 'Post-Communist Accession States', which joined the EU in 2004

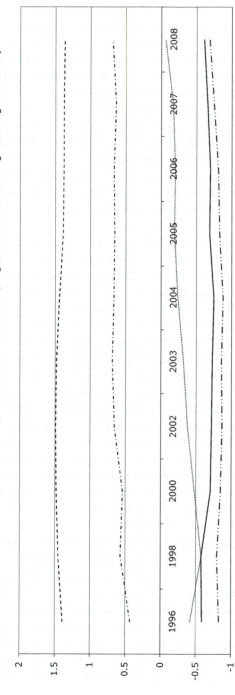

Figure 9.1 Governance Indicators, 1996–2008 (overall scale 2.5 to –2.5, higher scores indicating better governance)

--- Old EU   ---- Post-Communist Accession States   ······ The Southern Tier   —— The Eastern Marches   ---- Post-Soviet Space

Notes:
Indicators are calculated from measures for Voice and Accountability, Political Stability and Absence of Violence, Government Effectiveness, Rule of Law, Control of Corruption, and Regulatory Quality; data biennial 1998-2002, thereafter yearly. Old EU: Austria, Belgium, Denmark, Finland, France, Germany, Greece, Ireland, Italy, Luxembourg, Netherlands, Portugal, Spain, Sweden, UK. Post-Communist accession states: Bulgaria, Czech Republic, Estonia, Hungary, Latvia, Lithuania, Poland, Romania, Slovakia, Slovenia. The Southern Tier: Albania, Bosnia-Herzegovina, Croatia, Macedonia, Montenegro, Serbia, The Eastern Marches: Belarus, Moldova, Russia, Ukraine. Post-Soviet Space: Eastern Marches plus Armenia, Azerbaijan, Georgia, Kazakhstan, Kyrgyzstan, Tajikistan, Turkmenistan, Uzbekistan.
Source: World Bank Governance Indictors, http://info.worldbank.org/governance/wgi/index.asp (accessed 18 August 2010).

(Czech Republic, Estonia, Hungary, Latvia, Lithuania, Poland, Slovakia and Slovenia) and 2007 (Bulgaria, Romania). Second, there are scores for what we can call 'The Southern Tier'; these states – Albania, Bosnia-Herzegovina, Croatia, Macedonia, Montenegro, Serbia, and Turkey – form the southern border of the EU and are distinct in that they were either a part of Yugoslavia or were capitalist limited access orders in the past rather than state socialist (Turkey). Finally, scores for the Soviet successor states are recorded in two ways: there is a score for the whole 'Post-Soviet Space' – that is, for all of the successor states except for Latvia, Lithuania and Estonia (Armenia, Azerbaijan, Belarus, Georgia, Kazakhstan, Kyrgyzstan, Moldova, Russia, Tajikistan, Turkmenistan, Ukraine and Uzbekistan), and just for the 'Eastern Marches' – Belarus, Moldova, Russia and Ukraine – that is, for the successor states that border the EU and that are (at least in part) part of continental Europe.

The aggregated scores show the shifting of the European divide over the last two decades as the accession states have become open access orders: the 'Old EU' and the accession states score positively – that is, they have social orders that constrain elites and provide their citizens with the means to influence political life and gain access to state resources. As one might expect, there is still a difference between the levels of open access that the states in these two categories can achieve given the embeddedness of democracy in the 'Old EU' and the fact that the score for the post-Communist accession states is lowered somewhat by the poorer scores achieved by the later entrants, Bulgaria and Romania, on indicators to do with government effectiveness, corruption and regulatory quality. The aggregate score for the accession states has improved over time and since the scores were first taken in 1996, moving from 0.43 to 0.69. This improvement is significant, albeit not wildly dramatic. The significance of the move, but also that it has been relatively modest and not reached the 'Old EU' heights, shows a deepening of the open access orders created since 1989 in Eastern Europe but also that the basis of these orders lay very much in the forces and interests that the collapse of Communism released. Accession, the Copenhagen criteria for EU membership of 1993, the negotiation process and the adoption of the *acquis communautaire* – the conditions and conditionality of EU membership – did not create open access orders but interacted with what was already there with variable effects (Hughes *et al.*, 2004).[6]

At the other end of the spectrum the states of the 'Post-Soviet Space' clearly still lack the constraints on elites and citizen rights that create an open access order. Office-holding is proprietorial due to corruption, accountability and democratic rights are weak and the rule of law is still shallow. There are large and significant gaps between both the overall score of the region and the score for the 'Eastern Marches' and those of the 'Post-Communist accession states'; if we were to say that the aggregate score for the 'Post-Communist accession states represents something like a European open access minimum, the minimum necessary for entry to the EU, then both the whole set of successor states and the smaller set of successor states that border Europe are some way away from it. This represents the new European divide. Two further things are worth noting from Figure 9.1. First, that the states of the 'Eastern Marches' were doing a little better than the successor state average in the 1990s, but since the 2000s have reverted toward the post-Soviet mean. In other words, the divide between the open access orders of the enlarged EU and its neighbours widened and hardened in the 2000s. Gains for democracy/pro-European forces in Ukraine and Moldova, along with better scores for Georgia after the 'Rose' revolution, shifted both the 'Eastern March' and 'Post-Soviet space' scores back toward where they had been in the 1990s by 2008, but these gains have by and large been eroded politically since 2008. Second, although the gap between the 'Eastern Marches'/'Post-Soviet space' and the European open access minimum of the accession states has remained large, the gap between them and the 'Southern Tier' states of Turkey and the former Yugoslavia has narrowed considerably. This movement, from the 'Southern Tier's' low in 1998, is the largest shift of all, larger than that of the accession states between 1996 and 2008 (0.52 compared to 0.26). The 'Eastern Marches'/'Post-Soviet space' are thus falling behind other areas that have a claim on the EU's attention and that are prospective members. The divide that exists already might thus be extended and deepened as the 'Southern Tier' progresses and prospectively further marginalises the 'Eastern Marches' as it approaches possible EU membership.

Will the divide endure?

The divide in Europe that was hardened and made geographic by the post-1945 settlement has thus endured beyond the collapse of that settlement. The divide is an obvious source of tension as the natural states and the open access orders clash across an array of areas: trade openness, corruption and cross-border crime, human rights and electoral abuses, ability to implement international norms and treaty obligations, and foreign policy priorities. These tensions worsened as the natural state order hardened after 2004 in Russia under Vladimir Putin and began to contest the 'softening' of such orders elsewhere, most notably in Ukraine after the 'Orange' revolution, and Georgia after the Rose revolution (Ambrosio, 2009). The stabilisation of the natural state in Russia, albeit often under the guise of reform, was married with a more belligerent rhetoric from the Kremlin that gave voice to the bitterness that many Russians felt after the lost decade of the 1990s. This – on top of the second Chechen war of 1999 and subsequent destabilisation of the north Caucasus, the continued blatant flouting of democracy in Belarus, and increased fears about energy security caused by the lack of resolution of Middle Eastern political problems and high prices – highlighted the fact that the European project of integration of the 1990s had reached its limits. This has not, however, led to a rethink of how to deal with the remaining natural states of the East. Instead the EU has by and large managed its relations with the Eastern Marches using frameworks based on the accession process. Other processes that became associated with accession in the 1990s, such as the management of hard security relations across the continent through NATO structures, have also continued. The tensions that this causes are most often explained as a revival of the Cold War caused by Russian belligerence (Sakwa, 2008), rather than as a result of the application of models of relations that are inappropriate. Recognising this on Europe's part would mean limiting its ambitions, abandoning some of its grander claims, and negotiating its relationship with Russia to share approaches to the other Eastern March countries (Averre, 2009). There is not space here to deal with these issues in depth for each of the countries of the Eastern Marches. What we can do, however, is note, first, that there is a tension between the EU approach to these matters and Russia's and, second, that there is a wavering over which approach to go along within the region.

The EU's approach has progressed through Partnership and Cooperation Agreements (PCAs) in the 1990s and early 2000s to the development of the European Neighbourhood Policy (ENP) since 2007. The latter treats the Eastern Marches countries (except Russia and Belarus[7]) and the former Soviet states in the Caucasus (Georgia, Armenia and Azerbaijan) as a group, the 'Eastern group'. The aim of ENP remains the same as for previous EU initiatives. Like the PCAs before it ENP is to encourage the creation of open access orders in the area in the belief that so doing will be in the interests of the EU since this will export democratic stability and economic prosperity. Documents about the 'Eastern Partnership' are full of statements about the partnership's intention to 'promote democracy and good governance', create 'gradual engagement with the EU economy', and 'convergence towards the EU' (see, for example, Council of the European Union, 2010). Russia creates what Schimmelfennig and Sedelmeier (2004: 666) call 'cross-conditionality' for the other Eastern

Marches countries: while there might be rewards for following the EU path and moving toward the norms associated with open access orders through ENP, there are counter-pressures from Russia to maintain their regimes and political stability. The contradiction between promoting 'democracy and good governance' and regime and political stability is, of course, the same choice that has been before the countries of the region for the last twenty years. The obvious question to ask, then, is will they be able to make a choice in favour of 'democracy and good governance' when they have not in the past? Or in other words, will the divide that we have described endure? The answer to this is 'yes, but'. The 'yes' part of the answer is easy to comprehend. The divide will prove durable because it has been in place for twenty years since the end of Communism and overcoming it will take a considerable amount of time even if the effort to break it down began unambiguously and immediately (from the time of writing at the end of 2010) and were to progress without any major hiccups.

The 'but' part of the answer to the question is more complicated. The divide between natural states in the Eastern Marches and the open access orders is not a stable one because the Eastern Marches states have different capacities to continue to compromise on state building in favour of regime – natural state – stability. There is thus a constant tension within most of them between regime and state building. This makes for a schizophrenic attitude toward the West of the continent, one that is often expressed in frustration and anger by some politicians in the East (most noticeably by Vladimir Putin).[8] The capacity to resist greater state building in favour of regime stability and the natural state differs across the area both spatially and temporally. The pressure to state build has, as the Governance Indicators in Figure 9.1 imply, been weak overall but is still there due to financial weakness, security issues, external pressures and some domestic demand. The result is that reform is never off the political agendas in the Eastern Marches, but is never able to capture it either.

This creates high levels of political ambiguity and uncertainty, even in Belarus: its supposed closeness to Russia and antipathy to Europe has been marred by spats with Russia over the costs to Russia of sustaining Belarus' unreformed economy, energy prices and the crudity of Belarusian dictatorship. In Russia we can see this in the ambiguity of the Putin and Dmitry Medvedev Presidencies. Putin's aim was to develop state power for economic reform ends and this led him to take actions that many in the West had viewed as necessary correctives to the chaos of the Yeltsin era. It was necessary to rein in regional leaders, for example, to end the fragmentation of Russia as a legal space. This was necessary to ensure the rule of law, which is, of course, a fundamental requirement of open access and of the economic growth and common citizenship rights that such orders strive for. However, reining in regional elites strengthened Putin's personal power as much as it reformed state administration; we can record similar ambiguities in other areas too (see the case studies in Colton and Holmes, 2006). Under Medvedev 'modernisation' has become the key term defining both domestic politics and relations with Europe (a 'Partnership for Modernisation' between Russia and the EU was announced in June 2010). Again, however, the practical results of this call to reform are not clear and the prospects of reform are surrounded by uncertainty: is this call supported by now Prime Minister Putin, and will it last beyond his possible re-election as President in 2012? What are the actual policies that support modernisation beyond more anti-corruption campaigns? Can Russia pay for modernisation while dealing with the economic decline caused by international financial crisis? What is more important, modernisation or military expenditure, which is also set to rise over the next few years? Can Russia afford both?

In Ukraine and Moldova similar issues over reform arise. In both cases the interests of elites and the cause of reform clash and lead to uncertainty over the pursuit of state building that will lead to further engagement with Europe. In Moldova, efforts at moving closer to Europe have been balanced by both Russian interests and the interests of domestic elites in maintaining relations with Russia for economic advantage (Korosteleva, 2010). This has led to a seesawing in relations with Europe and problems for all political parties as they try to stabilise their rule. In Ukraine a similar seesawing took place, albeit over a longer period. The 'Orange' revolution created hopes for closer relations with Europe, in part because the EU tried to play a role in resolving the electoral crisis that provoked the revolt (Kubicek, 2005). The revolution obviously foundered since it could not construct a stable coalition of pro-reform forces from among Ukraine's elites, and the loser in the revolution of 2004–5, Viktor Yanukovych, was elected President in 2010. This does not mean that the uncertainty is over, however, since Yanukovych has had to deal with the ongoing economic crisis in Ukraine and take on further loans from the IMF to stabilise its fiscal position. This means a balancing act between regime, elites and people as conditions attached to loans have to be balanced against pressure from elites and the populace to continue resource flows to them, or to reform in such a way as to spread the cost of conditionality and impose some of it on elites. Some assistance from Russia – such as renewed lower gas prices that followed Yanukovych's election and a loan that filled some of the fiscal gap while negotiations with the IMF were going on – ameliorates the pressure to choose between these options, but does not remove them entirely. As a result, uncertainty over reform continues, with both pressure from elite interests to protect their sources of wealth and popular protest over the perceived injustice of reform measures such as reform of the tax codes.

Conclusion

Uncertainty about the future in the East of Europe means uncertainty about the future of the West of Europe, too. That natural states have endured in the East shows the ambiguity of the EU's power. Its model could only travel to countries that wanted it for their own reasons; it cannot by force of its economic weight pull other countries to that model simply and easily. At best these other countries have an ambivalent and shifting relationship to Europe. This has damaged the very idea of EU power as a force for regional assimilation – it is incomplete – and has done so at a time when that power was damaged anyway by the crisis of the eurozone that has followed in the wake of the wider international financial crisis. Questions therefore arise about the future of the EU as well as about the Eastern Marches because of the gap between them. How the EU deals with the Eastern Marches will likely have an effect on how it develops. Putting aside EU ambitions to transfer democracy and good governance to its neighbours runs the risk that calling for common standards within the Union becomes less legitimate since it shows that the universality of 'European' open access norms is in fact a particularistic phenomenon of the West. Insisting on building relations solely on the basis of the norms of open access means antagonism between the EU and East, particularly Russia, and this antagonism can be used by leaders in the Eastern Marches (and also in the Caucasus and Central Asia) to play off Russia and the EU, and moderate reform by seeking advantage from both. This, of course, adds to the longevity of the area's natural states so that history continues to repeat itself – again.

Notes

1 Or for a quicker introduction see North *et al.* (2009b).
2 The exception might be where they are imposed, as they were in post-Second World War Europe in West Germany and Italy.
3 For example, in the USSR '[as] of 1985, courts ... remained weak, dependent bodies that lacked public respect, and the career of judge had low status and

few rewards. Jurisdiction in matters of political import was limited. Judges were subject to multiple lines of dependency, including to local party leaders' (Solomon, 2008: 272).

4 On these and other features of democracy see Linz and Stepan (1996: 7–15).

5 For an analysis of the impact of factors such as nationalism on reformism in the former USSR see Darden (2009).

6 On the accession processes more generally, see Henderson (1998) and Pridham (2009).

7 Russia insists on being treated differently, Belarus is to a large extent outside of the process because of its unambiguous breaches of democratic conventions.

8 Perhaps most (in)famously in his speech of 10 February 2007 at the 43rd Munich Conference on Security Policy (available at www.isn.ethz.ch/isn/Digital-Library/Primary-Resources/Detail/?ots=69f57a17-24d2-527c-4f3b-b63b07201ca1&lng=en&ots627=fce62fe0-528d-4884-9cdf-283c282cf0b2&id=28802).

References

Ambrosio, T. (2009) *Authoritarian Backlash: Russian Resistance to Democratization in the Former Soviet Union*. Aldershot: Ashgate.

Averre, D. (2009) 'Competing Rationalities: Russia, the EU and the "Shared Neighbourhood"', *Europe-Asia Studies*, Vol. 61 (10), 1689–1714.

Colton, T. and Holmes, S. (eds) (2006) *The State after Communism: Governance in the New Russia*. Lanham, MD: Rowman & Littlefield.

Council of the European Union (2010) 'Conclusions on Eastern Partnership', 3041st Foreign Affairs Council meeting Luxembourg, 25 October 2010, www.consilium.europa.eu/uedocs/cms_Data/docs/pressdata/EN/foraff/117327.pdf (accessed 20 November 2010).

Darden, K.A. (2009) *Economic Liberalism and its Rivals: The Formation of International Institutions among the Post-Soviet States*. Cambridge: Cambridge University Press.

Geddes, B. (1994) *Politician's Dilemma: Building State Capacity in Latin America*. Berkeley, CA: University of California Press.

Heather, P. (2010) *Empires and Barbarians: Migration, Development and the Birth of Europe*. London: Pan.

Henderson, K. (ed.) (1998) *Back to Europe: Central and Eastern Europe and the European Union*. London: Routledge.

Hughes, J., Sasse, G. and Gordon, C. (2004) *Europeanization and Regionalization in the EU's Enlargement to Central and Eastern Europe: The Myth of Conditionality*. Basingstoke: Palgrave Macmillan.

Korosteleva, E. (2010) 'Moldova's European Choice: "Between Two Stools"?', *Europe-Asia Studies*, Vol. 62 (8), 1267–90.

Kubicek, P. (2005) 'The European Union and Democratization in Ukraine', *Communist and Post-Communist Studies*, Vol. 38 (2), 269–92.

Linz, J. and Stepan, A. (1996) *Problems of Democratic Transition and Consolidation: Southern Europe, South America, and Post-communist Europe*. Baltimore, MD: Johns Hopkins University Press.

North, D. C., Wallis, J. J. and Weingast, B. R. (2009a) *Violence and Social Orders: A Conceptual Framework for Interpreting Recorded Human History*. Cambridge: Cambridge University Press.

North, D. C., Wallis, J. J. and Weingast, B. R. (2009b) 'Violence and the Rise of Open-access Orders', *Journal of Democracy*, Vol. 20 (1), 55–68.

Pridham, G. (2009) *Designing Democracy: EU Enlargement and Regime Change in Post-Communist Europe*. Basingstoke: Palgrave Macmillan.

Robinson, N. (2002) *Russa: A State of Uncertainty*. London: Routledge.

Robinson, N. (2004) 'Path Dependency, Global Economy and Post-Communist Change', in Robinson, N. (ed.), *Reforging the Weakest Link: Global Political Economy and Post-Soviet Change in Russia, Ukraine and Belarus*, Aldershot: Ashgate, 106–26.

Sakwa, R. (2008) '"New Cold War" or Twenty Years' Crisis? Russia and International Politics', *International Affairs*, Vol. 84 (2), 241–67.

Schimmelfennig, F. and Sedelmeier, U. (2004) 'Governance by Conditionality: EU Rule Transfer to the Candidate Countries of Central and Eastern Europe', *Journal of European Public Policy*, Vol. 11 (4), 661–79.

Solomon, Jr., P. H. (2008) 'Judicial Power in Authoritarian States: The Case of Russia', in Ginsburg, T. and Moustafa, T. (eds), *Rule by Law: The Politics of Courts in Authoritarian Regimes*. Cambridge: Cambridge University Press, 261–82.

Staniszkis, J. (1992) *The Ontology of Socialism*. Oxford: Clarendon Press.

Urban, M. (1985) 'Conceptualizing Political Power in the USSR: Patterns of Binding and Bonding', *Studies in Comparative Communism*, Vol. 18 (4), 207–26.

Walker, R. (1992) 'Language and the Politics of Identity in the USSR', in Urban, M. (ed.), *Ideology and Systems Change in the USSR and Eastern Europe*. Basingstoke: Macmillan, 3–19.

World Bank (2010) Governance Indicators, http://info.worldbank.org/governance/wgi/index.asp (accessed 18 August 2010).

Conclusions: critical analysis, war of manoeuvre, war of position – neoliberalism and the prospects for a renewed Left politics in the EU

Ray Silvius and Randall Germain

Politics across the EU, marked for decades by relatively consistent patterns of democratic negotiation and compromise, have entered a period of deep turbulence. The politics of debt, austerity and fear occasioned by the 2008–9 financial crisis have challenged long-held assumptions about what citizens can expect from their governments, eroding or turning back many long-settled arrangements around which Europe's prosperity and its unsurpassed quality of life have long been organised. Of course, these assumptions and arrangements have been under stress for the better part of the past two decades, but the financial crisis has crystallised the pressures pushing for change and galvanised those who wish to reset the political landscape. Oddly, in this period of turbulence, while the Left has not been mute, its agenda has been unable to attract popular support beyond its traditional constituencies. Left politics in the EU has become strangely neutered and muzzled under conditions which, in the past, have generated an immense outpouring of energy and ideas about how to achieve a progressive political future.

The chapters in this volume, in different ways, explain why this has occurred. Our task in this concluding chapter is twofold: (1) to draw these explanations together and link them into a workable framework of analysis; and (2) to step back and ask what lessons from Europe's experience might be drawn for a more general understanding of the politics of the global economy. Our argument is that the explanations provided in this volume fall neatly into a conceptual schema that frames our understanding of the possibility of Left politics in terms of a historically sensitive version of critical political economy, albeit one that is sociologically deep without being reductionist in its materialism. Particularly significant here is the articulation of ideas, political parties and social movements (or civil society) as the key set of axes around which the possibility of Left politics is structured. A renewal of Left politics in Europe, on this reading, will gather steam if it returns to a previously abandoned intellectual terrain in order to move forward and engage with newly organised social forces animated by political concerns that are different from those traditionally expressed by the Left in western European societies.

Beyond this, we also believe that the experience of Europe's Left political forces hold important lessons for our understanding of the global political economy. For a considerable period now, scholarship in International Relations (IR) and IPE has enthused about the explanatory significance of ideas – under the banner of constructivism – as an antidote to the rump materialism of mainstream approaches such as realism and historical materialism. Even rationalism and liberalism, to the extent that they focus on the actions of institutions, remain wedded to a fundamentally materialist articulation of interests as the principal determinants of institutional behaviour. As contributors to this volume recognise, institutions are also ideational battlegrounds, and past achievements can continue to resonate even when the material conditions engendered by those achievements have withered and eroded. Similarly, new ideational formulations can wreak havoc with existing material political, economic and social arrangements, just as the demise of Communist regimes after 1989 released a pent-up demand for national expression which in central and eastern Europe has accommodated itself unevenly to the achievements of social democracy as articulated in western Europe. Our understanding of the global political economy can benefit from this recognition, especially where it points us towards an appreciation of emerging challenges to prevailing normative formulations such as neoliberalism. The disarticulation of the Left in Europe thus presents us with an example of how a well-entrenched social framework can unravel, and we can use the lessons from this experience to search for analogues that might presage the erosion of neoliberalism at the global level.

The chapter is organised in three sections. First, we use the arguments presented by the contributors to categorise the possibilities open to Left politics in Europe across the integrated spectrum of ideas, political parties and social movements. This deep sociological classification allows us to consider the dilemmas of the Left across a continuum of forms of action, and suggests that although the renewal of Left politics in the EU will not be easy, it is possible. Such a renewal will in turn demand careful assessment of the prospects of Left politics across the very different social formations prevailing in the EU, with the likelihood that an uneven war of position will develop.[1] Second, we shift our analysis to the global level in order to consider how the analytical lessons from Europe might shed light on developments in the global political economy. Central here is the contested role of neoliberalism as the central ideational or ideological glue of global capitalism. To the extent that neoliberalism is coming under question, we are able to make some clear arguments about the political spaces open to those who seek to temper corporate capitalism in its global search for accumulation. Finally, we stand back and reflect on how the contributions in this volume might be received by scholars working in the tradition of critical political economy. While there is much critique of critical political economy in these pages, there are also the grounds for a fruitful engagement that could strengthen the analytical power of critical political economy as an avenue of understanding within the discipline of IPE. Understanding why the Left in Europe is currently stalled, and what it might do to renew itself holds important lessons for many who do not study EU politics but are intensely interested in what is going on in the world around them.

Constructing analytical frameworks: ideas, political parties and civil society

As the Introduction by Gerard Strange and Owen Worth suggests, the EU emerged within the context of the historical trajectories of a number of national political economies as they became progressively embedded within a broader American-led multilateralism after the Second World War. The story of how this global multilateral order unravelled, together with the way in which the economic and political possibilities associated with Keynesianism have become constricted, occupies the core of this volume. These possibilities include the achievements of full employment, mass political participation, a generally accepted negotiated settlement between labour and capital and a generous welfare system. The contributors follow common practice among critical scholars and identify this breakdown and erosion as associated with the triumph of neoliberalism (as defined succinctly by Bieler in his Chapter 6).

Central to their concerns are the questions of how we are to understand the place of the EU within the rising tide of neoliberalism, and what prospects if any remain open for labour, Left and progressive political forces to resist the expansion of neoliberalism within a post-national Europe. In other words, to what extent can the EU and the wider process of European integration be considered to further consolidate neoliberalism, and how might the EU and Europe serve as a venue in which progressive forces can combat and challenge the norms and practices associated with neoliberalism? Does the advent of neoliberalism and its corresponding accumulation strategies represent the passing of the social democratic moment, which for decades was tied to the growth in European productivity and the associated compromises struck between labour and capital, and mass enfranchisement and political representation?

The generalised answer to these questions is essentially that the neoliberal turn is neither inevitable nor irreversible, and that Left strategies are not without prospects. Different contributors highlight different dimensions of such prospects, and we categorise them in terms of the dimensions of ideas, political parties and social movements. That is to say, the Left in Europe needs to address three kinds of challenges in order to generate the kind of 'opportunity structures' that will enable its political project once again to resonate more widely than at present. The first challenge is to revitalise its ideational core, namely the set of ideas and beliefs that in the post-war period served to attract support beyond the organised base of the working class.

Here there are two areas in which the contributors largely agree. The first area concerns the appropriate set of political institutions in which the Left should invest its aspirations for achieving progressive political advances. 'Progressive' in this sense implies a political order in which citizens have a rough equality of participation and representation in their political institutions, and where these institutions can facilitate actions that promote the ability to fashion a work/life balance that sustains both individual and societal growth. Historically this political order has been national in scope, but in the early years of the twenty-first century this scope has been widened to encompass the institutions of the EU. It is EU institutions that increasingly demand the Left's attention as the pre-eminent locus of political order. What the EU offers to the Left is a new and substantive terrain where claims on behalf of social citizenship and political representation can be pursued.

But as different contributors to this volume also make clear, the EU is not always a receptive terrain to these claims. For one thing, as Neil Robinson suggests in Chapter 9 the nature and depth of a specifically *European* sense of identity is truncated and in many ways stalled. There is a significant divide between 'old' EU states and those of what he calls the 'Eastern Marches', and their very different forms of institutional ordering mean that a genuine and integrated political terrain remains undeveloped. For Robinson, this suggests that appeals to Europe rather than to nation-states fall into an ambiguous and sometimes contradictory void. Furthermore, the *discursive* construction of a European economic space is far from a completed project, as Ben Rosamond's Chapter 2 demonstrates.

Yet, as Lawrence Wilde suggests in his Chapter 8, the absence of a strong European identity is not to be lamented, as this would be representative of a slide into the type of strong identity politics that represents parochialism on a new scale, a mentality that impedes the development of a robust cosmopolitanism. If the EU is to serve a progressive function, for Wilde, it must reject the types of exclusive claims inherent in national–territorial states and instead accommodate emerging multiple publics and a cosmopolitan consciousness.

Another way of making this point is provided by Michael Holmes and Simon Lightfoot in Chapter 4, who suggest that European political parties on the Left have yet to embrace fully their own Europeanisation, although they have made substantial progress over the past two decades. The main parties of the Left in Europe can see where they need to go, on this reading, but have not yet arrived there.

But as Wilde in Chapter 8 maintains, just because the EU remains deeply nation-state-centric (and in a liberal–constitutional mode) does not also mean that it provides no institutional support for a progressive politics. Gerard Strange in his Chapter 3 suggests that the euro and its associated institutions remain open to deep political contestation, and therefore also to Left political programmes, even if these institutions are themselves also conservative in parts of their orientation. And Owen Worth in his Chapter 7 on the Third Way argues that one of the enduring strengths of this otherwise maligned 'progressive' development is its clear-sighted focus on the transnational component of effective political action. If Europe is indeed a collection of (liberal) nation-states, the institutions of the EU at least offer a way to inflect Europe's nation-states back towards a progressive path. As with Andreas Bieler in Chapter 6, Worth is convinced that this extra-national focus provides the road to successfully reassert the political values long associated with the Left.

But where do these values come from? This is the second dimension of revitalising the ideational core of beliefs operative on the left that the contributors of this book for the most part embrace. Worth in Chapter 7 offers one articulation of this when he argues that an updated version of Stuart Hall's 'Marxism without Guarantees' is the answer, but this is not the only position. As both Robinson in Chapter 9 and Holmes and Lightfoot in Chapter 4 remind us, the political values in eastern and central Europe run in many ways counter to the open form of social democracy advocated by Hall and many old-style progressive

Left forces. Yet they are also themselves deeply rooted in a political culture that accepts certain aspects of Europeanisation precisely because such a development provides the best defence against an encroaching atavism, complete with its 'small Europe' or 'fortress Europe' mentality. As Magnus Ryner points out in Chapter 1, albeit in relation to western Europe and drawing on the work of Poulantzas, in its deepest connections the globalisation and indeed Americanisation of Europe is unlikely to be fully successful; there remain in the European traditions of political economy a well-spring of resonance for the centrality and even necessity of a strongly grounded form of 'social citizenship'. These are present in a series of distinctly European institutions (both at the EU and nation-state level) that draw on a set of social formations that, although they have bent under significant neoliberal pressure, have yet to collapse. Like Bieler in his Chapter 6, Ryner notes that the history and traditions of Left politics in Europe have bequeathed a set of institutions and associated political beliefs that, while currently quiescent, do retain the capacity to motivate a renewed accommodation between working classes and labour with capital. Together with Rosamond in Chapter 2, who maintains that neoliberalism rests on weak pillars of legitimacy and continues to be challenged by counter-narratives and political projects, these contributors suggest that a renewal of the ideational basis of Left politics is the starting point.

Such a renewal can gain traction because of the existence of a strong set of political parties organised on a pan-European basis, even though not all contributors to this volume view the future of Left, or social democratic parties, as equally robust. They all agree, however, that party organisation presents the second key challenge to the future of left politics. David Bailey in Chapter 5 is perhaps the least sanguine of all here, as he casts doubt on the very ability of social democratic parties to square the circle of working within a capitalist social order and yet trying to reform it by ameliorating the dynamics of accumulation and by moving to redistribute wealth. He contends that a process of 'de-social democratisation' is taking place, whereby European social democratic parties have lessened their redistributive and reformist ambitions since the 1980s, accepting many neoliberal tenets in the process. Set against this pessimistic outlook is the rather more optimistic assessment of Holmes and Lightfoot in Chapter 4, who see Left political parties responding positively to the broader process of Europeanisation. This more optimistic reading of the role in Left politics of political mobilisation through parties is extended by Strange and Worth in their analyses of the euro and Third Way, respectively, in Chapters 3 and 7: while each of these developments has been subject to many pressures, they have been initiated and mediated by political parties in a manner that has reinforced at least some of the attractions of social democracy.

The point for our consideration here is that there is a wide range of institutions through which Left politics can be organised and pursued, and political parties are a key element of this precisely because they have traction at the EU level. It may be, as Bieler in Chapter 6 and Ryner in Chapter 1 suggest, that there are some very problematic tensions inherent in national social democratic parties as they compete for and engage with governmental power, yet as there are no EU-wide governing coalitions this particular problem is less acute at the EU level. This allows Left parties to advance broader conceptions of social democracy and welfare – social citizenship, in short – without the attendant complications of wielding power. More to the point, they are freer to pursue a war of position at the EU level.

To argue that the existence of EU-wide political party organisations enables the Left to pursue a war of position is to recognise, as the contributors to this volume imply but do not explicitly articulate, that the immediate future of the Left is to be forged outside government in Europe and at the grassroots level of society or, in other words, in the relations of civil society. This is the third challenge facing Left politics in Europe today. In his discussion in the *Prison Notebooks* of political strategies during the interwar period, Antonio Gramsci considered a war of position as inevitable given the relation of forces across western Europe: in some countries the bourgeois class was firmly ensconced in power, while in others a kind of deadlock – a passive revolution – had been achieved between classes in which authoritarian leaders had commandeered the institutions of government and had violently suppressed dissent (Gramsci, 1971: 108–10, 229–39). A war of manoeuvre, a frontal assault on the levers of political power by political parties, sometimes occurred in both the legislatures and on the streets, as Gramsci noted. More appropriate, however, was the slow and determined construction of political sympathy towards the values and interests represented by subaltern classes and their parties. This strategy, a war of position, conducted within the relations of civil society, was primarily about building a leading political position from the ground up, to bring into being the infrastructure and support structure that would ultimately be conducive to a bid for hegemony on the part of the working class. Political parties were and must be a critical component of this strategy, and their existence at the EU level today is a tremendous asset for left politics in Europe.

At the same time, Gramsci recognised that political parties can become detached from the social movements that spawn them, and turn into bureaucratic shells whose only purpose is to act as vehicles for the careers or clashes of elites. As many contributors to this volume point out, in Europe Left political parties and many of the Left's key civil society institutions such as unions, have come under withering pressure over the past decades from liberalising forces. Bailey, for example, in Chapter 5 rejects the possibility of Left political parties even remaining social democratic, while both Bieler and Ryner in Chapters 6 and 1 recognise the dynamic constraints that social democracy faces today when up against the forces of capitalist accumulation. Nevertheless, as indicated above, others see more room for manoeuvre and negotiation, or as styled here they see a stronger likelihood that a war of position can be entertained. The core base of support for Left politics in the states of the 'old' EU has not disappeared; what is needed is a kind of outreach by the Left to engage with the political concerns of subaltern classes in newer states, even though the political cultures in these states face their own historically unique demands. The point that Strange, Worth, Wilde and Robinson make in different ways in Chapters 3, 7, 8 and 9 is precisely that such a reservoir of receptivity exists, although it has to be engaged with through a European (and therefore EU) level because this is where the institutional infrastructure resides, even if it is sensitive to and adapted by existing national formulations. This of course is in keeping with Gramsci's observation that hegemony is always knotted together at the national level, even if the complete achievement of hegemony is also to a certain extent an international phenomenon (Gramsci 1971: 240–1).

Taken together, the framework for understanding Left politics in Europe suggested by the contributors to this volume directs our attention to three critical and connected axes of activity: the possibility of renewing progressive Left ideas, in particular at the European level but yet in a manner that is sensitive to national demands especially in the states of eastern and central Europe; the strength of the existing EU-wide organisation of political parties, especially as they are responding to the pressures of Europeanisation; and the reservoir of receptivity to Left political ideas and values among social movements and in the organs of civil society. Each of these elements, while in some respects weakened as a result of the advance of neoliberalism over the past several decades, retains a deep attachment to the values and ideas that have animated left politics in Europe for decades. They have not collapsed completely, nor are they about to do so. Yet it will be a fraught and contingent process to reassert and rebuild a progressive political project that responds as much to the concerns of the new EU as to those of the 'old' EU, and of course ultimately there is no guarantee of success. Perhaps a modified version of Stuart Hall's call to arms is applicable here: 'Left politics without Guarantees'.

Frameworks and their lessons: from Europe to the global order

While not all contributors to this volume agree on the precise parameters to Left politics in Europe, they are united in contextualising whatever goes on in European politics within the changing global order. Are there lessons from this analysis for how we might consider the on-going transformations in the global political economy? We believe there are lessons, and we wish to focus our attention on what for many will be a counter-intuitive and unheralded lesson, namely the possibility of neoliberalism itself unravelling. This is a counter-intuitive lesson because all of the contributors to this volume are primarily concerned with understanding how and why the social democratic gains in Europe since 1945 have come under threat. Neoliberalism for each author is the primary culprit, although the precise nature of how this culprit operates varies with each author. Here we turn the framework elaborated in the previous section on its head and consider where it suggests we should look to see weaknesses in the current moment of neoliberalism at the global level.

Here we shall consider the relationship between the EU, European political parties and European social forces and the global political economy, and the prospects for European actors to serve as a progressive force in combating global neoliberalism. Those authors that defend the prospects for a progressive Europe envision different manners by which Europe may facilitate the resistance to neoliberalism and the attainment of desirable social objectives. Defenders of the prospects of social democracy in the EU advance numerous arguments: Europe represents an opportunity to insulate weaker states and actors from the ravages of the competitiveness inherent in neoliberal globalisation and serve as a form of structural (monetary) power to challenge American-led neoliberalism (Strange, Chapter 3); the EU remains the appropriate scale for various progressive political engagements and a unified vision of socially progressive ends (Worth, Chapter 7); and the EU can build on its commitments to social welfare and develop a European social alternative to American-led neoliberalism (Wilde, Chapter 8).

To what extent do 'external' factors within the global political economy – the role of American capital and monetary power, broad trends of neoliberalism and the development of supranational structures – structure the EU? There are several grounds for pessimism. Ryner's suggestion in Chapter 1 is that European social democracy is imperilled due to Europe's emerging neoliberal regime of accumulation and the corresponding superstructure that it may legitimately support. Whereas European social democracy had benefited under post –Second World War Fordist conditions and a climate of national regulation, the collapse of Bretton Woods ushered in finance capital-centered, post-Fordist, flexible organisation arrangements inimical to the surplus value growth and redistribution needed to sustain labour's compromise with capital.

Does the consolidation of the neoliberal project within the EU constrain the conduct of contemporary progressive political actors to the extent that social democracy is impossible in Europe? As we shall demonstrate in the subsequent section on 'new constitutionalism', it is not clear that a neoliberal victory in Europe is foreordained. Rosamond suggests in Chapter 2, for example, that in spite of the fact that much effort and energy has been expended to naturalise neoliberal governance and political rationalities at the level of Europe, this has not effectively occurred. It may be that though disciplinary neoliberalism has made substantial gains in Europe in recent decades, new opportunities at the European level exist for progressive forces. Bieler in Chapter 6 argues that while unions have been disempowered through the rule-based power of neoliberal new constitutionalism – for example, ECB autonomy, low inflation dictates and macroeconomic decision making being made by the European Council – the EU level remains the appropriate level to coordinate labour strategy and resistance. Labour can contribute to the re-establishment of a European social model of capitalism to tame the excesses of neoliberalism.

The broad framework of ideas/political parties/social movements/civil society, when used to consider the strength of neoliberalism, suggests to us that it may not be quite as solidly entrenched as many scholars and analysts presume. For starters, the ideological attraction of neoliberalism has been challenged as a consequence of the 2008–9 financial crisis. Not only did this crisis seemingly start in the neoliberal heartland of global capitalism – the US and its financial markets – but the response to this crisis has almost everywhere brought a sharp focus on to the extent of state oversight of financial market activity. In response to the crisis, and in its aftermath, states have become more interventionist in their economies: capital ratios are rising; barriers to capital mobility are increasing; and regulatory restrictions are multiplying. When coupled with the continuing strength of state capitalism in China,

India, Russia, Brazil and many other emerging market economies, some are now suggesting that the high point of neoliberalism has been reached (Germain, 2010). As a default ethos across the global political economy, liberalisation is under pressure as national and regional barriers to capital mobility strengthen.

Some on the global periphery have perceived neoliberalism as a material and ideational phenomenon brought about by a combination of coercion and consent from an American state aspiring to hegemony. For example, pressure for liberalisation in post-Soviet Russia came from the American state and IMF, who worked in tandem with domestic reformers to transform the Russian national political economy from statist–redistributionist to an open market economy. While one may have to look hard to find the redistributive commitments Vladimir Putin and a dominant but embattled United Russia Party, the statist element remains powerful in the contemporary period. In fact, the post-Yeltsin period has been coloured by Russian state efforts to shift the discursive and ideational terrain away from Western hegemonic neoliberal intervention and democracy support to something more accommodating of 'sovereign' states that are free to develop national development models with a corresponding political architecture (Silvius, 2012). Neoliberalism is anything but a benign force to such Hobbesian contender states who have not yet fully integrated into a pacified 'Lockean heartland' of capitalist and pluralist political orders (van der Pijl, 1998) and its dominance as global common sense is being challenged with new ethical–ideational models for global political life.

This ideational challenge to neoliberalism is reinforced if we consider the rise of populist and on occasion Left political parties around the world. In Europe, populist and sometimes overtly nationalist political parties are making significant electoral gains, often at the expense of mainstream parties that have long-established accommodations with corporate capitalism. Across Scandinavia, for example, anti-immigrant and nationalist political parties have made spectacular electoral breakthroughs over the past several years that threaten to raise any number of barriers to the movement of capital, goods and especially people across borders.[2] But it is not just Right-leaning parties that are making electoral inroads. In Brazil and Canada, for example, 2010 and 2011 saw Left-leaning parties – nominally social democratic in orientation – consolidate themselves or make significant electoral breakthroughs. Dilma Rousseff led the Brazilian Worker's Party to re-election in 2010, while Canada's Left-leaning New Democratic Party won a major breakthrough in that country's 2011 federal election. And while all of these political parties are subject to many of the same constraints identified by Bailey and Ryner in Chapters 5 and 1 in this volume, their continued resistance to the most excessive aspects of neoliberalism surely indicates that Left politics has not yet been routed.

Some of course may question the depth of these indicators of neoliberal erosion. One of the strongest of such challenges appears to be the way in which the on-going eurozone debt crisis is being addressed. Greece, Ireland and Portugal have all turned to the EU for assistance in meeting debt payments that have ballooned since the financial crisis of 2008–9. In exchange for access to fresh EU/IMF funds, they have agreed to austerity measures that involve privatisation, fiscal retrenchment, taxation reform and public sector restructuring, much of which is set to proceed in the direction of further liberalisation. A similar package of liberalising reforms is arguably underway in the UK. However, the interesting development here is the response of citizens to these developments. Despite the prevailing consensus that austerity is the only option, popular unrest and organised demonstrations in Greece and Portugal have suggested that there is considerable support to resist such measures. If we also consider the extent of popular antipathy in countries like France to efforts to restructure social security payments such as pensions, or the 'No' vote in Iceland's referendum to sanction the IMF 'rescue' of its banking system, then we can see how resentment against liberalisation and popular resistance to a neoliberal version of capitalism has not lost its resonance with wider populations. We may say that across a wide cross-section of nation-states there is a deeply embedded antipathy to extreme liberalisation efforts, and this places a formidable constraint on the ability of neoliberalism to maintain its grip as the primary ethos of global order. Civil society both nationally and globally has refused to sanction neoliberalism as an organic element of its anatomy.

One important lesson from this volume in relation to thinking about the power of neoliberalism at the global level, therefore, is that neoliberalism's 'power' is a far cry from being complete, or what in the literature is often identified as hegemonic. Whether in terms of ideas, the operation of political parties, or even the broader formulation of the organs of civil society, neoliberalism falls short of exercising leadership in the manner that Gramsci often associated with 'hegemony'. It was perhaps closest to doing this at the height of the Bretton Woods period after the Second World War, and maybe again in the mid to late 1990s, but today there are too many weak areas in the overall structure of global order to confirm its hegemonic status. Just as with the erosion of social democracy in Europe over the 1990s, neoliberalism has eroded from within, and has been challenged in terms of its ideational supremacy, its political form of organisation and the depth of its penetration into the organs of civil society. While there are nation-states and societies in which neoliberalism as an ethos remains powerful – the US and UK stand out here – in many if not a majority of the societies around the world this is not the case. As with Europe, we must pay close attention to individual national social formations if we want to be able to assess the strength of a regional or global phenomenon.

'New constitutionalism' and resistance: refocusing the debate

One of the strengths of this volume is that it brings together specialists in critical IPE (such as Bieler, Ryner, Strange and Worth), European politics (Bailey, Rosamond, Robinson and Holmes and Lightfoot) and social theory (Wilde) to consider the many angles of Left politics in Europe. Not all of these authors take their point of departure to be broader debates in critical IPE, but they have all made a contribution to this debate by focusing on the possibilities open to Left politics in Europe. We want to use this last section to reflect on how these considerations can push forward the agenda of critical IPE. For us, the chief consideration here lies in thinking about the relationship between the variant of critical IPE known as 'new constitutionalism' and the broad organisation of resistance that critical IPE seeks to apprehend (and foster). In particular, we ask here whether and how the strictures of 'new constitutionalism' need to be relaxed or adapted.

'New constitutionalism' is the term coined by Stephen Gill (1998) to denote the key features of the neoliberal order, or what he has also called 'disciplinary neoliberalism' or market civilisation (Gill, 1995). The enduring analytical strength of this framework is that it focuses attention on the complex relationship between political forces and institutional developments. 'New constitutionalism' directs our attention to how the political forces that have embraced liberalisation have been able to structure key political institutions so that they are effectively insulated from popular political pressures. Central banks are a principal example, but the trend identified by 'new constitutionalism' is at play within the operation of critically important regulatory institutions such as finance ministries and the many agencies that oversee financial activities. The main insight here for Gill and others who utilise this approach is that neoliberalism has moved from an ideology with clear material anchors to become inflected in the organisation of the institutional infrastructure of national (and global) capitalism. The advent of 'new constitutionalism' strengthens the hold of neoliberalism as the organic glue of global capitalism; understanding how 'new constitutionalism' works advances our understanding of how the capitalist global order functions.

While several of the contributors to this volume work quite comfortably within the broad parameters of 'new constitutionalism', others suggest that its explanatory capacity with respect to appreciating the full spectrum of possibilities open to Left politics is constricted. Our own view, in line with the remarks in the preceding section, is that while 'new constitutionalism' is very helpful in outlining the material and rhetorical support that neoliberal political forces may have to shape institutional configurations for a time, it both underestimates the opposition that neoliberalism generates to its programme, and overestimates its ability to capture completely the very levers of power which 'new constitutional' theorists attribute to the institutions which remain at the heart of its focus. Together, these deficits suggest a fruitful terrain of engagement between scholars who occupy different strands in the multiple traditions that make up critical IPE.

'New constitutionalism' underestimates the opposition that its policies and programmes generate. We earlier argued that one of the consequences of the earlier triumph of neoliberalism in Europe has been the emergence of Far-Right nationalist and anti-immigrant political parties that have gained unanticipated political traction within the political systems of northern Europe. The success of these parties represents what in many respects are atavistic impulses in these societies, but they are impulses that reflect a significant level of popular support. Intriguingly, they are in a certain sense also anti-corporate in their orientation, which means they have a very ambiguous relationship to corporate capital. What this tells us is that neoliberalism, as the political expression of corporate capital, has failed to accommodate itself to an important element of the electoral public, which sees itself as under threat from the advance of global capitalism. To generate overt hostility to open borders among 20 per cent of the voting public across the most globalised part of Europe should be seen as a sign of social weakness, not a by-product of hegemony. And although it may be a while before the Left in Europe recognises this and incorporates it into their political strategies, it is an important social fact in the political assessment of the possibilities for the renewal of Left politics that must be considered. 'New constitutionalists' rarely examine the rise of the Far Right as a sign of neoliberalism's organic weakness, and we argue that the insights generated by the contributors to this volume at least open this possibility up analytically, even if they themselves do not follow this up explicitly.

Equally importantly, we argue that 'new constitutional' scholarship systematically overstates the power of the institutions it focuses on, and tends on the whole to offer a uniform view of how power in these institutions operates. This is clearest in the way that 'new constitutionalists' consider independent central banks such as the ECB. For 'new constitutionalists', the ECB is the archetype of a political institution insulated from popular political pressures, and in its design it clearly is insulated from any sort of popular and democratic pressure. However, what is key here is the way that this institution not only conceives of itself (as independent from political pressure) but reacts to and reflects such political pressure. A good example of this – which reinforces Strange's argument in his Chapter 3 that rules stipulating EMU self-regulation have been successfully challenged by member states, particularly in times of crisis – lies in the manner in which the ECB began to purchase government bonds during the eurozone debt crisis since 2009. This was specifically forbidden in its mandate, but was in fact undertaken precisely to support political efforts by the EU to grapple with the Greek, Irish and Portuguese debt crises. In other words, here we have a quintessentially 'new constitutionalist' institution acting in a manner that compromises its neoliberal ethos. From this we take the insight that neoliberalism is not as robust as its institutional form suggests, which is a further indication that its ideational or ideological core is not as powerful and extensive as 'new constitutionalism' assumes.

Holmes and Lightfoot in Chapter 4 echo the sentiment that neoliberal rule-based power is far from a foregone conclusion in the EU. As Left parties have become increasingly supportive of the EU after profound initial scepticism, the authors conclude that there is now the potential for a progressive European-level response to the growth of Right-wing Euro-scepticism and national populism. Within the EU (and its constituent member states), Left parties (and forces) may counter the neo-liberal turn by institutionally embedding progressive regimes. We agree with Holmes and Lightfoot's suggestion: the EU serves as the terrain in which representatives of competing 'constitutionalisms' battle – those representing neoliberal new-constitutionalism and seeking to embed budgetary discipline and those representing a more progressive variety. The result of this battle is not foreordained. This is similar to Worth's suggestion in Chapter 7 that a post-Fordist, post-national politics at the regional level is not merely a 'new constitutionalist' portrait of a consolidated and inescapable neoliberalism. European integration does not signal the definitive consolidation of neoliberalism, but rather constitutes a new reality and the necessary point for progressive interventions.

For us this opens up an engagement among critical IPE scholars that helpfully calls attention to the complex question of how we actually measure hegemony. 'New constitutionalism' directs our attention to the form and function of certain institutions, but we also need to consider how the rules held up by 'new constitutionalists' are indeed conceived and honoured by those holding the levers of power, and how they may in fact be used in ways that are different from or undermine their initial coherence. Institutionally negotiated settlements can erode in many different ways, and we need to pay attention to the modalities of these erosions if we are to understand the full spectrum of political possibilities at any one moment in time. Having an engagement among critical IPE scholars over the manner and import of these erosions would be a very constructive way to think about the strength of neoliberalism, both within Europe and beyond.

Conclusion

We have outlined in this summary chapter both a framework for conceiving of the future of the Left in Europe that is suggested by the contributors to this volume, although articulated fully by none of them. We then considered how this framework might add some analytical value to our consideration of the strength of the neoliberal order at the global level. Finally, we offered a reflection on how the insights generated by the contributors to this volume might engage with broader currents of thinking in critical IPE.

The enterprise of critical IPE is a vibrant branch of enquiry that offers a way of apprehending the structural conditions of our contemporary global capitalist order. But it is not yet an enterprise fully mapped out and ring-fenced by a set of precepts which must be rigidly adhered to in order to gain entry into its theoretical fraternity. This we think is a good thing. Each contributor to this volume has in their own way also contributed to the 'war of position' in Europe by debunking the myths associated with neoliberal globalisation, even if their conclusions vary. Further engagement among the practitioners of critical political economy, who share a point of entry but not perhaps a final destination, can improve the terms of debate and open up further opportunities to consider new and innovative ways of thinking about the world we inhabit. And where we can act on this thinking to bring into being a future that is both kinder and more attentive to the fullest expression of our human possibilities will make not just a scholarly contribution to our world, but a useful and practical contribution as well. This is the promise of critical IPE, and it is why thinking about the future of the Left in Europe has something to tell everyone interested in what we can all do to make the world a fit and better place to be.

Notes

1 The terms 'war of position' and 'war of maneuver' are associated with the writings of Antonio Gramsci, the celebrated Italian Marxist whose *Prison Notebooks* (1971) have become a major theoretical inspiration for critical political economists. Although not used explicitly in this volume, we believe these concepts are useful descriptions of possible Left strategies in Europe. These concepts are developed throughout this chapter.
2 The success of the True Finns, Sweden Democrats, Danish People's Party and Norway's Progress Party over the past several years has brought them into governing arrangements that have seen long-held (neoliberal) assumptions about mobility challenged. For example, Denmark resurrected border controls in May 2011 (*New York Times*, May 12, 2011).

References

Germain, R. (2010) *Global Politics and Financial Governance*. Basingstoke: Palgrave.

Gill, S. (1995) 'Globalisation, Market Civilisation and Disciplinary Neoliberalism', *Millennium: Journal of International Studies*, 24 (3), 399–423.

Gill, S. (1998) 'European Governance and the New Constitutionalism: Economic and Monetary Union and Alternatives to Disciplinary Neoliberalism', *New Political Economy*, Vol. 3 (1), 5–26.

Gramsci, A. (1971) *Selections from the Prison Notebooks*. London: Lawrence & Wishart.

New York Times (2011), www.nytimes.com/2011/05/13/world/europe/13iht-border13.html (accessed 13 May 2011).

Van der Pijl, K. (1998) *Transnational Classes and International Relations*. London and New York: Routledge.

Silvius, R. (2012) *Russian State Visions of World Order and the Limits to Universal Liberalism*. PhD thesis, Carleton University.

Index